The Leg [illegible] usiness World

The Legal Environment of the Business World

R. B. Buchanan, BA (Law) Hons., Barrister

Stanley Thornes (Publishers) Ltd

First published in 1982 by Stanley Thornes (Publishers) Ltd,
Educa House, Old Station Drive, off Leckhampton Road,
CHELTENHAM, Glos. GL5 3 0DN, England.

British Library Cataloguing in Publication Data

Buchanan, Robert
The legal environment of the business world.
1. Associations, institutions, etc. – Law and legislation – Great Britain
I. Title
344.106′6 KD2040

ISBN 0-85950-305-4

Typeset by Tech-Set, Unit 3, Brewery Lane, Felling, Gateshead, Tyne and Wear.
Printed and bound in Great Britain at the Pitman, Press, Bath.

Contents

Preface

This book provides the basic Law content for the Learning Objectives of the Business Education Council's National Award, Common Core Module 3 and 4, and the Business Law Option.

The subject is presented in such a way that the book will also be suitable for a variety of courses where Law is studied at a *foundation* or *introductory* level. These courses include: GCE 'A' and 'O' level law; BEC General – Law and the Individual/Consumer Law; BEC Higher – Bankers' Conversion, Institute of Legal Executives. It is hoped that the book will also appeal to a general readership.

Where appropriate and convenient, *authorities* (cases/statutes) are listed in selected chapters, so as to facilitate easier reference and use. Many sections (SS or S) in statute laws are also referred to.

The assignments are grouped together on pages 198–209, and may be undertaken on an assessed or non-assessed basis. It is within the discretion of individual lecturers to set assignments at a time which ultimately will be decided by the knowledge and progress of their students.

Every effort has been made by the author and publisher to be as accurate and up to date as possible within the constraints of a textbook of this type. However, no responsibility can be accepted for any inaccuracies or misstatements howsoever caused.

List of Cases

(Page references in bold type denote the main or full reference to an authority.)

List of Statutes

(Page references in bold type denote the main or full reference to an authority. S or SS refers to a section or sections of the appropriate Act.)

STATUTORY ORDERS

Acknowledgements

Thanks are given to the following for assistance and the necessary permission to produce or reproduce material:

The All England Law Reports
The Law Society
Lloyd's Bank Ltd
HMSO
The Registrar of Companies
Wildman and Battell Ltd.

1

Law Defined

CRIMINAL AND CIVIL WRONGS

Law can be defined as a set of rules regulating the conduct and behaviour of a person in society.

These rules are divided into two types:

1. Rules regulating the conduct of persons as a whole, i.e. criminal laws: anyone who breaks these rules commits a *crime* and is *prosecuted* by the people in the name of the *Queen*. The rule-breaker, if found guilty, is punished, for example, by a fine or imprisonment.
2. Rules regulating the conduct of persons to each other, i.e. civil laws: anyone who breaks these rules commits a *civil wrong* and can be *sued* by the other party. If the rule-breaker is found *liable*, he will be made to pay compensation known as *damages*.

Examples of Crimes	*Examples of Civil Wrongs*
Murder	A food supplier's failing to deliver goods to a shop as promised (a breach of contract).
Burglary	Doing harm to someone by carrying out a job carelessly (a tort).
Theft	Dismissing a person unfairly from his employment (a breach of contract).
Assault	A motorist injuring a pedestrian by driving badly (a tort).

All civil wrongs can be classified as either breaches of contract or torts.

BREACH OF CONTRACT

A contract is a legally enforceable agreement. Most persons make contracts every day: for example, buying goods from a shop, travelling on a bus or train, or taking a job. Many contracts are made in writing but most contracts do not need to be; they can be created orally or by conduct.

Every contract creates express or implied rights (known as terms) between the parties to the contract. For example, in a contract for the sale of a car, the parties may *expressly* agree that the buyer will pay for the car by instalments. The law would *imply* that the car is roadworthy.

TORTS

Torts are wrongs established by law. Torts create duties owed by persons to others without the need for any contractual agreement between them. For example, a surgeon who carries out an operation carelessly causing injury to a patient commits the tort of negligence; a person going on someone's land without permission commits the tort of trespass. There are only a specified number of torts (the main ones being negligence, nuisance, trespass and defamation), and unless an injured party can bring a claim for compensation within one or more of the existing torts he will be unsuccessful in his action.

COURTS OF LAW

Separate courts of law decide, by way of a trial, whether a crime or a civil wrong has been committed, namely:

Criminal Courts	and	*Civil Courts*
Magistrates' Courts		County Courts
Crown Courts		The High Court
The Court of Appeal (Criminal Division)		The Court of Appeal (Civil Division)
The House of Lords		The House of Lords

See page 185.

Sometimes, the rule-breaker by his conduct commits both a crime and a civil wrong.

E.g.: A taxi-driver called John Smith may carelessly crash his vehicle injuring a passenger, Bill Brown.

1. Smith commits the crime of reckless driving and will be punished in a criminal court; society prosecutes Smith: *R.* v. *Smith.*

2. Smith commits a civil wrong against Brown (both a breach of contract and a tort) and will be sued for compensation in a civil court by Brown: *Brown* v. *Smith*.

In most cases the actual decision of the court (as to the guilt of the accused or the liability of the defendant) can be challenged by way of appeal to a higher court (see page 189), the exception being in criminal cases where the prosecution cannot challenge a jury's "not guilty" verdict.

SEEKING LEGAL ADVICE

When a person wants help on the lawfulness of some conduct, he will often consult a lawyer. Lawyers are either solicitors or barristers. Their job is to advise and assist clients on legal problems, and if necessary to represent them in court. When consulted on a legal problem a lawyer will obtain the *facts* of the case, then apply the *law* (the rules of conduct) to those facts when giving advice. Lawyers are trained to discover where the precise laws upon any particular problem can be found.

SOURCES AND CONTENT OF LAWS

Acts of Parliament

Acts of Parliament contain the rights and duties of persons within the community. The process by which an Act becomes law is by way of a bill being introduced into Parliament (House of Commons or House of Lords). If a majority of Members of Parliament are in favour of the bill becoming law, it passes through various stages before being given the Royal Assent by the Queen, at which time the bill becomes an Act.

So much new legislation is needed annually that Parliament gives to others (government ministers, public bodies, local authorities) powers to create rules, regulations and orders (e.g. statutory instruments) to enable an Act of Parliament to be workable. "Delegated legislation" is the phrase used to describe law-making power sanctioned by an Act of Parliament.

Note: In international trade and "company laws" the institutions of the European Economic Community (EEC) issue "regulations" and "directives" which can bind member states. If a conflict arises between English domestic law and EEC law, the latter takes precedence.

The Common Law

The phrase "the common law" has a very wide meaning but can be defined as the rights and duties of persons, and these rights and duties are declared by judges in court disputes when there is no relevant Act of Parliament to decide a case.

The process by which the common law is created is called "judicial precedent", i.e. laws declared by judges. The value of a precedent depends greatly upon the court within which the law is declared.

A judge hearing a legal dispute in the Queen's Bench Division of the High Court (see page 186) will listen to the evidence presented by the lawyers for both parties to the dispute and their arguments that conflicting previous case precedents support their side. Evidence includes witnesses giving their version of the facts under oath. (A judge often decides cases in favour of one party on the basis that he believes the facts given by one or more witnesses for one side in preference to those on the other side.)

Once the judge has heard both sides he delivers a judgment. This judgment contains both the *facts* of the case he has heard, and as he finds them, and his *interpretation* of the *law* as it applies to the facts. The judge refers in his judgment to the previous cases argued before him in support of the arguments of the opposing lawyers, and then he selects the most appropriate precedent(s) from those previous cases to apply in the *present* case.

In many cases the judge *must* follow a previous precedent. So, for example, a previous precedent (formulated by a judge in an earlier case), decided in the Court of Appeal, which cannot be *distinguished* – because of factual similarity – from the new and *present* case, *must* be followed by the High Court judge. That is, precedents decided by the Court of Appeal are binding on the High Court and all lower courts in similar cases (see table of Hierarchy of Courts, page 185). Hence the phrase, "binding precedent".

If there is no similar precedent that can be followed by the judge, he must create a new precedent: i.e. he declares the common law.

The process of judicial precedent is unnecessary where:

1. There is an Act of Parliament that regulates a legal dispute. Parliament is the supreme law-making power, and where legislative rights conflict with common law rights, the former prevail.

   But even then in some disputes a court case may be necessary because there is a conflict as to the *meaning* of words used in an Act of Parliament. For example in *Evans* v. *Cross* (1938) a judge had to decide whether a white painted line in a road was a traffic sign as the Act applied to "all signals, warning signposts, direction posts, signs, or *other devices*". The courts have rules for interpreting statutes, and applying the *ejusdem generis* rule, the white painted line was not a traffic sign (see page 193).

2. The common law is clear and undisputed.

E.g.: A person is in conflict with a football pools company because he claims to have sent in a coupon with a winning entry, but the pools organisation refuses to pay him anything and he is considering suing the company. He would almost certainly be advised by a lawyer not to do so because there is clear and undisputed common law authority that his agreement with the pools company is "binding in honour only": *Jones* v. *Vernons Pools Co. Ltd* (1938) 2 All E.R. 626 (see page 25); followed in the case of *Appleson* v. *Littlewood Ltd* (1939) 1 All E.R. 464.

Equity

Non-lawyers are often very confused by the meaning of Equity, and its relevance in modern law. Although Equity *was* a separate system of law, nowadays it is part of the "common law system". Prior to 1875, English law was divided into Common Law Courts and Courts of Equity. It was possible to commence legal proceedings of a similar nature in either court system and sometimes obtain a different right and a different remedy depending upon which court an action started in. (A remedy is the award given to the party that wins a legal case.) The only common law remedy was, and still is, *damages* (monetary compensation). Equitable remedies are more versatile and include:

An injunction: A court order stopping a person doing something.

Specific performance: A court order compelling a person to do something.

The Judicature Acts 1873–5 merged the common law courts and the courts of equity and it became possible to obtain either a common law or equitable right and remedy in *any* court. But the present-day significance of the previously separate systems lies in the fact that whilst common law decisions were broadly decided by judicial precedent, equitable decisions were decided solely by principles of fairness – hence the word equity.

E.g.: In the sixteenth century a person who borrowed money by mortgaging his land was unable by common law to recover the land if he did not pay the money back on time. The courts of equity considered this unfair and introduced an equitable right enabling a borrower to recover land even if he did not pay the loan on time – the "equity of redemption". This principle is still the same in modern times.

However, equity nowadays is subject to the process of judicial precedent and there is no scope for a judge to create any new rights or remedies "in equity"; though if in a case a common law right is in conflict with an equitable right, the latter prevails: *Central London Property Trust Ltd* v. *High Trees House Ltd* (see page 24).

The essence of an equitable principle is that it arose only to correct unfairness in the common law; it put a "gloss" on the common law; further, an equitable remedy is entirely at the discretion of a judge (granted when he considers it fair) unlike a common law remedy, which is available "as of right" (see page 68).

DISCOVERING STATUTE LAW AND THE COMMON LAW (see pages 210–12)

Statute Law

Acts of Parliament and Statutory Instruments are published by Her Majesty's Stationery Office and are available for sale from there to the general public. Both Acts and Statutory Instruments are identified by the year they were passed and S.I.s will additionally have a reference number: see examples, pages 210–11.

Most good libraries have a section containing bound volumes of statutory law. The best and most important is *Halbury's Statutes.*

The Common Law

All the more important court decisions will be reported in "Law Reports", notably the Weekly Law Reports (W.L.R.), and the All England Law Reports (All E.R.). There are many different law reporters but these are the main ones. Each case that is reported will be cited by name, date and reference number; hence,

Jones	v. *Vernons Pools Ltd*	(1938)	2 All E.R. 626
Plaintiff	Defendant	Date reported	2nd volume of All England Reports for 1938, at page 626

Law reports are bound in annual volumes and by using textbooks and other reference material the relevant case(s) for an unresolved new problem can be found. Most libraries have a law section and the bound law reports (All E.R. or W.L.R.) are usually located there.

APPLYING LAWS TO BUSINESS DECISIONS

Whenever there is a business decision or problem involving law, the sources will always be the same, i.e. statute or common law. However, the *source area* may be different.

E.g.: A businessman is concerned about an allegation that he has sold defective goods. He would be advised to consider the "Sale of Goods Laws".

2

Legal Personality

A "person" is subject to the rules of the law, and only he (or she) has rights, obligations and duties under it. However, the law recognises and gives "status" to two types of person:

1. A "natural" (individual) person, i.e. an individual human being.
2. An "artificial" person, i.e. a personality or status attributable to an organisation or to a public office.

Note: Under the Congenital Disabilities Act 1976, certain rights are given to an unborn child.

BUSINESS STATUS

Every "person" concerned with the business world is given status. For example, a person working in business on his own account (usually called a "sole trader") has natural status; a large organisation will almost always have artificial status, e.g. a Public Limited Company.

By giving status or legal personality to an organisation (as well as to an individual) the parties to a legal conflict are easily identifiable. The legal system works on the basis that all disputes are between one person against (versus) another person. Hence:

A Person	v.	*Another Person*
(Natural or Artificial)		(Natural or Artificial)

ARTIFICIAL PERSONS

Artificial persons have many of the same rights, obligations and duties as natural persons. So,

A natural person	=	A legal person
An artificial person	=	A legal person

The significance of attributing "personality" or status to an organisation is tied to the historical development of business activity.

Buying and selling for gain (trading) by an individual, a partnership or a "company" of natural persons has progressed through the years. From early times to modern day, trading has been the common thread of business dealings.

Originally, risk-taking traders (businessmen) prospered in an atmosphere of individual endeavour through the anonymous nature of a partnership or of group activity. Royal Charters and Acts of Parliament identified and approved organisational business groups, but astute lawyers were able to devise schemes exempting personal loss to individuals connected with the promotion of such groups. This was done by businessmen when entering into legally binding arrangements (e.g. contracts) limiting their personal loss if any business venture happened to go wrong; hence the phrase, "limited liability". This is still the same nowadays.

Eventually it was recognised that control and regulation of a company of individuals was needed and a warning given to the public that company (or artificial) "personality" was to be identified with a particular group of natural persons who were at the same time protecting their private fortunes. Hence, a company (of persons) with limited liability, i.e. a company limited. The full consequences of this only became clear in 1896 in the leading authority of *Salomon* v. *Salomon and Co. Ltd* (see page 12).

Nowadays organisations with limited liability status are formed (registered) and governed by the Companies Acts 1948–81 (see page 132).

PRIVATE ENTERPRISE AND STATUS

Any person can engage in trading activities, i.e. buying and selling goods and services for gain, without him or her (the trader) complying with legal requirements for the *creation* of that "business".

E.g.: During her summer holidays, a student earns a living by selling home-made ice-cream to friends and neighbours. This is subject, of course, to the activity itself being lawful – selling stolen goods, for example, is not lawful.

Many "corner" shopkeepers are examples of persons occupied full-time in the "art" of trading: buying goods from a wholesale (cash and carry) and reselling them at a profit to the public. They are identified as businessmen or "sole traders".

Persons working together in "partnership" also need not comply with any formalities to create a "partnership"; the combination of two or more individuals trading together for a common purpose is deemed at law to be a partnership firm: see page 132 and the Partnership Act 1890, s. 1.

Both sole traders and partners have natural status and cannot be limited in their personal liability. If a business or partnership is in debt, the individual businessman or partner can be compelled to sacrifice his personal property and possessions to settle the debt.

Many sole traders and partners can choose to create a limited company to obtain the benefit of "limited liability" (see page 13) (although there are prohibitions on certain professional partnerships forming limited companies, e.g. doctors and lawyers.) But limitation of liability is not the only factor in deciding whether to change a business unit into a limited liability company.

An accountant may advise a businessman that there are good financial or tax reasons to alter or retain the status quo; further, the formalities and publicity attached to registration may well deter some people (see pages 134-5). Even when a business is changed (or sold) to a registered company, many people, especially potential creditors or investors, are wary of dealing with a limited liability organisation without obtaining personal guarantees from those connected with it. Nevertheless, when the decision to "incorporate" a company is taken, and formalities are complete, a new legal person is born. He is owned by shareholders (members) and managed by directors; and he is capable of all the normal business activities of a natural person:

Making contracts
Employing persons
Owning or renting property

He has "perpetual succession", i.e. exists indefinitely, but can be terminated either voluntarily or involuntarily. He is, in short, a corporate body.

The formalities of registration and the types and structure of limited liability companies are shown on page 135.

PUBLIC ENTERPRISE AND STATUS

Statute law often creates either:

1. A "commercial corporation" designed to run an industry, e.g. the National Coal Board; or

2. A "social services corporation" designed to carry out a particular social service, e.g. the Health and Safety at Work Executive.

Such a public enterprise is created by, or under, an Act of Parliament and is not subject to the Companies Acts requirements, nor the principle of *Salomon's case.* It is financed by and accountable to the taxpayer; it is usually run by appointed directors and ultimately controlled by a government minister. However, for the purposes of legal identification such an organisation has a distinct legal personality or status.

Naming and Recognising Legal Personality

		Method of Creation
A Registered Corporation	A Limited Company →	Registration under the Companies Acts 1948–81
A Public Corporation	A Nationalised Industry →	By Act of Parliament
A Statutory Corporation	A Statutory Company →	
A Local Authority or County Council	London Borough of Hammersmith and Fulham →	
A Chartered Corporation	BBC →	By Royal Charter
A Government Department or Government Minister	The Home Office → Secretary of State for Employment	The Courts attribute them with status
An Unincorporated Association	A Partnership → A Trade Union →	Special status
A Businessman	A Sole Trader →	
A Consumer	Buying goods to consume →	

Identifying an Artificial Person

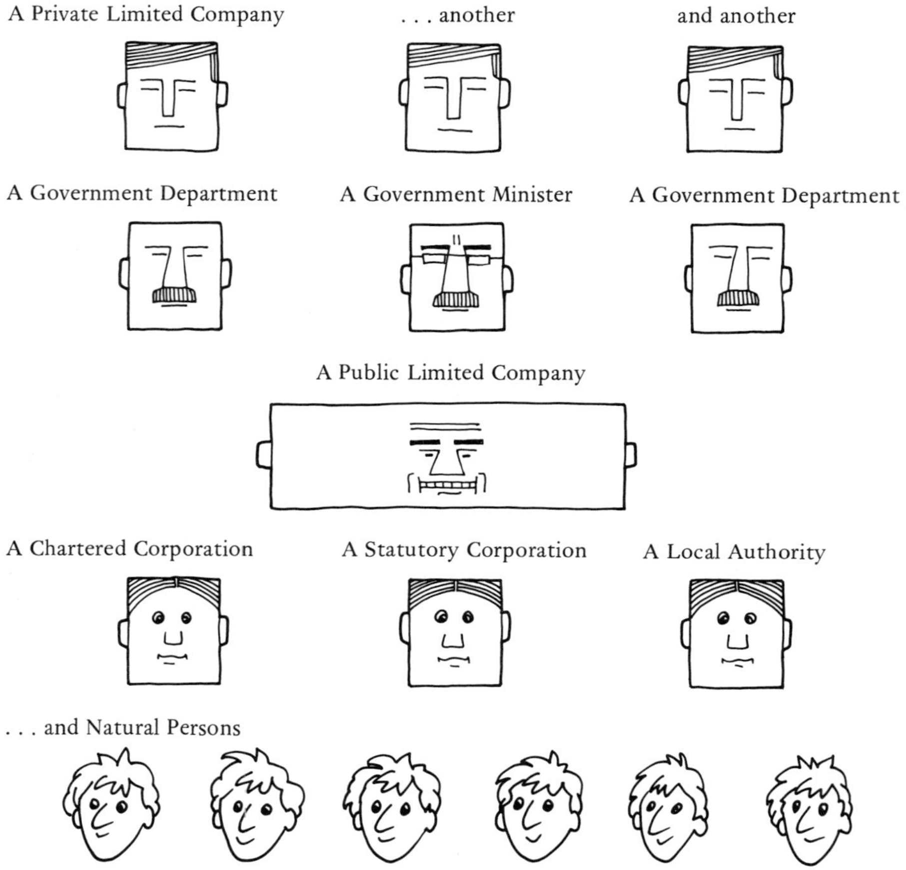

All legal disputes are between: Natural/Artificial persons v. Artificial/Natural persons. For an example, see *Congreve* v. *Home Office*, page 180.

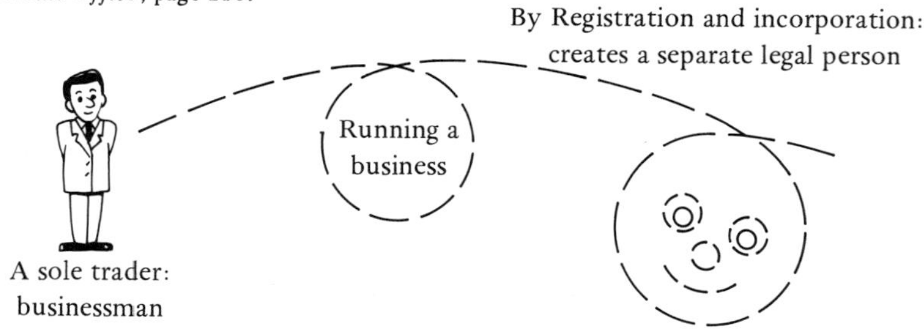

Salomon v. *Salomon and Co. Ltd* (1897)

A Mr. Salomon had carried on a boot-making business for several years. He called himself a "leather merchant". In 1892 he formed a registered limited liability company: Salomon & Co. Ltd. He was the majority shareholder with £20 001 in shares at £1 each; the other six shareholders (all members of his family) had one share each. The managing director of Salomon & Co. Ltd was Mr. Salomon.

The company purchased the boot-making business from Mr. Salomon. But it only had £21 007, and the price of the boot-making business was £39 000. The company borrowed the difference (i.e. £39 000 less £21 007) by entering into loan agreements; in particular, Mr. Salomon lent the company £10 000, by way of a "secured debenture" and this gives such a "secured" creditor a right to be paid *before* other (unsecured) creditors in the event of the company going into "liquidation" (see page 153).

The company did go into liquidation not long after it was formed; its liabilities were £18 000 (including the £10 000 owed to Mr. Salomon) whilst its assets were only £6000. This amount was paid to Mr. Salomon and the remaining creditors received nothing. These unsecured creditors claimed that to all intents and purposes Mr. Salomon *was* the company and so he could not owe money to himself.

The House of Lords *held* that Mr. Salomon and Salomon and Co. Ltd were two separate and distinct persons. There was *no evidence* that Mr. Salomon had behaved fraudulently. Had he done so, the case would have been decided differently.

This decision confirms two important principles:

1. *A registered limited company is a legal person:*
   - *a)* It can own property.
   - *b)* It has rights, obligations and duties.
   - *c)* It can defend and bring legal cases in its own name.
   - *d)* It has unlimited liability (*only* the members have limited liability).
   - *e)* It is possible to have a so-called "one-man company" whereby the person in charge is separate from the company.
   - *f)* A member (shareholder) can be a director and effectively control the company even though separate from it.
   - *g)* The law will "lift the veil of incorporation", i.e. treat an individual and a company as *one person* when a limited company is used to commit fraud, e.g. evasion of tax.

2. *The members of such a company have limited liability:*

   In the absence of proven fraud a shareholder is only liable to pay to the company the amount of money he has put into it.

3

Contractual Obligation and Tort Duty

THE LAW OF CONTRACT

THE CONTRACT OBLIGATION

A contract is a legally enforceable agreement. Two or more persons must agree to perform some task or activity and so create an exchange of obligations and hence a contract.

In the business world people agree and disagree, argue and negotiate all the time. Many of these transactions and dealings lead to and are recognised as creating legal rights under the law of contract.

THE NEGOTIATION PROCESS

It is possible to classify everyone (especially those connected with business) as either buyers or sellers, trading in goods and services, making bargains and concluding deals.

CAVEAT EMPTOR

Many of these transactions are dominated by an established principle called *caveat emptor* – "let the buyer (or seller) beware"; the effect of the *caveat emptor* principle can be illustrated by the following examples:

E.g. 1: A car dealer agrees to sell a second-hand car to a young man for £2000. A legally enforceable contract is made. After purchasing the car the buyer sees another vehicle, identical in every respect, being sold elsewhere for £1000.

E.g. 2: A salesman employed by a large company has agreed to sell goods on a $2\frac{1}{2}$ per cent commission on-sales basis; he later discovers that one of his colleagues (of equal rank and status) has negotiated a 5 per cent commission on sales.

E.g. 3: A customer browsing through an art shop discovers an old painting and the shopkeeper sells the painting to him for £10. It is later discovered that the painting is worth £10 000.

In *all* these examples there is a legal contract and the first mentioned price is binding on the parties. If a person makes a "bad" bargain, that is not a question of law but of business judgement and the law is not concerned with bad bargains.

This attitude greatly benefits a business person who is unable to compete with another, perhaps larger, business selling the same goods or services.

E.g.: A retailer sells winter coats at £75 each; a nearby department store sells exactly similar coats at £55 each. If a customer purchases a coat from the shopkeeper and then discovers the much lower price of the same type of coat at the department store, he has no legal right to claim that his agreement with the shopkeeper is invalid. The customer failed to "shop around" for the best bargain available.

Note: Many organisations nowadays make it a part (term) of the agreement (contract) that a customer will have *some* rights in law if goods can be bought more cheaply elsewhere. For example, a notice in a store may read: "If any goods displayed in this store can be purchased for less than the price shown, we will refund the difference in price."

BARGAINING POWER

The principle of *caveat emptor* has, in many respects, dominated the business world for hundreds of years. The philosophy is that a person should be freely entitled to enter into whatever arrangement he wishes: freedom to negotiate and enter into contracts.

If it later transpires that a person regrets *the quality of the bargain* negotiated, then (as in the examples above), there is no legal claim available.

However, in recent times, the law has recognised that in many negotiating relationships one of the parties is in such an inferior bargaining position that it cannot be said he is able to freely negotiate his rights, and the law is prepared to give the person in the inferior position a legal claim: *Lloyds Bank Ltd* v. *Bundy* (see page 31).

It is also recognised that large-scale organisations, perhaps dominating the supply of goods and services to the public, have a great advantage in the negotiating process, compared with the individual person (the "consumer") who, in reality, is obliged to accept whatever terms the superior party dictates. This in turn has led to numerous "consumer protection" laws including the concept of the unfair contract term (see page 43).

THE TORT DUTY

The legal relationships created by an agreement under the law of contracts may at the same time *or independently* create rights under the law of torts. The word "tort" (a civil wrong) signifies a right in the civil law not deriving from a contractual agreement but imposing a legal duty upon a person towards others generally.

Only certain types of "tort" duties are recognised by law (see page 50), and unless it can be proved that a duty does exist, there will be no legal responsibility; i.e. "no right, no remedy".

E.g.: A family grocer, in business for several years, discovers that a large supermarket is due to open near to his shop. It is very probable that this will damage his "trade" as many of his customers will do their shopping at the supermarket. Nevertheless, there is nothing in law, i.e. no duty owed, which would prevent the supermarket being opened.

Alternatively, there are certain kinds of torts (e.g. trespass to land; libel – under defamation) that not only impose legal rights but do so without the need for a person proving he has actually suffered any loss or harm; these are called torts "actionable *per se*"; i.e. a legal claim is possible without any proof of damage.

Nevertheless, a most important practical difference between a right in the law of contract and a right under the law of torts is the requirement for a claimant (plaintiff) in tort to prove that a defendant was *at fault* (unlike in contract): *Frost* v. *Aylesbury Dairy Co.* (see page 128).

E.g.: A person is knocked down in the street by a motor vehicle and is crippled for life. There is no contract between him and the driver of the vehicle so the only claim the injured party can bring is for the tort of negligence. Unless he can *prove* that the "accident" was the driver's fault, which may be very difficult to establish, there is no remedy (right) in tort.

DUTIES AND LIABILITY

In both the law of contract and the law of torts, the primary purpose of deciding whether, respectively, an agreement or tort obligation or duty exists is to establish a person's claim for damages, i.e. monetary compensation (see page 67).

In the commercial world the failure of a businessman to anticipate properly, and hence plan for (e.g. by insurance), the legal responsibilities and liabilities arising from his business activities, particularly in contract and tort, can have serious and sometimes financially disastrous consequences.

The Contract Obligation

Essentials of a Valid Contract

Offer and acceptance	Consideration	Intention to create a legal relationship	Genuine consent	Legal capacity	Lawfulness of agreement

A valid contract = A legally enforceable agreement.

A void contract = An agreement giving no contract law rights.

A voidable contract = A valid contract which can be declared void by a court of law.

An unenforceable contract = A valid contract which cannot be successfully enforced in the courts.

OFFER AND ACCEPTANCE

Offer

Definition: a proposal to give or do something. An offer may be expressed (by word or mouth or in writing) or implied from conduct.

E.g.: A customer enters a supermarket, obtains a wire basket, selects food items, which he places in the wire basket, and presents the goods at the "check-out". This action of the customer is an "offer" by conduct to purchase goods: *Pharmaceutical Society of Gt Britain* v. *Boots* (1953) (see opposite). The person who makes the offer is called "the offeror"; the person to whom the offer is made is called "the offeree".

A proposal will be recognised as an offer if it conforms to the following:

1. It is made to a definite person, class of person or the world at large.
2. It is firm and definite. If the "terms" of an "offer" are unclear or not precise, then there is no offer and the parties are still at the negotiating stage.
3. It is not simply a trade boast, or merely a supplying of information or an invitation to a person to enter into negotiations.
4. The offer is made known (communicated) to the offeree.

E.g.: A business places an advertisement in a newspaper claiming: ". . . a fantastic job offer . . . opportunity to travel . . . highest rates of pay." An unemployed person reads the advertisement and immediately "accepts" the "offer". The law would say that the advertisement was, at best, an invitation to make an offer. See the leading case of *Carlill* v. *Carbolic Smoke Ball Co.*; see also: *Gibson* v. *Manchester City Council*; *Butler Machine Tool Co.* v. *Ex-Cell-O Corp.* (pages 19-21).

An offer comes to an end (terminates) if any of the following occurs:

1. It is accepted.
2. The offeror withdraws (revokes) it.
3. The offeree rejects it.
4. The offer lapses. An offer lapses when the time given for acceptance passes; if no time is given, the offer lapses after a reasonable time.
5. Either party dies before acceptance.

Acceptance

Definition: unqualified positive assent to the offer.

E.g.: After a job interview an employer says to an interviewee: "We offer you the job at £5000 per annum". The applicant says: "I accept your offer if you will pay me £6000 per annum." There is a positive assent to the offer, but it is qualified, so there is no contract.

The acceptance must be made known (communicated) to the offeror and must conform to the terms of the offer. In certain exceptional cases the terms of the offer may do away with the need for communication of the acceptance; and sometimes a contract is formed when a letter of acceptance is put in the post, regardless of it reaching the offeror: the so-called "post rule".

E.g.: After a job interview an employer writes to an applicant offering him the job "at £5000 per annum". The offeree writes a letter accepting the offer on the terms given and posts the letter. There is a contract when the letter is posted: *Adams* v. *Lindsell* (see page 21).

Authorities on Offer and Acceptance

Pharmaceutical Society of Gt Britain v. *Boots* (1953)

The defendant owned a self-service shop in Edgware. On entering the shop each customer passed a barrier where he obtained a wire basket. In the main part of the shop, shelves displayed various drugs and medicines. Certain of these drugs were controlled by the Pharmacy and Poisons Act 1933. The Act said it was a criminal wrong to sell these controlled drugs when the "sale" was not supervised by a qualified pharmacist. A qualified pharmacist was employed by Boots in the store. He was located behind the cash desk and supervised all transactions that took place there. The Pharmaceutical Society *claimed*: Boots were guilty of selling controlled drugs without supervision. The display of drugs on the shelves constituted an offer. When the customer selected the items he wanted and placed them in his wire basket, the offer was accepted by the customer and a "sale" contract of goods arose. This "sale" was in contravention of the Act as at the time it was made a qualified pharmacist was not in attendance.

Boots *defended*: it was the customer who made the offer (at the cash desk). This being so, no offence was committed as the "sale" took place under the supervision of a qualified pharmacist. The court *found* in favour of Boots. Somervell L.J. said: "Is a contract to be regarded as being completed when the article is put into the receptacle (wire basket), or when the customer, having free access to what is in the shop and having looked at the different items says to the shop assistant 'I want this'? The assistant in 999 times out of 1000 says 'This is all right,' the money passes and the transaction is completed. In the case of an ordinary shop, although goods are displayed and it is intended that the customers should go and choose what they want, the contract is not completed until the customer having indicated the articles he needs, the shopkeeper, or someone on his behalf, accepts that offer."

Carlill v. *Carbolic Smoke Ball Co.* (1893)

The defendants were the owners and sellers of a medical preparation called the "Carbolic Smoke Ball". They inserted an advertisement in a newspaper: "£100 reward will be paid by the Carbolic Smoke Ball to any person who after using the smoke ball as directed for two weeks, catches influenza." It went on to say that £1000 was deposited with the Alliance Bank, Regent Street showing their "sincerity" in the matter.

The plaintiff, Mrs. Carlill, on the faith of the advertisement, bought one of the smoke balls, followed the instructions, but nevertheless went down with the "flu". She sued the defendants for breach of contract because they failed to pay her the £100. The company argued in court that there was no legally binding agreement.

The court decided that the advertisement was a valid legal offer, accepted by the plaintiff when she purchased the smoke ball. All the other essentials of a contract were present and the company was ordered to pay Mrs. Carlill £100. The court made the following observations:

1. *A Legal Offer*

   a) An offer can be made to the whole world; if it is conditional on some event, then when, and only when, the "condition" is fulfilled, there will be a binding contract. In the *Carbolic Case* the "condition" was following the directions on the smoke ball.

   b) Advertisements which suggest that there is a legal offer will be given that effect; depositing £1000 with a bank is strong evidence of a legal offer.

   c) Most advertisements are not legal offers but are merely "commercial boasts".

2. *A Legal Acceptance*

   It is a rule of the law of contract that an acceptance should be notified to the offeror (the person making the offer). But communication of an acceptance is not necessary where the offeror indicates, expressly or by implication, that the performance of a condition is a sufficient acceptance without notification. This was the position in the *Carbolic Case.*

Gibson v. *Manchester City Council* (1979)

A city council circulated a letter to its council house tenants. In the letter they said that the council "may be prepared to sell [your] house to you". A tenant called Mr. Gibson treated this as a legal offer and accepted it. The council denied that the words in the letter were a valid offer and so could not be accepted; the House of Lords agreed, the crucial words being "may be prepared"—which stopped the proposal being a legal offer.

Butler Machine Tool Co. v. *Ex-Cell-O Corporation* (1979)

A machine-maker wrote to the defendants quoting a price of £75 535 for a machine. On the back of the quotation were "terms of sale". One of these terms included a clause enabling the seller to increase the price (a price variation clause) in certain circumstances.

The defendants wrote and ordered the machine with the words "on our terms only". There was no mention of provision for price increase in the order. A "tear-off" acknowledgement form was attached to the order with the words: "We accept your order – on the terms stated." This was signed by the machine-maker and returned to the defendant.

A dispute arose upon the question of which party made the offer and so whose terms applied. It was *held* that on the evidence it was the buyer who made the offer and his terms were accepted by the seller in the acknowledgement.

The court said that the modern commercial practice of giving quotations and placing orders produces a "battle of the [standard] forms". In most cases there is a contract as soon as the last form is sent and received (i.e. the acknowledgement) without objection being taken.

Adams v. *Lindsell* (1818)

The defendant wool-dealers made an offer by letter to sell wool to the plaintiffs, requiring an answer "in course of post". The letter was delayed in reaching Adams but when he received it he accepted immediately. In the meantime, Lindsell sold the wool to someone else. The court *held* that there was a binding contract between Adams and Lindsell. The contract was made when Adams posted the letter of acceptance.

The existence of the "post rule" is a question of evidence in each case, looking at the intention of the parties. An offeror who says he expects an acceptance "by notice in writing" does *not* attract the post rule; i.e. the letter must be *received* by the offeror before there is a contract: *Holwell Securities* v. *Hughes* (1974).

Dickinson v. *Dodds* (1876)

On Wednesday, 10 June, the defendant delivered to the plaintiff a written offer to sell certain property. The offer was to remain open until "9.00 a.m. Friday, 12 June."

On Thursday, 11 June, the plaintiff was informed by a Mr. Berry that the defendant had sold the property to someone else. At 7.00 a.m. on 12 June the plaintiff "accepted" the offer.

The court *held* there was no contract between Dickinson and Dodds. The offer was effectively revoked (withdrawn) before "acceptance" by communication of the withdrawal by a reliable third party.

Note: In such a case an offeree may protect himself by paying a deposit to keep an offer open for a certain time.

CONSIDERATION

Definition: Consideration is the so-called *quid pro quo*. Something given, promised or done in exchange as part of the same bargain. The judicially accepted definition of consideration is: "some right, interest, profit or benefit accruing to one party, or some forbearance, detriment, loss or responsibility given, suffered or undertaken by the other": *Currie* v. *Misa* (1875).

E.g.: A wholesaler promises to deliver goods to a retailer who promises to pay £100 for them. The exchange of promises is the "consideration" making the agreement an enforceable contract.

"Consideration" is essential for all contracts and must comply with all the following:

1. Consideration must be legal.
2. Consideration must not be past, i.e. it must be part of the same bargain: *Re McArdle* (see below).
3. Consideration must be sufficient, i.e. capable of money value: *White* v. *Bluett* (see page 23).
4. Consideration must be more than a promise to perform an existing contractual obligation: *The Rule in Pinnel's Case* (see page 23).
5. Only a party giving consideration can claim contractual rights: *Tweddle* v. *Atkinson* (see page 24).

Exceptionally the courts will dispense with the need for consideration:

1. Where the promise is contained in a deed.
2. Where under an existing contract it would be "unfair" to allow a party to go back on a promise but for the absence of "consideration"; this is called the principle of Equitable Estoppel: *Central London Property Trust Ltd* v. *High Trees House Ltd*; *D. and C. Builders* v. *Rees* (see page 24).

Re McArdle (1951)

The occupant of a house made certain improvements to the house at a cost of £488. *After* the work was done, a number of the occupant's relatives entered into written agreement promising to pay the cost of the improvements. But they never fulfilled their promise and were sued for breach of contract.

Held: The claim to recover the £488 failed. At the time the promise to pay was made, the improvements were already completed (past) and the promise was therefore not binding.

There are three cases in which "past" consideration does make a promise binding:

1. Under the Bills of Exchange Act 1882 cheques and other bills of exchange issued to pay existing debts will be valid.
2. A later written promise to pay a long outstanding debt is enforceable.
3. If a person, expressly or by implication, *requests* another to perform services for him *and* after the services are rendered promises to pay for the services, the promise is binding; (and see the Supply of Goods and Services Act 1982).

White v. *Bluett* (1853)

A father was owed money by his son. The father promised his son that if he would "stop complaining" that his brother was better treated than himself he would not have to pay the debt. The son agreed but sometime later an action was brought against him to pay the debt. He claimed he was not liable as his promise to "stop complaining" *was* consideration and created a contract to release him from his obligation to pay the debt.

The court disagreed and the son was *held* bound to pay the debt. "Consideration" – to be valid – must usually be capable of having a monetary value placed upon it. It is not possible to put a value on a purely moral claim, i.e. to "stop complaining".

Pinnel's Case (1602)

A creditor sued a debtor for £8.50 due on 11 November 1600. The debtor claimed that at the creditor's request he had paid £5.25 on 1 October and that this was accepted in "full settlement".

The court *held* that a promise to perform less than an existing obligation is not sufficient consideration. But where a debtor makes an earlier payment or alters the mode of payment or adds something of value this will be "new" consideration.

Note: If under a contractual debt a creditor agrees to accept less than the sum due from a third party, this promise binds the creditor: *The Rule in Temple's Case.*

Tweddle v. *Atkinson* (1861)

Two parties entered a written contract promising to pay money to a third party, Tweddle, when he married. The agreement expressly stated that Tweddle had rights to sue for non-payment. When Tweddle married, one of the parties failed to make the payment and Tweddle sued him. The court *held* that as Tweddle had given no consideration for the exchange of promises he had no rights under the contract.

Note: Only a person who gives or promises to give "consideration" *and* is party to a contract, obtains rights and obligations under that contract. The principle of "Privity of Contract".

Central London Property Trust Ltd v. *High Trees House Ltd* (1947)

A block of flats was let for £2500 per annum by the plaintiffs to the defendants. Because of wartime conditions the plaintiffs agreed to accept a reduced rent of £1250 per annum for the duration of the war. At the end of the war the plaintiffs claimed to be entitled to the arrears of rent for the war years.

Held: Although the defendants had performed less than their contractual obligation, i.e. paid £1250 per annum instead of £2500 per annum, it would be unfair to allow the plaintiffs to go back on the promise. They were stopped (estopped) from doing so.

D. and C. Builders v. *Rees* (1966)

A firm was owed £482 under a building contract. The debtor was aware that the building company was in financial difficulties. He offered them £300 "in full settlement" of the debt, which the firm reluctantly accepted. They then sued for the remaining balance of £182.

Held: They were entitled to it. The rule in *Pinnel's Case* applied. It was argued by the defendant that it would be "unfair" to allow the creditor to go back on his promise. The court disagreed. It was the defendant who was unfair by exploiting the builders' financial difficulties.

Note: This case illustrates that where there is a conflict between a common law rule (*Pinnel's Case*) and an equitable rule (*High Trees*) the latter applies *unless* the court decides, as it did, not to exercise its equitable discretion.

INTENTION TO CREATE A LEGAL RELATIONSHIP

"All contracts are agreements but not all agreements are contracts."

An agreement is only a *contract* when the parties to the agreement intend to create a legal relationship. The "intention" of the parties is a question of fact to be discovered from all the evidence.

When parties enter into a commercial or business arrangement there is presumed to be a binding contractual agreement unless evidence displaces this presumption.

Simpkins v. *Pays* (1955)

Simpkins was a lodger in a house belonging to Mrs. Pays, who lived there with her granddaughter. The three of them *agreed* to share the stake money in a magazine's weekly fashion competition. The coupon was entered in Mrs. Pays' name and one of the entries on it won a prize of £750. She refused to share the prize with Mr. Simpkins, who sued her for £250. The outcome of the case depended on whether the agreement was intended to create a legally binding contract.

The court said the agreement was an enforceable contract; the evidence suggested there was a joint enterprise and the parties expected to share any prize won. It was not merely a "domestic" arrangement carrying no rights in law.

Jones v. *Vernons Pools Ltd* (1938)

Jones sued Vernons Pools claiming breach of contract. He had sent to them a completed pools coupon with a "winning" line but Vernons said they had never received the coupon.

The court *held* that even if they had received the entry there would be no valid contract as the words on the coupon expressed that the arrangement would not give rise to a legal relationship: it was "binding in honour only". The precedent in this case was followed in another dispute (where the facts were similar): *Appleson* v. *Littlewood Ltd* (1939).

GENUINE CONSENT

Definition: An agreement will *not* be a "contract" unless both parties have genuinely consented to it.

There will not be genuine consent if the agreement is brought about (induced) by a fundamental misapprehension or by improper pressure. Such inducements are called "vitiating" (cancelling) factors and are classified in three ways:

1. Operative Mistake

Generally a mistake will have no effect on the validity of a contract. But in extreme cases the courts are prepared to hold that a mistake of fact "operates" to nullify an agreement.

E.g.: Two parties enter an agreement for the sale of goods. It is later discovered that the buyer had in mind one quantity of goods, the seller a completely different quantity. The contract is void for mistake: *Raffles* v. *Wichelhaus*, (see page 28).

A mistake on the law will not usually nullify an agreement.

E.g.: A householder enters a number of trading contracts with a view to running a business from his home. He is later refused planning permission to use domestic premises for business purposes. The householder *cannot* claim the trading contracts are void: "Ignorance of the law is no excuse."

There will *not* be genuine consent if it is proved that the identity of one of the parties was *material to the formation* of the contract.

E.g.: A businessman agrees to sell and deliver goods to a firm ordering goods under the name of Marks and Spencer. It is then discovered the buyers are really "Mark and Spence" – street traders. This is an operative mistake and there is no contract: *Phillips* v. *Brooks* (see page 29).

A mistake as to the quality of the subject-matter will not avoid a contract.

E.g.: A customer buys a vase for £25 from a junk shop. He mistakenly believes it to be worth £5000. The contract to buy the vase is valid: *Bell* v. *Lever Brothers* (see page 29).

A person who signs a contractual document *will* be bound by the agreement contained within it *unless* there are exceptional circumstances enabling a court to release the signor from his obligation: *Saunders* v. *Anglia Building Society* (see page 30).

Conversely, the courts do have certain powers to *correct* a written contract which by mistake omits to contain part of an agreement: *Joscelyne* v. *Nissen* (see page 30).

2. Misrepresentation

An agreement can be avoided if it is proved that the "contract" was induced by a misrepresentation.

Definition: A misrepresentation is a false statement about a material fact inducing a negotiating party to enter a contract: *Smith* v. *Land and House Property Corporation* (see page 31).

In the course of business dealings many statements are made between bargaining parties. From the decided cases *the knowledge* of the representor appears to decide whether a pre-contract representation amounts to a misrepresentation.

E.g.: A car dealer represents to a prospective buyer that a second-hand car's mileage is 20 000. After the purchase is completed the buyer discovers the true mileage of the car to be 80 000. The dealer, as a man of business, ought to have known the car's true mileage. If the buyer can prove the statement was made, he can have the contract voided by the court for misrepresentation.

The silence of a negotiating party will never amount to a misrepresentation.

E.g.: A consumer examining a pair of shoes says to a salesman: "I assume these shoes you are selling are fit for disco-dancing." The salesman says nothing. The consumer purchases the shoes but later discovers they are not suitable for disco-dancing. He cannot claim misrepresentation: there was none. The principle of *caveat emptor* applies.

In certain negotiating situations the law does impose a duty to disclose all material facts. The best example is where the bargaining leads to a written contract for insurance. The insured is said to owe a duty of "utmost good faith". If it is later discovered that the insured failed to inform the insurers fully on material facts in his application, the contract can be cancelled by them.

Originally the law only recognised fraudulent misrepresentation, but fraud is very difficult to prove and the Misrepresentation Act 1967 introduced an action for non-fraudulent misrepresentation.

3. Duress and Undue Influence

There is no true consent if:

1. A person is induced to enter an agreement by force or the threat of it. This is called "duress".
2. A person is improperly pressurised into entering an agreement. This is called "undue influence". The law presumes that in certain relationships resulting in contracts there is undue influence. Such a relationship arises where one party is in a stronger bargaining position *and* the other party would place confidence and trust in him.

E.g.: A solicitor learns that one of his clients is looking for a house to buy. The solicitor offers to sell *his own* house to the client. The client accepts and makes a binding agreement. The law presumes that by the relationship of the parties to the agreement, i.e. solicitor and client, there was undue influence. But there is generally no presumption of undue influence between a businessman and his customer.

E.g.: A customer enters a department store and is persuaded by the "sales talk" of one of the staff to buy a suite of furniture. The buyer later regrets his decision as he did not need the goods and he now realises that an identical suite was being sold for half the price at a rival store. There is no undue influence. *Caveat emptor* applies. (But see *Lloyds Bank Ltd* v. *Bundy*, page 31.)

The presumption of undue influence may be resisted (rebutted) if it is proved that "free judgement" was exercised in making the contract. This would usually arise if the weaker party was advised to take independent advice, and adequate "consideration" was given for the resulting contract.

E.g.: Before a solicitor sells *his own* house to his client, he suggests the client seeks separate advice from another unconnected solicitor on the proposed deal. It is also proved that the price paid for the property was the true market value. The presumption of "undue influence" is displaced.

In cases where duress or undue influence arises the innocent party has the right to avoid the contract.

Authorities on Genuine Consent

Raffles v. *Wichelhaus* (1864)

There was a business contract for the sale of cotton that would arrive in England from Bombay on a ship called the *Peerless*. Coincidentally, there were two ships arriving from Bombay, both containing cotton and both called the *Peerless*. One would arrive in October, the other in December.

When the contract was made the buyer believed he was buying the December cargo, the seller that it was the October cargo. The buyer refused to take delivery of the October cargo and was sued for breach of contract.

Held: There was no genuine consent. One party believed he was buying one thing, the other party something else. The mistake operated to void the contract.

Phillips v. *Brooks Ltd* (1919)

A customer entered a jeweller's shop and selected various goods to purchase. The jeweller agreed to sell him some items including a ring. The customer then paid by cheque claiming to be a Sir George Bullough. This was not true: the customer was really a fraudulent person called North.

The jeweller allowed the customer to leave the shop with the ring. The customer then "sold" the ring to the defendant pawnbrokers, Brooks Ltd. Later the cheque given to the jeweller was "dishonoured".

The jeweller sued the pawnbroker for the return of the ring. The court had to decide whether the agreement between *the jeweller and North* was valid. If it was, then so was the agreement between North and the pawnbroker and hence the jeweller could not then recover the ring from him.

The validity of the jeweller's "contract" depended upon whether the identity of North was material *at the time* the contract *to sell* the ring was made.

Held: On the evidence available the jeweller intended to sell the goods to the person who came into his shop whether or not he claimed to be Sir George Bullough. The identity of the buyer was therefore not material when the contract was made. It was *at the time* of the agreement a valid (though voidable) contract, and the jeweller was unable to recover the ring from the pawnbroker.

Note: This case was followed in *Lewis* v. *Averay* (1971). The facts were similar though the subject-matter of the agreement was a car and not a ring. The defrauder had claimed to be a famous television actor, but the court decided that this did not influence the seller in parting with the car.

Bell v. *Lever Brothers Ltd* (1932)

A company dismissed two employees, Bell and Snelling, before the end of their five-year fixed term contract. Each employee entered an *agreement* to accept £30 000 and £20 000 respectively as compensation for the early termination of their employment contracts.

Subsequently, the company discovered that the employees had committed serious breaches of contract during the course of their employment. Such behaviour *would have* justified their dismissal without paying them compensation. The company claimed that the agreement to pay compensation was entered into under an operative mistake and was hence void.

Held: The court said the compensation agreement was valid. There was no operative mistake.

Lord Atkin said the company got exactly what they bargained for: the release of Bell and Snelling from their employment contracts. He gave an example: "A buys a roadside garage business from B abutting a public thoroughfare: *at the time* of the agreement, unknown to A, but known to B, it has already been decided to contract a by-pass road which will divert substantially the whole of the traffic from passing A's garage. A has no remedy."

Lever Brothers were in the same position as A.

Saunders v. *Anglia Building Society* (1971)

A 78-year-old widow, Mrs. Gailee, wanted to transfer her house to her nephew, Mr. Parkin. Mr. Lee, a friend of Mr. Parkin, prepared the document of transfer but fraudulently inserted his own name instead of Mr. Parkin's as the transferor. He took the document to Mrs. Gailee and told her it was a transfer of the house to Mr. Parkin. Her glasses were broken and she signed the document without reading it.

From the document, Mr. Lee appeared to be the owner of the property. He took it to the Anglia Building Society and mortgaged the house to them. They lent him £2000.

Neither Mrs. Gailee nor Mr. Parkin received any money. The Building Society claimed they owned the house. Mrs. Gailee argued that her signature was induced by an operative mistake and in support raised the ancient, but relevant, plea of *non est factum* ("it is not my act").

The case eventually reached the House of Lords, by which time Mrs. Gailee had died and Mr. Saunders had become her representative.

Held: A plea of *non est factum* will only succeed if:

1. There is a *fundamental* difference between the legal effect of the document signed and the effect the signor believed it to have; and
2. The signor's mistake has not been made carelessly.

In this case Mrs. Gailee failed on both counts. She believed she was signing a transfer of the house and this was so; and she signed the document without reading it. The building society owned the house.

The court did indicate that if in a similar case the signor were senile, blind, illiterate or suffering from some other disability, they would be prepared to allow the person "equitable relief". In the present dispute there was no evidence to this effect.

Joscelyne v. *Nissen* (1970)

The owner of a car hire business agreed orally to transfer it to his daughter. Part of her "consideration" was a promise to pay the owner's household expenses: gas, electricity, coal, etc. The agreement was then expressed in a binding written form. By mistake, the written agreement failed to refer to the daughter's liability to pay the household expenses.

The court exercised its equitable powers and ordered that the contract should be rectified (corrected) and this enabled the owner to enforce his daughter's promise to pay the household expenses.

Smith v. *Land and House Property Corporation* (1884)

The plaintiff offered for sale a hotel, stating it was let "to Mr. Frederick Fleck (a most desirable tenant)". The defendants agreed to buy the hotel but later discovered that Mr. Fleck had not paid his rent for five months. They claimed the right to avoid the contract for misrepresentation. The plaintiff argued that the description of the tenant was merely an expression of opinion.

The court allowed the contract to be avoided, finding that the description was a statement of fact. It was an assertion that nothing had occurred in the relationship between landlord and tenant to make the tenant an unsatisfactory one. The plaintiff knew this assertion was untrue.

Lloyds Bank Ltd v. *Bundy* (1975)

An elderly farmer and his son had been customers of the plaintiff bank for many years. The son had founded a company which also had an account with the bank. The company was overdrawn and Bundy senior acted as a guarantor for the company's overdraft.

In 1969 the manager from the bank visited Bundy senior and told him that continuance of the company's overdraft depended upon him guaranteeing it, with his farm as security.

The bank manager did not advise Bundy senior to seek independent advice, and the farmer signed a contract guaranteeing the overdraft. Later, a dispute arose. Bundy claimed that this was a case of undue influence.

The Court of Appeal *held* that the contract could be avoided for undue influence; a "special relationship" of confidence existed between the defendant and the bank.

Lord Denning said: "English law gives relief to one who, without independent advice, enters into a contract upon terms which are very unfair or transfers property for a consideration which is grossly inadequate, when his bargaining power is grievously impaired by reason of his own needs or desires, or by his own ignorance or infirmity, coupled with undue influence or pressures brought to bear on him by or for the benefit of the other."

LEGAL CAPACITY

An agreement will not be a valid contract if one of the parties lacks the legal competency, power or fitness to enter into and be bound by it. Such a party does not have contractual capacity (ability).

Usually, persons (human and "artificial") do have the capacity to enter into and be found by agreements. However, there are two types of persons who do not have this capacity:

1. Minors (formerly called infants)

A minor is a person under the age of 18: Family Law Reform Act 1969. A minor cannot make a binding contract: Infants Relief Act 1874.

The law does not prevent a minor entering into an agreement, but the agreement can only be enforced *by* and not *against* the minor.

E.g.: A 16-year-old makes an agreement to buy a television on credit terms. The shopkeeper fails to enquire as to the age of the purchaser. After the television is delivered, the credit payments are not made. Because of the age of the buyer no action can be brought for breach of contract. (The television set cannot be recovered unless obtained by fraud or misrepresentation, which is not the case here.)

There are two exceptions when minors will be bound by agreements:

1. *Agreements for Necessaries*
   A minor must pay a reasonable price for necessary goods and services. "Necessaries" are goods and services supplied at a time when *needed* for the "lifestyle" of the minor.

   E.g.: A 17-year-old homeless person enters separate contracts to rent a flat, buy food and hire a music centre. He is bound by the first two agreements, and must pay reasonable prices under them, but not by the third agreement, as a music centre is not necessary: *Nash* v. *Inman* and *Chapple* v. *Cooper* (see page 33).

2. *Agreements Beneficial to the Minor*
   Agreements of services concerned with employment, apprenticeship and education are said to be beneficial to the minor and enforceable against him: *Chapple* v. *Cooper.*

   E.g.: A minor enters an agreement with a college to follow an educational course for 12 months. The course fees are due by instalments, but the student defaults on the payments. He is liable to pay as the agreement is for his benefit. *Doyle* v. *White City Stadiums* (see page 34).

Agreements connected with trading (buying and selling) are not included within this exception even if beneficial to the minor: *Cowern* v. *Nield* (see page 34).

2. Insane or Drunk Persons

A person who is insane, or under the influence of drink or drugs will not be bound by an agreement if at the time:

1. He is incapable of understanding the nature of the agreement; and,
2. The other party knows or ought to know of his incapacity.

Authorities on Legal Capacity

Family Law Reform Act 1969

A minor is a person under the age of 18 and he attains 18 "at the commencement of the (18th) anniversary of his birth". (Previously the age of majority was 21.)

Infants Relief Act 1874

All agreements entered into by minors, whether for money lent or goods (and services) supplied, other than necessaries, are unenforceable against the minor.

Nash v. *Inman* (1908)

A Savile Row tailor supplied clothing to a minor. The clothes included eleven "fancy" waistcoats. When the goods were supplied the minor was a student. The court heard evidence from his father that his son was amply supplied with clothes at the time of the sale.

Held: The goods were not needed for the lifestyle of the minor. The agreement, not being for necessaries, could not be enforced.

Chapple v. *Cooper* (1844)

A widow, who was also a minor, entered an agreement with an undertaker for his services in carrying out the funeral of her deceased husband. After the funeral, she refused to pay him, claiming "minority" as her defence. The undertaker sued on the basis that the work done was necessary. The case was decided in favour of the undertaker. A decent burial was the right of every man and necessary to him and his close relations.

The court added that everyone needs food, lodgings, education or training, the extent of such goods and services depending on the status or lifestyle of the minor. Articles of mere luxury are never necessary but "luxurious articles of utility" (usefulness) may in some cases be necessary.

Doyle v. *White City Stadiums Ltd* (1935)

A minor, who was a professional boxer, entered into an agreement to fight "win, lose or draw" for payment of £3000. The agreement bound him to the rules of the British Boxing Board of Control. The rules stipulated that any boxer who was disqualified, forfeited his "purse". In the match he was disqualified for hitting below the belt. He brought an action claiming that as a minor the agreement was not enforceable *against* him but was enforceable *by* him, hence he was entitled to the £3000.

The court *held* that the agreement (and so the rules) amounted to a valid contract. Taken as a whole it operated for his benefit as a professional boxer. The rules encouraged "clean fighting" and this enabled him to pursue his career.

Cowern v. *Nield* (1912)

A minor carried on a business selling hay and clover. He was paid in advance for a consignment, but he failed to deliver any hay and the buyer refused to take delivery of the clover, which was "rotten". The buyer claimed breach of contract.

It was *held* that the agreement was unenforceable against the minor. The fact that the agreement benefited him did not make him liable on it. Only certain agreements could be enforceable against a minor: for necessaries or for apprenticeship or services. A trading agreement did not come within these categories.

LAWFULNESS OF CONTRACT

An agreement cannot be enforced in the courts if it is against the law.

Agreements against the law can be classified as follows:

Agreements Unenforceable by Statute

Parliament has designated certain kinds of agreements against the public interest. These include:

1. *Restrictive Trade Practices*

   Agreements to restrict the manufacture, supply or distribution of goods.

   E.g.: Two firms of coat wholesalers agree to limit the supply of coats to retailers to keep the prices high. Such an agreement is void.

2. *Resale Price Maintenance*

   Agreements between suppliers and retailers of goods to fix minimum resale prices to consumers.

E.g.: A chocolate supplier wishes to enter into separate agreements with retail outlets imposing minimum resale prices. Such agreements would be void.

For 1. and 2. see the Resale Prices Act 1976 (see page 36).

3. *Waging and Gaming Agreements*

Under the Gaming Act 1845 and subsequent legislation a betting dispute cannot be challenged in the courts.

E.g.: A customer has placed a bet on a horse race with a firm of bookmakers ("turf accountants"). The bookmakers refuse, without reason, to pay the customer his alleged winnings. The courts would not recognise the transaction as legally enforceable.

Agreements Unenforceable under Common Law

The courts have decided that certain kinds of agreements are against "public policy". This can be defined as a principle of law which says no person can do that which tends to injure the public good.

Examples of agreements against "public policy" include:

1. *Agreements to Commit Criminal or Civil Wrongs*

E.g.: A businessman, in order to collect insurance money, pays a criminal £1000 to burn down his business premises. The criminal takes the money but fails to carry out the crime. The businessman would be unsuccessful in suing the criminal for the return of the money.

2. *Agreements for Immoral Purposes*

E.g.: A married but childless company director agrees to promote one of his female staff if she will bear him a child. She agrees, but after the child is born, she refuses to give the baby to him. He sues her for breach of contract. Such an agreement is regarded as immoral and unenforceable: *Pearce* v. *Brooks* (see page 36).

3. *Agreements in Unreasonable Restraint of Trade*

Any restriction on a person's normal freedom to carry on a trade, business or profession is called a restraint of trade and is contrary to public policy.

E.g.: An 18-year-old college-leaver enters an agreement with a firm of accountants. He agrees that in return for them training him as a qualified accountant he will then stay with the firm for 10 years. Five years after he is qualified he leaves the firm to work for himself. He is entitled to do so as the agreement is in restraint of trade: *Morris* v. *Saxelby* (see page 36).

A restraint of trade agreement can be a valid enforceable contract if it is proved to be reasonable. A restraint will be reasonable if it protects a legitimate business interest *and* is not excessive.

E.g.: A businessman buys a shop, and part of the price includes a sum for "goodwill' (see page 163). The agreement stipulates that the vendor (seller) will not set up in competition with the purchaser within "half a mile" of the business premises. After the sale is completed the vendor attempts to set up a similar shop next door to the purchaser. It is probable that many of his previous customers will transfer their business to him. In such a case the court is likely to consider the restraint of trade reasonable and hence valid. There was a legitimate business interest to protect (goodwill) and the restraint was not excessive (half a mile): *Home Counties Dairies* v. *Skilton* (see page 37).

Authorities on Lawfulness of Contracts

Resale Prices Act 1976

This consolidates provisions formerly contained in the Restrictive Trade Practices Act 1956 and the Resale Prices Act 1964. Agreements between dealers based on the withholding or refusal to supply goods are void, as are agreements maintaining minimum prices at which goods are to be resold. Exceptionally, the Restrictive Practices Courts has the power to exempt such arrangements if proved to be in the public interest.

Note: Regulations made under Article 85 of the Treaty of Rome prohibit (with some exceptions) arrangements which restrain or prevent competition.

Pearce v. *Brooks* (1866)

A firm of coachbuilders let a carriage to a prostitute. The firm knew she was a prostitute and that she intended to use the carriage as a means of soliciting clients. She had agreed to purchase the carriage when she had enough money. But she failed to pay the agreed price and was sued for breach of contract. The court had to decide whether the agreement was enforceable. It decided that it was not. Although to let a carriage is not unlawful, to do so for an *immoral* purpose causes the agreement to be unenforceable.

Herbert Morris Ltd v. *Saxelby* (1916)

A skilled draughtsman worked for an engineering company. In his contract of employment he promised that for seven years after leaving his employment he would not engage in any similar business to that of his employers in any part of the UK.

The court had to decide whether this restraint of trade agreement was enforceable. The crucial question was the type of restraint sought by the company. They were attempting to restrain the employee from using his own technical skill and knowledge acquired in the service of the organisation – a restraint effectively preventing the employee competing with his employer. This was unenforceable. It was also unreasonably wide.

The court may have come to a different conclusion had the restraint protected trade secrets (secret formulae, processes or lists of information) or the employer had acquired influence over the employer's clients or customers.

Home Counties Dairies Ltd v. *Skilton* (1970)

A milkman agreed that for one year after leaving his employment he would not sell "milk or dairy produce" to customers to whom he had supplied his employers' goods during the final six months of his employment. The court had to decide whether the restraint was reasonable. The words "dairy produce" were too wide and were hence excessive as this would prohibit the employee engaging in a different trade, e.g. that of shopkeeper. If a restraint is too wide, the agreement is unenforceable as it is not the job of the courts to rewrite agreements. However, in limited cases the courts are prepared to conclude that the parties do not intend the words used as to impose such a wide restraint. This was the case here. The purpose of the restraint was to protect milk sales to the company's customers and the restraint was enforceable in respect of *milk* only.

TYPES OF CONTRACT

The purpose of examining the law of contract is to determine when a legally enforceable agreement exists and what are the rights and duties arising from such an agreement.

In *every* type of transaction where there exists a valid agreement it will be subject to the law of contract, e.g. supplying goods or services, employing people, owning property, etc.

By identifying various transactions that involve the law of contract it is also possible to identify different statutory laws that may apply to each activity *in addition* to the law of contract.

E.g.:

In Business Activity	*Law of Contract?*	*Additional Statutory Laws*	*Terminology*
Buying and selling goods	√	Sale of Goods Legislation	A contract for the sale of goods
Getting and keeping a job	√	Employment Legislation	A contract of employment
Renting shop premises	√	Law of Property Legislation	A contract for a lease

Sometimes a statutory law may modify the Law of Contract. The best example concerns land. Under the Law of Property Act 1925 a contract for the sale of land is not enforceable in the courts unless there is written evidence of the main terms of the contract.

E.g.: A trader agrees orally to sell his business premises to B. In breach of contract the trader sells the property to C. There is nothing B can do as his contract with the trader is unenforceable.

Note: Under the equitable doctrine of "part performance", where there has been a sufficient act of part performing a contract for the sale of land, the absence of written evidence will be disregarded by the courts.

Standard Form Contracts

A standard form contract can be defined as a contract in printed form containing standardised terms used for many contracts of the same kind. (See the example on page 213.)

SFCs are used extensively in all kinds of activities: transport, insurance, banking, financial services, trade, consumer sales, credit agreements, etc. All types of business organisations used standard forms, including nationalised industries, and there is even provision for "standard form" by statute, e.g. Table A of the Companies Act 1948.

By using an SFC, time spent negotiating separate arrangements is saved. Such a contract can also allocate contractual liability in advance, e.g. by placing certain responsibilities upon one party to insure against loss.

A TERM IN A CONTRACT

Definition: A provision or limitation in a contract creating an obligation.

E.g.: A buyer says to a seller, "I promise to pay you £500 for that car." It is a term of the contract that: (1) the buyer pays £500; (2) the seller gives him the car.

If one party to a contract fails to comply with a term, the other party has a *right* to claim damages for breach of contract.

Terms are of two types:

1. *An Express Term*: an obligation contained in a contract which is expressed in writing or orally.

   E.g.: A buyer writes or says to a seller: "I agree to pay £500 for your car".

2. *An Implied Term*: an obligation imposed by common law or statute into a contract.

   Terms will be imposed to give business effect to a contract: *The Moorcock* (see page 41); The Supply of Goods and Services Act 1982; and the Sale of Goods Act 1979, ss. 12–15 (see page 123–5).

   E.g.: A builder agrees to do some emergency repair work for a shopkeeper. After the work is completed the shopkeeper refuses to pay the builder as he "never agreed to pay in the first place". The law would imply a term that the shopkeeper pays a reasonable price for the work done.

An express term in a contract takes preference over an implied term except where statute law says otherwise. (See "Taking Responsibility and Disclaiming Liability", page 42.)

The Significance of a Contract Term

Parties to an agreement are free to make whatever terms they wish. However, if a term is against the law (criminal or civil) then the term, though not necessarily the contract, will be unenforceable in the courts.

A term, express or implied in a contract, is classified by the common law as either:

A Condition	or	*A Warranty*
A major obligation under the contract going "to the root" and fundamental to it.		A minor obligation under the contract, neither going "to the root" nor fundamental to it.

Breaking a term, whether a condition or a warranty entitles the innocent party to claim damages. However, the importance of the distinction between a condition and a warranty is that unless the parties agree otherwise, the law will only give a *right* to a party to end (discharge; see page 45) a contract when the other party has broken a condition: *Bettini* v. *Gye* (see below); *Poussard* v. *Spiers and Pond* (see page 41).

Sometimes contracting parties will refer to terms as conditions or warranties, e.g. "conditions of sale"; if the parties *intend* such terms to have effect as "conditions" in the *legal* sense, the courts will give effect to that intention, apart from exceptional cases: *Wickman Ltd* v. *Schuler A.G.* (see below).

Authorities on Contract Terms

Wickman Ltd v. *Schuler A.G.* (1974) (HC)

A term in a distribution agreement said that it was "a condition" of the contract that the distributor would visit six named customers once a week. The number of visits under the contract was to be about 1400.

In breach of contract the distributor failed to make a visit on one occasion and the innocent party claimed to be entitled to end the whole agreement.

The court said the effect of the breach was so trivial there was no right to end the contract. The breach was of a "warranty".

Bettini v. *Gye* (1876)

The plaintiff, an opera singer, entered into a written contract with the defendant, the director of the Royal Italian Opera in London. Under the contract the plaintiff agreed to sing in concerts and operas in the UK from 30 March 1875 to 13 July 1875, and "to be in London without fail at least six days *before* the commencement of his engagement, for the purpose of rehearsals".

The plaintiff was prevented by illness from arriving in London before 28 March, but he did arrive on that day and was ready and willing to perform his agreement. The defendant declined to accept the plaintiff's services, and put an end to the agreement.

The court had to decide whether the term had effect as a "condition" or as a "warranty". It said that this depended upon an interpretation of the contract taken as a whole, in the absence of any express declaration. The obligation of the plaintiff was to sing (in concerts and operas) for 15 weeks, and his failure to attend at rehearsals could only affect the performances during the first one or two weeks.

This did not go to the "root of the matter", so as to classify the obligation as a condition. The plaintiff was therefore entitled to damages for the defendant's wrongful ending of the contract.

Note: If a contract of employment is only for a short time, attendance for the whole period of the employment would then be a vital part of the agreement.

Poussard v. *Spiers and Pond* (1876)

Madame Poussard made a contract to sing at various operas. The first performance was announced for 28 November 1874. On 23 November Madame Poussard was taken ill and the defendants engaged another artiste, Miss Lewis, for the part. On 4 December Madame Poussard, having recovered from her illness, offered to take the part but was refused; she then brought this action.

The court *held* that the illness was a serious one, of uncertain duration, and that in the circumstances the defendants were justified in treating the breach as fundamental (a condition) *and* ending the contract with Madame Poussard.

The Moorcock (1889)

The defendants owned a wharf and made a contract to allow the plaintiffs to unload their ship at the wharf. The ship was damaged by settling at low water on a ridge of hard ground. It was *held* that the defendants were liable for this damage as they were in breach of an implied term that they would take reasonable care to see that the berth was safe.

There are a number of occasions when the court, subject to the express terms and statute law, will imply a term (condition or warranty) into a contract, i.e.

1. If this is to give effect to the presumed intentions of the parties; or
2. In accordance with trade usage; or
3. Because of a pattern of previous dealing between the parties; or
4. Where the court regards it as "just" to do so.

THE LEGAL EFFECT OF CONTRACT TERMS

1. A person who signs a contractual document is bound by the terms of it. In *L'Estrange* v. *Gracob* (1934) the court said failure by one party to read an agreement is no defence. But if the effect of the term is to take away a legal right this may be so. (See "Taking Responsibility and Disclaiming Liability", page 42.)
2. A pre-contract representation (e.g. an oral statement) may be treated by the court as a term of the contract.

E.g.: A dealer selling a car tells a customer the vehicle is "of excellent quality"; the buyer is convinced and buys the car; soon afterwards the engine explodes due to an obvious defect in it. Because the dealer ought to have known the true position, the statement by the dealer would be treated as a term of the contract.

A written contract will often disclaim any responsibility for pre-contract statements (but see below). A pre-contract which is false and which is not a term may be a misrepresentation (see page 27).

3. A term cannot be introduced into an agreement *after* the contract is formed. In *Olley* v. *Marlborough Court Hotel Ltd* (1948) a guest at a hotel was not bound by a notice in the hotel room after making the contract at the reception desk.

4. An essential term which is uncertain means there is no contract.

5. A term which is unclear or ambiguous (i.e. capable of more than one interpretation) and is not essential to the agreement will not end the contract. A meaningless term can be ignored; a vague term can be clarified by previous dealings or trade custom. An ambiguous term is *interpreted* (by the courts) against the person imposing it, providing "this works no wrong". This is called the *contra preferentem* rule.

TAKING RESPONSIBILITY AND DISCLAIMING LIABILITY

Introduction

E.g.: A person who owns land will often put a warning sign on the land: "Trespassers will be prosecuted."

A person in business premises will regularly do the same in suitably modified form: "Customers must not go beyond this point," or "Staff only".

Such warnings or restrictions can arise in *all* types of business relationships, not just those connected with land. For instance, activities connected with the supply of goods and services may carry a warning. Goods that are being sold may be labelled: "Use with care – follow attached instructions."

Alternatively the goods may carry a restriction: "It is the sole responsibility of the buyer to follow the instructions when using the goods."

Sometimes, as in the above examples, a warning or restriction will refer to the apportionment of responsibility. However, on other occasions the extent of one party's legal *liability* will be expressed as restricted *or* non-existent. A label on goods may read: "The manufacturer is not liable for loss, damage or injuries caused by these goods for whatever reason." In such a case the manufacturer is attempting to *disclaim* any liability at all.

When a party in business or other activities (e.g. under a contract) attempts to so disclaim liability, perhaps by a term in a standard form contract or by a notice given to persons generally, the disclaimer is known as an "exemption clause".

Most exemption clauses are nowadays subject to the Unfair Contract Terms Act (UCTA) 1977 (summarised below). Broadly, the effect of this Act is to declare void any clause which purports to remove an obligation or duty resulting from negligence (liability) or which tries to take away a right to a claim for failing to perform a contract as agreed (i.e. disclaiming responsibility).

E.g.: A standard form of employment might state that the employer is "not responsible for injury to employees howsoever caused, whether or not by the employer's fault, neglect, breach of contract or other breach of duty".

An employee is injured in the course of his job by the careless behaviour of the employer. The employee can disregard this term and bring a claim for damages.

As its title reveals, the 1977 Act was created to tackle "unfair" contracts. The history of exclusion clauses reveals an abuse of "freedom of contract". Certain powerful persons, e.g. large organisations, drafted contracts mainly in standard form in a way that the less powerful person had little or no choice but to submit to exclusion (of liability) clauses. These so-called "take it or leave it" terms meant that an individual had to agree to the terms or do without the goods or services.

Not every contract will be subject to the UCTA 1977; in such cases the courts will usually interpret an exemption clause against the party relying on it, as they did before the Act: the *contra preferentem* rule (see page 42).

THE UNFAIR CONTRACT TERMS ACT 1977

S1

Generally, this Act only applies to business liability, i.e., activities in the course of a business or from the occupation of premises used for business purposes of the occupier.

"Negligence" in this Act means:

The breach of an obligation or duty to take care imposed by contract or tort, *or*,

The breach of the common duty of care imposed by the Occupiers' Liability Act 1957.

S2(1)

A person cannot by a contract term or a notice given to persons generally exclude or restrict his liability for death or personal injury resulting from negligence.

S2(2)

In the case of other loss or damage a person cannot exclude or restrict liability for negligence unless the term or notice is "reasonable".

S3

A party cannot by a contract term: exclude or restrict liability for breach of contract, or claim to render a substantially different performance from that reasonably expected, or render no performance at all, unless in all cases just mentioned the term is reasonable.

This section only applies where one party deals as a consumer or on the other's written standard terms of business.

S5

In the case of goods ordinarily supplied for private use or consumption the terms of a "guarantee" of goods cannot exclude liability for loss or damage caused by defects in those goods.

S6(1)

A person cannot by a contract term exclude or restrict liability for s. 12 of the Sale of Goods Act 1979 or the corresponding thing in relation to hire-purchase.

S6(2)

In a consumer sale a person cannot by a contract term exclude or restrict liability for ss. 13–15 of the Sale of Goods Act 1979, or the corresponding thing in relation to hire-purchase. In a non-consumer sale or non-consumer hire-purchase there can be no exclusion or restriction of liability unless the term is reasonable.

S7

In contracts for the supply of goods implied terms as to title cannot be excluded or restricted. The implied terms concerning description, merchantable quality, fitness for purpose and sample cannot be excluded or restricted except in non-consumer sales if the exclusion is reasonable.

S11

In deciding what is reasonable all the circumstances known or which ought to have been known by the parties at the time of the contract or "notice" are considered. These include:

Schedule 2: *a)* the bargaining positions of the parties;

b) whether the customer knew or ought to have known of the exemption clause.

S12

A party to a contract "deals as consumer" if:

1. He does not make the contract in the course of a business; and
2. The other party does make the contract in the course of a business; and
3. In the case of a sale of goods or hire-purchase contract the goods are of a type ordinarily supplied for private use or consumption.

S14

"Business" includes a profession and the activities of any government department or local or public authority. "Notice" includes an announcement, whether or not in writing.

Schedule 1. Sections 2–4 of this Act do not apply to any contract of insurance, creation or transfer of land, patent, trade mark, copyright, registered design, formation or dissolution of a company, partnership or rights of its members.

ENDING A CONTRACT

Contractual rights give rise to corresponding contractual obligations, i.e.

RIGHTS = DUTIES

When all the duties under a contract come to an end, so do the rights. The contract is said to be "discharged", i.e. ended.

The ending of a contract can be classified under four headings:

Discharge by Performance

The complete performance of the obligations under a contract will bring it to an end.

Discharge by Breach

The breach of a condition under a contract gives the innocent party a right to treat the contract as at an end (see page 39).

Discharge by Agreement

A contract may:

1. Contain a term providing for the ending of the agreement at any time; or,
2. Come to an end before time by both parties agreeing to it being ended.

If one party seeks to end a contract prematurely, without performing his obligations, he is in breach of contract.

Discharge by Frustration

In exceptional cases a contract can be ended in law by frustration (subsequent impossibility) when an event occurs making the contract impossible to perform.

An event will only frustrate a contract if:

1. It causes the contract to be radically different in nature; and
2. Neither party caused this; and
3. There was no provision in the contract for such an event.

E.g.: An employee, due to a serious and permanent illness is unable to continue to perform his contract of employment.

E.g.: A commercial vessel is "requisitioned" by the Government (due to outbreak of war) hence frustrating holiday voyage contracts between a travel firm and its passengers.

A contract will not be frustrated purely because it has become unprofitable. In *Davis Contractors Ltd* v. *Fareham UDC* (1956) a builder was unsuccessful in claiming "frustration" due to an increase in the cost of labour and materials.

By ss. 1–2 of the Law Reform (Frustrated Contracts) Act 1943, where frustration occurs money paid can be recovered and money payable ceases to be payable. The court has a discretion to allow either party to recover expenses or to retain money already paid.

CONTRACTS AND AGENCY

Agency – The relationship where a person called an agent, "A", makes a contract on behalf of someone else called a principal, "P", with a third party, "T".

E.g.: A film actor (P) engages a theatrical agent (A) to negotiate an agreement on his behalf with a film company (T).

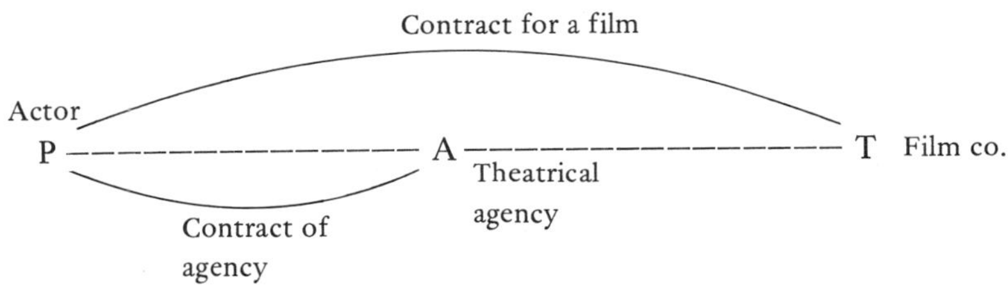

There is a contract between P and A providing both have legal capacity and the other essentials of a valid agreement exist. The agent usually collects a fee or payment from his principal for services rendered.

There is *also* a contract between principal and agent called a contract of agency.

Contracts of agency arise in a variety of business transactions: an employee often acts as an agent for his employer, bringing the latter into contractual contact with customers; a travel agent acts for a traveller; a partner in a firm may be an agent of that firm; and a company director often acts as agent for his company.

A person may be an agent without using the word "agent", e.g. a broker. Conversely it is unlikely that a person calling himself a "motor agent" is really an agent in the *legal* sense.

Formation of a Contract of Agency

1. *Express Agreement* – The agent is appointed in writing or orally by the principal.
2. *Implied Agreement* – The courts imply into a relationship that a contract of agency exists.
3. *"Estoppel"* – In some cases a principal is stopped (estopped) by law from denying that a particular person is his agent.

   In *Watteau* v. *Fenwick* (1893) the court decided that although the manager of a public house had been told not to order goods on credit, the owner of the public house was stopped by law from denying to the supplier his employee had such authority by virtue of his position as manager. The manager had apparent authority.

4. *Ratification* – Sometimes a contract made by "A" on behalf of "P" may be confirmed (ratified) even though at the time of the agreement "A" had no authority to bind "P". The effect of a valid ratification is retrospective, i.e. the contract from the start becomes one not between "A" and "T" but between "P" and "T".
5. *Necessity* – In exceptional cases the law may rule that "A" acted as "P"s agent where "A" was placed in a position of "urgent necessity". "A" is deemed an agent of necessity.

Obligations of Agent and Principal

The significance of a contract of agency is that the law imposes obligations upon both agent and principal, default enabling the innocent party to claim breach of the contract of agency.

An agent must:

1. Carry out his instructions within his express or implied authority.
2. Display proper skill and care.
3. Act honestly, i.e. in good faith towards his principal.
4. Account to the principal for money and property received.

The principal must:

1. Pay the agent for his services unless agreed otherwise.
2. Indemnify (reimburse) the agent for expenses incurred.

The agent has a right of:

3. *Lien* – a right to retain property belonging to his principal as security for unpaid services.

The Position of the Third Party

Generally a third party (T) can only claim against an agent upon *the contract between T and P* if:

1. The agent (A) fails to notify the third party (T) that he is acting as agent, i.e. the principal (P) is undisclosed; *or*
2. The agent gives a personal undertaking to be responsible on that contract.

If an agent discloses he is acting for a principal but exceeds his authority, the third party may claim "breach of warranty of authority" against the agent.

Termination of Contract of Agency

The agreement may be ended by either party notifying the other of its termination or they may agree to this collectively. Otherwise the agreement can be automatically ended by law, e.g. the death or insanity of either principal or agent.

THE LAW OF TORTS

THE TORT OF NEGLIGENCE

The modern basis of the legal duty to take care arises from the ruling of Lord Atkin in the leading case of *Donoghue* v. *Stevenson* when he said: "A duty of care is owed to our neighbour, and our neighbour is anyone we can reasonably foresee would be likely to be injured by our acts or ommissions."

To succeed in an action for the tort of negligence a plaintiff must prove:

1. The defendant owed him a legal duty of care; and
2. That the legal duty of care was broken; and
3. As a result of breaking the legal duty of care the plaintiff suffered damages.

A business owes the legal duty of care to its employees, customers, clients and other businesses. In particular, a manufacturer of products which are sold in such a way as to show that the manufacturer intends them to reach the ultimate consumer in the form in which they left him owes a duty to the consumer to take reasonable care.

The duty of care extends to careless acts, omissions or statements.

The duty of care will *not* arise in certain relationships, e.g. by an occupier of land to a trespasser (see under the tort of Occupiers' Liability, page 53).

The task of proving negligence is placed upon the person who asserts it, though the burden of proof sometimes shifts to the defendant to disprove negligence.

Authorities on Negligence

Donoghue v. *Stevenson* (1932)

Two women went into a cafe and ordered ginger beer. The bottle which Mrs. Donoghue received was bought for her by her friend from the proprietor (the retailer), who in turn had purchased the beer from the manufacturer, Stevenson. When pouring out her second glass of ginger beer Mrs. Donoghue saw the remains of a decomposed snail which had been at the bottom of the bottle. In consequence she became seriously ill and claimed damages for negligence against the manufacturer.

The Law of Torts

Torts create duties:	upon persons generally, including business persons	EXAMPLES
A general duty of care	Negligence	Making goods
A duty in occupying land	Occupiers' liability	Occupying business premises
A duty to land	Trespass to land Nuisance *Rylands* v. *Fletcher*	Using land
A duty to goods	Trespass to goods Conversion	Using goods
A duty to other persons	Trespass to the person	Respecting customers and the public
A duty to tell the truth	Defamation	Respecting customers and the public
A duty to be original	"Passing off"	Creating new products

The House of Lords *held* Stevenson liable in negligence in allowing a snail to get into the bottle.

Note: The retailer could not be said to be negligent as it was not his fault that there were the remnants of a snail in a sealed opaque bottle. Mrs. Donoghue had no claim for breach of contract as any contractual relationships were between the buyer and seller of the ginger beer.

Wilsons and Clyde Ltd v. *English* (1938) – see also page 88

A coal miner employee was injured whilst working in his employer's mine. He contended that this was due to the negligence of his employers. The employers claimed that they were not liable as the responsibility of taking care of employees had been delegated to a competent colliery agent.

The court *held* that the employers could not delegate their duty in this way. It is the sole responsibility of an employer to provide a safe system of work, competent fellow workers and adequate materials. The employers had not discharged their duty and were liable to pay damages to the miner.

Hedley Byrne & Co. Ltd v. *Heller and Partners Ltd* (1963)

A company selling advertising obtained a written credit reference from a bank: the latter stated that a limited liability company called Easipower Ltd were good for credit. The statement proved to be incorrect and as a result the advertising company lost £17 000. They sued the bank for negligence. The court *held* that as the bank had stated at the time of giving the reference it was made "without responsibility on their part" and so they had excluded their duty. But if they had not issued such a disclaimer there would have been a duty owed by the bank to the advertising company.

Where damages are claimed for a purely negligent statement there must be a "special relationship" between the giver and receiver of the statement. Such a relationship would arise when a professional person gives advice in his professional capacity, e.g. as a lawyer, an accountant, a chartered surveyor, etc.

Mutual Life & Citizens' Assurance Co. Ltd v. *Evatt* (1971)

Evatt was a policy-holder in the defendant company. He obtained advice from them about investing money in a subsidiary company of theirs. On the basis of the information received he invested money which he lost as the information was wrong.

ırt decided that Evatt was not entitled to damages for the ; statement. There was no special relationship: an insurance ıny is not usually in the business of giving advice to policy- :rs *on investment.*

Dutton v. *Bognor Regis UDC* (1972)

In 1958 a local council building inspector negligently approved the foundations of a house subsequently built on a filled-in rubbish tip. The house was eventually sold to a Mrs. Dutton. Because of the inadequate foundations, cracks appeared in the house, and the internal walls started to subside. It was alleged that the defendant's inspector owed a duty to Mrs. Dutton.

The court *held* that in such circumstances a duty is owed not only to the original owner of the house but to all subsequent purchasers, and the defendants were vicariously liable for their building inspector's negligence.

Haley v. *London Electricity Board* (1965)

Haley, a blind man, was walking to his work in south-east London. He tripped over an obstacle placed by the LEB on the pavement beside a trench that the LEB had excavated. Haley fell into it and was badly injured. The obstacle consisted of a hammer hooked in the railings and resting on the pavement at an angle of thirty degrees. Haley was using a white stick as a guide, but the stick did not encounter the obstacle, with the result that instead of the obstacle warning him, he fell over it.

The court decided that although the hammer was adequate warning to sighted people, it was not adequate for unsighted or partially sighted persons. Furthermore, it was reasonable to expect blind persons to use this particular pavement and so in the circumstances the LEB had broken their duty of care to Haley and had to pay him damages.

Barnett v. *Chelsea and Kensington Hospital Management Committee* (1969)

A night watchman, Barnett, arrived at the defendant's hospital in the early hours of the morning and complained of vomiting after drinking tea. He was sent home without being examined and was told by a member of the hospital staff to contact his own doctor later that day. A few hours later Barnett died of arsenic poisoning. The defendants were sued for negligence. The court *held* that although there was a duty of care owed and a breach of it, the carelessness of the hospital did not *cause* Barnett's death. Even if he had been examined and treated by a doctor it would, on the medical evidence, still have been impossible to save his life.

Scott v. *London and St Katherine Dock Co.* (1865)

The plaintiff was standing near the door of the defendant's warehouse when he was injured by some bags of flour which fell onto him from the upper part of the warehouse. He sued the owners who claimed that there was *no evidence* that they were negligent.

The court said the "facts speak for themselves" (the doctrine of *res ipsa loquitur*) and it was the defendants who had to disprove negligence and if they could not do this they would be liable.

So, if a person controls something (e.g. a warehouse) and an accident occurs which clearly suggests lack of control, then – in the absence of an explanation – it is presumed that there was negligence *unless* proved otherwise.

OCCUPIERS' LIABILITY

There is a legal duty owed by an occupier of land to visitors. By the Occupiers' Liability Act 1957, s.2, an occupier of premises owes a common duty of care to all his visitors.

The common duty of care is a duty to take such care as in all the circumstances is reasonable to see that the visitor will be reasonably safe in using the premises for the purposes for which he is invited or permitted by the occupier to be there. The occupier must be prepared for children to be less careful than adults.

The occupier may expect that a person, in the exercise of his calling, will appreciate and guard against any special risks ordinarily incidental to it.

An "occupier" is a person who has control of land, e.g. tenant or owner. A "visitor" is a person who, expressly or impliedly, is invited or permitted to be on land. The common duty of care is *not* owed to a trespasser, but nevertheless an occupier does owe to a trespasser a duty of common humanity: *British Railways Board* v. *Herrington* (see page 54).

Fisher v. *C.H.T. Ltd* (1966)

Crockford's, a London club, obtained the services of an independent company to manage their restaurant and club premises. Fisher was employed by the independent company to replaster the restaurant and whilst doing this he was injured. A question arose as to who were the "occupiers". The court decided that it was *both* Crockford's and the restauranteurs; although the latter controlled the restaurant, the former had sufficient control over the premises *as a whole* to make them "occupiers".

British Railways Board v. *Herrington* (1972)

A fence separated an electrified railway line from a children's playground. The fence was in a state of disrepair and adults often climbed through it as a "short cut". Children frequently did the same and this fact was known to the station-master, but nothing was done to repair the fence.

Herrington, a six-year-old boy, climbed through the fence and was injured by a live rail. He claimed damages for negligence against British Railways. They said they owed no duty of care to a trespasser.

The House of Lords *held* that a trespasser is not owed by an occupier the same duty of care as a visitor. But there is a duty to trespassers to take such steps as common sense or common humanity dictates. This will depend on what a humane person could reasonably be expected to have done before an accident. If he knew there was a probability of trespassers coming onto his land and did nothing to prevent it, he is liable; this was the case here.

THE TORT OF NUISANCE

This is a legal duty not to interfere wrongfully with another person's enjoyment of land.

Definition of the Tort of Nuisance: the unlawful interference with another's use or enjoyment or rights in relation to land. There are two types of nuisance, public and private:

1. *Public Nuisance*: unlawful interference or harm which affects the public generally. It is also a crime as well as a tort and the person responsible can be prosecuted.
2. *Private Nuisance*: If a plaintiff can establish that someone has interfered with his land unreasonably, he is entitled to claim damages under this tort: *Sedleigh-Denfield* v. *O'Callaghan* (see page 55).

Authorities on Nuisance

Tarry v. *Ashton* (1876)

Ashton was the tenant of a house which had a large lamp fixed to the outside wall overhanging the road. He employed a contractor to repair the lamp but due to the negligence of the contractor the fittings were not properly repaired and the lamp fell on the plaintiff. It was *held* that the defendant was liable (vicariously) as he was in breach of his duty not to create a public nuisance.

A private individual is entitled to sue for public nuisance where he can show that he has suffered some loss or harm over and above that suffered by the public at large.

Halsey v. *Esso Petroleum Co. Ltd* (1961)

Smoke and smut were emitted from the defendant's chimneys causing damage to the plaintiff's clothes which had been hung out to dry on a clothes line. His car, which was parked on a public road, was also damaged. Halsey won his claim in private nuisance for the damage to the clothes. The damage to the car – though not being an interference with the enjoyment of his land – was actionable in public nuisance.

Sedleigh-Denfield v. *O'Callaghan* (1940)

"A balance has to be maintained between the right of an occupier to do what he likes with his own land, and the right of a neighbour not to be interfered with. It is impossible to give any precise formula, but it may broadly be said that a useful test is *what is reasonable* according to the ordinary uses of mankind living in society": Lord Wright

Christie v. *Davey* (1893)

Christie, a music teacher, used her house for frequent practice and musical evenings. Davey lived in adjoining semi-detached premises and the music coming from Christie's house annoyed Davey to a great extent. Whenever lessons were in progress he banged trays on the party wall, whistled, shrieked and shouted. Christie obtained an injunction against Davey, who acted maliciously and unreasonably, and was therefore liable.

Polsue and Alfieri Ltd v. *Rushmer* (1907)

The plaintiff lived in Fleet Street next door to the defendant company, who had installed some printing machinery in their premises. The noise of the machinery kept the plaintiff and his family awake at night. He was granted an injunction: a court order compelling the company to cease the noise at night.

In some areas a certain amount of noise must be expected, though in this case the company had made a serious and unacceptable addition to the noise.

Robinson v. *Kilvert* (1889)

The defendants manufactured paper boxes in the cellar of a house, and leased the floor above to the plaintiff. The cellar was heated by the manufacturers with hot dry air. This raised the temperature of the plaintiff's premises, which were used for storing brown paper. Because of its special sensitivity and quality the paper was affected by the hot dry air and lost its value. The plaintiff claimed damages for nuisance.

The court decided that the defendant was not liable. The heating of the premises would not have damaged ordinary brown paper and the real cause of the damage was the extreme delicacy of the paper stored by the plaintiff.

Bliss v. *Hall* (1838)

The defendant used his tallow factory for making candles. The factory emitted noxious fumes for about three years. The plaintiff, who had recently purchased a house nearby, claimed private nuisance. The defendant contended that he could not be liable as the plaintiff "came to the nuisance". The court *held* this was no defence, and damages were awarded accordingly.

THE TORT OF TRESPASS

This is a legal duty not to interfere wrongfully with land, goods or another person.

The Tort of Trespass to Land

The unjustifiable, direct and immediate interference with another person's possession of land, e.g. walking on land without permission or legal authority; "every invasion of private property, be it so minute, is a trespass": *Entick* v. *Carrington* (1765).

The Tort of Trespass to Goods

See the Torts (Interference with Goods) Act 1977, page 57.

The Tort of Trespass to the Person

A wrong suffered by a person in the nature of either assault, battery or false imprisonment.

1. *Assault*: a crime and a tort resulting from an act by which a person intentionally, or possibly recklessly, causes another to fear the immediate application to himself of unlawful physical violence, e.g. a person who – in a threatening manner – lifts an office chair above the head of another person. The word "assault" often includes "battery".
2. *Battery*: a crime and a tort involving the actual and intended use of unlawful physical force on a person without his consent. It includes the slightest force; no actual harm need result. (Merely touching a person to draw his attention to something is not a battery.)
3. *False Imprisonment*: the direct and intentional infliction of some bodily restraint which is not expressly or impliedly authorised by law.

E.g.: A shopkeeper wrongly detains someone in his premises mistakenly believing the person to be a "shoplifter".

Authorities on Trespass

Gregory v. *Piper* (1829)

An employer ordered his employee to put some rubbish near to, but not touching, a neighbour's wall. The employee did this as carefully as possible but some of the rubbish fell on the wall and the owner successfully sued for trespass to land, i.e. to his wall.

Stephens v. *Myers* (1830)

The plaintiff was at a parish meeting seated some seven or eight places from the defendant, who was disagreeing with the remarks made by the plaintiff. The defendant started to shout at the plaintiff and go towards him with a clenched fist, but was stopped by the vicar who was sitting nearby. The defendant was liable for assault.

Meering v. *Grahame White Aviation Co.* (1919)

The plaintiff, Meering, worked in a factory owned by the defendant. Meering was asked to accompany two works security officers to the works office to answer some questions about certain thefts at the factory. He did so voluntarily and was unaware he was suspected of being involved in the crimes. When he was being questioned in the office he did not know that the two security officers were waiting outside and they would have stopped him from leaving the office if necessary. He later discovered that he was suspected of the crimes and learnt about the "guards" on the office.

Meering brought an action for "false imprisonment" and won his case. This tort protects freedom of movement and it was irrelevant that Meering was unaware *at the time* of the restriction put upon him.

Torts (Interference with Goods) Act 1977

This Act brings together and redefines various torts affecting goods, in particular the tort of trespass to goods and the tort of conversion.

Trespass to Goods: the wrongful interference with the *possession* of goods of another person.

E.g.: In *Fouldes* v. *Willoughby* (1841). Willoughby was the manager of a ferry boat. Fouldes embarked on the ferry with his horses. The parties had an argument and in order to get Fouldes to leave the boat, Willoughby turned the horses off the boat. Fouldes remained on the boat and crossed to the other side of the river. The court said that Willoughby would be liable for trespass to goods, i.e. the horses.

Conversion: The wrongful interference with the *ownership* of goods of another person.

E.g.: In *Consolidated Co.* v. *Curtis* (1892) an auctioneer was handed by his client goods to sell. The client was not the owner; the auctioneer was unaware of this and sold the goods. He was held to be liable in conversion to the true owner.

THE TORT OF DEFAMATION

This is the legal duty to publish the truth.

Definition of Defamation: the publication of a false statement which tends to injure the reputation of a "person", or lower him in the eyes of reasonable people.

The two types of defamation are libel and slander.

Libel

The publication of a defamation in permanent form. This would usually be printed words, but radio and television broadcasts for general reception are treated as publications in permanent form.

Slander

The publication of a defamation in transient form. This would usually be spoken words, but includes gestures and mimes.

The main differences between libel and slander are as follows:

1. A plaintiff claiming libel need not prove he has suffered financial loss as a result of the defamation; a person claiming slander must prove he has suffered financial loss because of it, unless the publication suggests a person is unfit or incompetent for their work, or that a person is suffering from a contagious disease or that a woman is "unchaste".
2. Libel is a crime as well as a tort if it provokes a breach of the peace; slander would not amount to a crime.

The tort of defamation arises when it is proved that:

1. *The statement was defamatory*: mere insults or abuse do not amount to defamation.
2. *The statement refers to the plaintiff*: defamation is a tort against an individual's reputation and would not apply to remarks made about a group of persons, e.g. "All lawyers are crooks".

3. *That the statement was published*: a person's reputation will only suffer if the defamation is communicated to a third party: *Theaker* v. *Richardson* (see page 60).

Defences to Defamation

A defendant can escape liability if he can show one or more of the following:

1. *Justification*: If a statement is true or substantially true it cannot be defamatory.
2. *Fair comment*: opinion or comment on matters of public interest cannot be defamatory: e.g. "The Prime Minister is carrying out unfair policies".
3. *Privilege*: Statements made in the course of Parliamentary or Judicial proceedings are protected from defamation claims. Such statements are said to be "absolutely privileged" (protected) from successful claims for defamation. Certain other statements made and received to protect moral, legal or business interests often attract "qualified privilege" (protection). This means the statement cannot be defamatory unless made maliciously.
4. *Offer of amends*: Section 4 of the Defamation Act 1952 protects a person who innocently defames another. The defamer must apologise with a suitable correction and publicise the withdrawal of the statement, e.g. a newspaper which innocently defames a person would publish an apology and a correction.

Authorities on Defamation

Youssoupoff v. *MGM Pictures Ltd* (1934)

A film made by the defendants falsely suggested that the plaintiff had been raped by the monk Rasputin. The court decided the film was a libel and that the plaintiff was entitled to damages. The false suggestion in the film would tend to cause her to be shunned or avoided by reasonable people.

Lewis v. *Daily Telegraph Ltd* (1964)

The defendant newspaper stated that police officers (from the Fraud Squad) were making enquiries into the affairs of a certain company and mentioned the name of the Chairman. He claimed libel on the basis that the article was capable of meaning that he was guilty of fraud. The court *held* that the words were not capable of bearing that meaning. There is a distinction between a suggestion of guilt and a mere suspicion of it.

Theaker v. *Richardson* (1962)

A defamatory letter was written by the defendant. He sealed the letter in an envelope, addressed it in typescript to the plaintiff and put it through her letter-box. Her husband opened the envelope (believing it to be a circular) and read the contents. The court decided that there was a "publication" of the defamation and the question of whether the husband believed the accusation in the letter was irrelevant.

Watt v. *Longsdon* (1930)

The overseas manager of a company wrote a letter to a director (the defendant) making false and serious allegations about the plaintiff's morals. The defendant showed this letter to the other directors of the company and to the plaintiff's wife. The court decided that he was entitled to damages, as the publication of the letter to the plaintiff's wife was not made upon a "privileged" occasion; there was no interest or duty (moral, legal or business) to make the communication. The communication to the fellow directors was, however, "privileged".

Somerville v. *Hawkins* (1851)

The defendant told two of his employees that he was dismissing the plaintiff for "robbing him". When sued for defamation the defendant successfully claimed that the statement was protected by "qualified privilege" as he was protecting an interest in his property.

Bridgeman v. *Stockdale* (1953)

At an examination the invigilating officer, the defendant, told those taking part in the exam that Bridgeman had "cheated" and would get no marks. The defendant was mistaken and was sued for slander.

Because it was accepted in evidence that the remarks were not made maliciously and that Stockdale had a common interest to protect with those taking part in the exam, i.e. for a fair examination, Stockdale was protected by qualified privilege.

BREACH OF STATUTORY DUTY

Definition of statutory duties: legal duties created by Acts of Parliament.

To succeed in this tort a person must prove:

1. A statutory duty was owed *to him.*
2. The injury suffered must be of the type the statute was intended to prevent.

3. The defendant has broken the statutory duty.
4. The breach has caused the injury.

Authority

Clarkson v. *Modern Foundries Ltd* (1958)

A Factories Act said that factory owners should provide adequate ventilation to render harmless any impurities in the air (the atmosphere in the factory).

Clarkson worked in the defendant's factory for 10 years when it was discovered he was suffering from a lung disease (pneumoconiosis). He was able to prove the four elements of the tort (above) and was awarded damages.

THE TORT OF *RYLANDS* v. *FLETCHER* (1866)

The facts:

Fletcher employed an independent contractor to construct a reservoir on his land. Under the land were some disused mineshafts. These connected with Rylands' mines on neighbouring land, though no one was aware of this. The contractor did not fill in the shafts and when the reservoir was filled, the water burst through the old shafts and flooded Rylands' land.

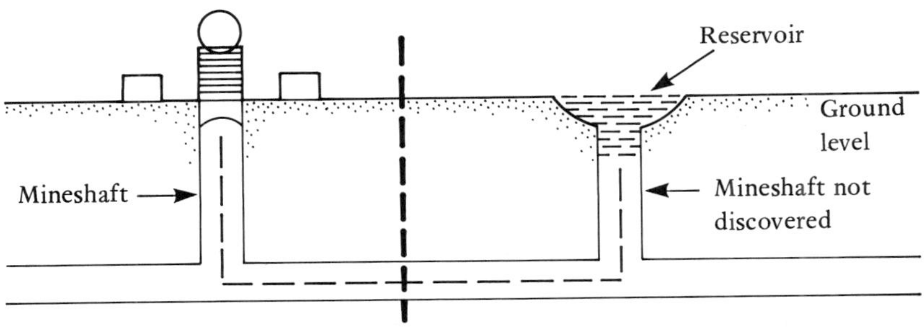

There was no evidence to show that Fletcher had been negligent. Nevertheless, he was held responsible and the court ruled: a person who for his own purposes brings onto his land and collects and keeps there anything likely to do harm if it escapes, must keep it at his own risk. If he does not do so, he is answerable for all the damage which is the natural consequence of its escape.

The rule has been applied to various kinds of things, including electricity, wire fencing and explosives. A landowner is said to be strictly liable, and it is no defence for him to claim he was not negligent or that the damage was caused by an independent contractor.

The rule only applies to things which the occupier brings onto his land and keeps there, and the courts have interpreted it in such a way that it only applies to things brought onto land that are used in a dangerous way.

A landowner is not liable if the "escape" of something is due to:

1. An Act of God – e.g. an exceptional storm or rainfall which would not have been reasonably anticipated.
2. An act of a *stranger* — the unlawful act of a third party over whom the defendant had no control.

Perry v. *Kendricks Transport Ltd* (1956)

A transport company parked a coach on their land. A young boy threw a lighted match into the petrol tank of the coach which caused an explosion and badly injured a person walking nearby. The plaintiffs were not liable under the rule in *Rylands* v. *Fletcher* as the explosion was caused by the act of a stranger over whom the plaintiff had no control.

In such a case there may be liability in the tort of negligence.

THE TORT OF "PASSING OFF"

Definition: a tort committed by one person who, in a manner calculated to deceive, passes off his goods or business as those of another; e.g. by imitating their appearance or selling them under a similar name or trade mark.

Authority

Wright v. *Wright* (1949)

A Mr. Wright was not allowed to carry on a cosmetic business in his own name; nor could he sell any toilet goods, so long as there was a risk that his products might be confused with a firm marketing "Coal Tar Soap".

THE PRINCIPLE OF VICARIOUS LIABILITY

Definition: imposing liability (responsibility) on one person (vicariously) because of his relationship to another person.

E.g.:

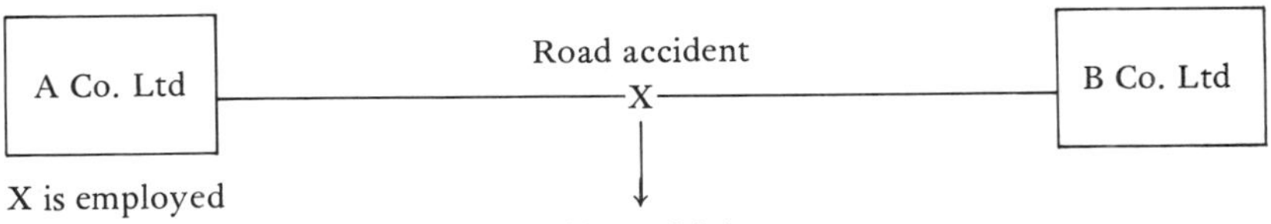

X is employed as a van driver to deliver goods to B Co. Ltd

Xs negligent driving causes injury to another road user – Y. Y may sue A Co. Ltd *vicariously* for the tort committed by X

In the law of torts an employer can be held responsible for torts committed by his employee if:

1. *There is a master and servant relationship*

   A person employed under a contract *of* services is a "servant". But someone who is employed under a contract *for* services is not a servant and he is called (for present purposes) an independent contractor (who is often "self-employed").

   It is a question of evidence to decide whether a person is either a servant or an independent contractor, e.g. method of payment, whether times of working are specified, membership of a company pension scheme, etc.

   In a contract of service a person is employed as part of the business and his work is done as an integral part of the business; under a contract for services, his work – although done for the business – is not integrated into it, but is only accessory to it: *Ready Mixed Case* (see page 64).

   Even if a person is an independent contractor, the courts will sometimes find an employer liable for torts committed by the "employee", e.g. if the employer authorised the tort.

2. *The tort was committed in the course of the employment*

   For a claim of vicarious liability against an employer to be successful it must be shown that a tort was committed in the course of the employment.

   An employer will be liable even though the employee carries out his job in a negligent or criminal way; though if the tort is unconnected with the job, or if the tort is committed in an "outrageous" way, the employer is not responsible: *Warren* v. *Henlys Ltd* (see pages 64-5).

Note: The imposing of liability vicariously does not affect the responsibility of an employee personally, regardless of the question of employment: *Lister* v. *Romford Ice Case* (see page 65).

Authorities on Vicarious Liability

Ready Mixed Concrete Ltd v. *Ministry of Pensions* (1968)

In this case the driver of a lorry worked for a company delivering concrete to building sites. The driver provided his own lorry and was responsible for its repair and maintenance. He was free to provide a substitute driver. Payment for work done was made by gross amounts (i.e. no tax deducted at source) on the basis of mileage and quantity of concrete delivered.

The driver described himself as a self-employed contractor, but it was argued by the Ministry that he was an employee. However, on the evidence the court decided he was a self-employed "transport contractor" and not an employee.

Hardaker v. *Idle District Council* (1896)

The defendant council employed a contractor to construct a sewer. Due to the negligence of the contractor a gas pipe was fractured and the escaping gas exploded, damaging the plaintiff's property.

Even though the contractors were "independent", the council were held responsible vicariously for the negligence; the defendants should have been more careful in who they employed.

Rose v. *Plenty* (1975)

A milkman was expressly told not to engage anyone to assist him in the performance of his duties. Nevertheless, he employed a boy to help him on his milk round. *Whilst delivering milk* the employee negligently drove the milk float causing injury to the boy, who later sued the employer, claiming he was vicariously liable. The court upheld the claim as the injury was caused at a time when the milkman was doing his job and it was irrelevant that he was doing it in a careless way.

If the milkman had caused the accident when *not* delivering milk, e.g. driving the milk float to visit a friend ("on a frolic of his own"), the employer would not then have been responsible.

Warren v. *Henlys Ltd* (1948)

An employee of the defendant garage owners thought that the plaintiff was going to drive away without paying for the petrol he had just been given. There was a heated argument and the defendant hit the plaintiff, knocking him to the ground.

The employer was *not* vicariously liable for the tort (of trespass to the person – assault) as it was not committed in the course of the employment; the behaviour was "outrageous" and dictated by personal malice.

Lister v. *Romford Ice and Cold Storage Co. Ltd* (1957)

Mr. Lister and his father were both employed by the same company. The son was a lorry driver and whilst carrying out his work he knocked down his father, who was injured. The father recovered damages from the employers, who were vicariously liable for the tort committed by the son.

The company claimed they were entitled to recover damages from the son, who was in breach of his duty to them. The House of Lords agreed and Mr. Lister was liable to pay the company the amount of money they had paid his father.

GENERAL DEFENCES IN TORT

A frequent form of defence in tort is a *denial* of the facts alleged; sometimes the defence is on a point of law, e.g. that no duty of care was owed by the defendant to the plaintiff.

Certain special defences are available for *particular* torts, e.g. "qualified privilege" in defamation.

The following are *general* defences available to a defendant in every tort where they are appropriate:

Volenti non fit injuria

No injury is done to a person who *consents.*

This defence will only be successful if it is proven that a person, expressly or impliedly, consented to run the risk of injury and so waive any claim for negligence.

Imperial Chemical Industries v. *Shatwell* (1965)

George and James Shatwell were qualified shot-firers employed by ICI; disregarding their employer's instructions the two were injured by an explosion. The court accepted evidence that the Shatwells were fully aware of the risks involved and the defence of *volenti* applied.

Knowledge (as opposed to consent) of the risk of injury is not enough.

Smith v. *Charles Baker & Sons* (1891)

The plaintiff was employed by the defendants on the construction of a railway. He was drilling holes in rocks in a quarry, and at the same time a crane on top of the embankment was removing stones overhead.

Smith knew that this work was being carried out but continued his drilling. On one occasion some stones fell from the crane and injured him. When he sued for negligence his employers claimed *volenti non fit injuria*.

The court *held* that the defence would not succeed. Although the plaintiff *knew* of the danger and still continued to do his work, there was no evidence that he had *voluntarily* agreed to run the risk of injury. Merely carrying on his work was not an indication of consent.

Apart from exceptional cases it is unlikely that the defence will succeed where there is an employer–employee relationship. The defence of *volenti* does not apply when a dangerous situation has been created by the defendant's negligence and a person is placed in a situation of emergency, and has to decide how to act to save or protect the lives of others.

Baker v. *T. E. Hopkins & Sons Ltd* (1959)

Two employees were overcome by fumes caused by their employer's defective petrol-driven pump. A doctor was called and, although worried by the danger, he went to the assistance of the men and was himself overcome by fumes and later died.

The question arose as to the employer's liability for the doctor's death, the defence being that he was *volenti*. But the court decided the defendants had created the dangerous situation and the doctor had acted under the compulsion of a moral duty: the defence of *volenti* was inapplicable.

Statutory Authority

It is a defence to an action in tort to show that a statute authorises the alleged wrong. But the courts are reluctant to *interpret* statutes in such a way as to enable Parliament to authorise a wrongful act *unless* the statute is quite clear *and* the authority is exercised reasonably.

Metropolitan District Asylum Board v. *Hill* (1881)

A hospital board was given the power to erect a smallpox hospital. The hospital was being built in a residential area where it caused danger of infection to residents nearby. It was claimed that the hospital constituted a nuisance; the hospital board defended by claiming statutory authority.

The court, however, decided that whilst there was power to erect a hospital, the Act did not sanction the erection in a place which would cause danger. The statutory authority was therefore exercised unreasonably and an injunction was granted against the board.

Self-Defence

A person may use reasonable force to defend himself (or [illegible] person) against unlawful force. A defendant will not be liab[illegible] the amount of force is reasonable and proportionate to the harm suffered.

Contributory Negligence

By s.1 of the Law Reform (Contributory Negligence) Act 1945 any person who recovers damages shall have those damages reduced to such an extent as the court thinks just and equitable having regard to the claimant's share in the responsibility for the damage. In other words, damages recoverable by a plaintiff are reduced in accordance with his own degree of default. This defence is usually raised against negligence claims, but may be applied to other torts.

Sayers v. *Harlow UDC* (1958)

Mrs. Sayers entered a public toilet owned and operated by the defendant local authority. Owing to a defective lock without a handle she could not get out of the cubicle. She was in a hurry and she tried to climb over the door. She placed her foot on the revolving toilet roll, fell to the ground and was injured.

Her claim for damages in negligence was successful. However, in response to a defence claim the court found that she had contributed to her injuries by attempting to balance her foot on a revolving object. This contributory negligence reduced her damages by one quarter.

Froom v. *Butcher* (1976)

A car driven by the plaintiff collided with a vehicle driven by the defendant. The accident was caused by the defendant's negligence but the injury to the plaintiff would have been avoided had he worn a seat belt. The court reduced the award of damages made to the plaintiff by one quarter.

A driver (or front seat passenger) in a motor vehicle must bear *some* responsibility for the injuries received if the wearing of a seat belt would have reduced or avoided them.

REMEDIES IN CONTRACT AND TORT

A "remedy" is the means provided by the law to recover rights or to obtain redress or compensation for a wrong.

The main remedy to a person who has suffered a breach of contract or a tort is an action for damages.

Damages

The court's estimated compensation in money for detriment or injury sustained by a plaintiff in contract or tort.

Damages for Breach of Contract

A contract-breaker is always liable for the loss which arises naturally from the breach, *or* loss the parties to the contract might reasonably be supposed to have contemplated, in making the contract, as the likely result of the breach: the rule in *Hadley* v. *Baxendale* (1854).

E.g.: *The Heron II* (*Koufas* v. *Czarnikow*) 1969: There was a contract for the shipment of sugar. Because of delay caused by the shipowner, the cargo arrived nine days late and the market value of the sugar had fallen. The innocent party claimed and was awarded damages for the loss due to the fall in the market value.

The Common Law Principle of Contract Damages

The aim of an award of damages is to compensate a party for the loss he has suffered by putting him, as far as money can, in the position he would have enjoyed if the contract had been performed.

E.g.: A wholesaler agrees to supply a retailer with 100 crates of oranges at £5 per crate. The wholesaler fails to deliver as agreed and the retailer is forced to buy in the open market at £7 per crate. He is entitled to £200 in damages.

The above common law principle is affected by the duty placed on an innocent party to mitigate his loss, i.e. to take any reasonable steps that are necessary to reduce the damages caused by the breach.

E.g.: A football club manager is wrongfully dismissed after 1 year of a 3-year contract at £20 000 per annum. He is entitled to damages for the amount he would have received for the remaining 2 years of his contract; but he must take reasonable steps to find another job. If he does not do so, his damages can be reduced.

Assessment of Damages by Contracting Parties

The parties to a contract will sometimes attempt to assess in advance the damages payable upon a breach. This pre-assessment of damages does *not* exclude the common law principle above.

A clause in a contract pre-assessing damages will only be valid if it represents a *genuine attempt* to pre-estimate the loss. This is called a "liquidated damages clause".

If a clause in a contract attempts to penalise one of the parties, i.e. attempts to force him to pay damages in excess of the actual loss, the clause is known as a *penalty clause* and is void.

The party relying upon a pre-assessment of damages clause will obviously argue that the clause is a genuine attempt at estimating loss; whatever way the parties describe such a clause it is for the courts to decide on its validity.

Ford Motor Company v. *Armstrong* (1915)

The defendants were retailers of cars from the plaintiff manufacturers. The defendant agreed not to sell any of the plaintiff's cars, or any part of such cars, below the listed price. The contract specified that for every breach of the agreement the defendant was to pay £250 as "agreed damages". This clause was later disputed and the court *held* that it was void as a "penalty". It did not genuinely attempt to pre-estimate the loss, as "any trifling" breach would compel the defendant to pay £250.

When a clause is void as a penalty, the damages awarded will be assessed in accordance with the common law principle. The courts have emphasised that where there is a *genuine attempt* to pre-estimate loss then even if the *actual* loss is greater or smaller this will not necessarily make void the clause. Certain standardised pre-estimate formulas have been accepted as valid, e.g. in standard form building contracts.

OTHER REMEDIES FOR BREACH OF CONTRACT

The courts have a discretion and may in particular circumstances award one of the remedies below.

Specific Performance or Injunction (see page 5)

In *Warner Brothers Incorporated* v. *Nelson* (1936) an actress agreed to work for a film producer for one year and not to work for anyone else. In breach of contract she attempted to work for another film company and the film producer sought an order compelling her to work only for him (specific performance) and an order restraining her from working for the other company (injunction). The court *held* that specific performance cannot be granted to compel the performance of a personal obligation, e.g. an employment agreement, but an injunction can be granted to stop the breaking of a negative stipulation in a contract, e.g. to restrain the actress from working for *another* film company.

Rescission

Cancellation of the contract. This remedy is available for misrepresentation, but is only possible if the parties can be restored to their original position.

Rectification

Where a written document does not accurately express an agreement between parties as the result of some mistake, the court has power to correct (rectify) that mistake: see *Joscelyne* v. *Nissen*, page 30.

DAMAGES IN TORT

The general principle is that in tort a plaintiff is entitled to such damages as will restore him to the position in which he would have been if the tort had not been committed, while in contract, he is restored to the position he would have been in had the contract been performed. Other remedies are available in tort, e.g. an injunction to stop a person committing a nuisance or from committing a trespass to land.

4

The Law of Employment

TRAINEE DRAUGHTSPERSON

To work for Civil Engineering Contractors. Interesting work, permanent appointment, salary negotiable, dependent upon age, experience and qualifications.

Write giving brief details to

Do not let redundancy depress you

A major British manufacturing company require personnel to be trained to sell their products. The company's comprehensive product and field training programmes will enable successful applicants to achieve an exceptionally high level of earnings in a permanent and satisfying career with excellent prospects for promotion. Selling experience is not required but applicants should own a car, have a telephone and be 25 to 45 years of age.

For further details contact the Sales Manager on:

WAREHOUSE STAFF

We have a vacancy for an experienced warehouse person for general packing and unloading work. The work is heavy and is more suited to a person in good physical condition.

Hours 8 am to 5 pm Monday to Friday with opportunities for occasional overtime.

We offer good rates of pay and working conditions. Staff canteen facilities.

WANTED PAPERBOYS AND GIRLS

THE CONTRACT OF EMPLOYMENT

The general rules of contract law apply to the formation of a contract of employment: offer and acceptance; consideration; intention to create a legal relationship; genuine consent; legality; capacity.

A contract of employment can be made in writing, orally or by conduct: no formalities are necessary to create the agreement. The parties to the employment contract are the employer and the employee; the employer is often a corporate (artificial) person, i.e. a company.

The employment contract is personal between the employer and the individual employee.

E.g.: A large company employs twenty new employees. At the time, each employee is issued with a "standard form" contract. The company has, in law, entered into twenty separate contracts.

The employment contract is a bargain. In exchange for labour or services payment is given.

E.g.: LABOUR ⟷ PAY (Wages/Salary)

A distinction exists between employees and self-employed persons: the employed person works under a contract *of* service; the self-employed person works under a contract *for* service, see pages 62-3.

The parties to a contract of service are sometimes referred to as Master (Employer) and Servant (Employee). When this contractual relationship is established:

1. The principle of vicarious liability applies; i.e. the employer can be held responsible for any wrongs committed by the employee causing injury to others in the course of the employment: *Rose* v. *Plenty* (1975) (see page 64).
2. Statutory protection is given to most employees, e.g. compensation can be awarded for "unfair dismissal" and redundancy: Employment Protection Consolidation Act (EPCA) 1978.

TERMS IN AN EMPLOYMENT CONTRACT

The terms (rights), expressed and implied in an employment contract arise in the same way as in contracts generally.

The personal nature of each employment contract means that it is often necessary to discover the particular terms that apply to a contract and then the effect of those terms.

Usually, many of the main terms will be expressed in written form, providing for: wages, salaries, commissions, bonuses, hours of work, nature of employees' work, holiday entitlement, overtime, sickness, sick pay, pensions, trade union rights, etc. These terms can be discovered from various sources, including:

1. A written contract.
2. Work/staff rules: many employers issue booklets or post notices containing the rules of the work place.

3. Job description: defining by title or nature the duties of an employee. It can limit the extent to which an employer can require an employee to change his duties.
4. A "collective agreement": this results from bargaining between trade unions and employers, or their associations, in relation to the terms of employment. It will often contain arrangements for correcting misconduct (disciplinary procedures) or provide methods for an employee in dispute with his employer to seek an internal settlement (a grievance procedure). A collective agreement will often be incorporated into an individual contract of employment.
5. "Custom": sometimes terms are implied representing practices which are customary in a particular industry, local area, or even within a single firm.
6. The provisions of a wages order may sometimes form part of an employee's contract.

Every term of a contract gives rise to a duty.

DUTIES ARISING FROM AN EMPLOYMENT CONTRACT

The duties under a contract of employment arise from the terms. However, duties can exist independently from the terms although arising because of them. The main duties created by common law and statute law may be summarised as follows:

Duties of the Employer

1. To give the employee a written statement of the main terms of his contract: EPCA 1978, s.1.
2. To pay the employee sick pay, unless otherwise agreed: *Marrison* v. *Bell* (see page 87).
3. To permit an employee time off work to carry out public duties: EPCA 1978, s.29.
4. To reimburse an employee for expenses reasonably incurred in the course of the employment.
5. To insure employees against injury at work: Employers' Liability (Compulsory Insurance) Act 1969.
6. To take reasonable care of the employee at work: *Wilsons and Clyde Coal Co. Ltd* v. *English* (1938).
7. To maintain health and safety standards: Health and Safety at Work Act 1974.

8. To give equal treatment to a woman doing the same work as a man (and vice-versa): Equal Pay Act 1970; Sex Discrimination Act 1975.
9. Not to discriminate against a person in a way deemed unlawful: Sex Discrimination Act 1975 and Race Relations Act 1976 (pages 83-4).
10. To treat the employee with respect and trust and not in an unjust or vindictive manner: *Cox* v. *Phillips Industries Ltd* (see page 86).
11. Under the EPCA 1978 an employee who is dismissed is entitled to request and receive a written statement of the reasons for his dismissal from his employer. This right arises after 26 weeks of employment.

Duties of the Employee

1. To perform the contract properly.
2. To obey all lawful, reasonable and authorised instructions concerning his employment.
3. To take care of his employer's property.
4. To act honestly and in good faith.
5. To conduct himself properly.

For examples of 1–5, see *Alidair Ltd* v. *Taylor*; *Superflux* v. *Plaisted*; *Pepper* v. *Webb*; and see Health and Safety at Work Act 1974.

RIGHTS AND DUTIES ON TERMINATION OF THE EMPLOYMENT CONTRACT

The legal obligations (i.e. rights and duties) that arise upon ending of the employment contract can be summarised in the following way:

1. Termination with notice
2. Summary dismissal
3. Wrongful dismissal
4. Constructive dismissal
5. Unfair dismissal
6. Redundancy
7. Unfairness by reason of redundancy

Termination with Notice

A contract of employment is usually ended by one party "giving notice" to the other party of the termination. In the absence of a term, expressed or implied, in the contract, a "reasonable" period of notice must be given: *Hill* v. *Parsons*. The period of notice cannot be less than a statutory minimum: EPCA 1978, s.49 (page 85).

An employment agreement terminated without proper notice is a breach of contract unless the termination is justified: *Pepper* v. *Webb* (see page 87).

Summary Dismissal

Definition: where an employer dismisses an employee without giving notice.

If there is no justification for the summary dismissal, such dismissal is wrongful. Summary dismissal will be justified if there is gross misconduct, wilful refusal to obey a lawful or reasonable order, gross neglect, or dishonesty by an employee.

Wrongful Dismissal

Definition: an action brought by an employee claiming summary dismissal without justification or termination of his contract by the employer given to him with insufficient notice: *Hill* v. *Parsons* (page 86).

Constructive Dismissal

Definition: conduct of the employer which entitles the employee to resign with or without notice: *Western Excavating (ECC) Ltd* v. *Sharp* (see page 88).

Unfair Dismissal

If an employee is "dismissed" as defined by EPCA 1978, s.55, this dismissal will be regarded as "unfair" if in all the circumstances of the case an employer acted unreasonably in dismissing the employee: Employment Act 1980, s.6.

Section 57 of the EPCA 1978 lays down the following five categories of reasons which may make a dismissal "fair":

1. Capability or qualifications.
2. Conduct.
3. Redundancy.
4. Illegality of continued employment; i.e. for some reason it would be illegal to continue to employ the employee.
5. Some other substantial reason.

Even if an employer shows one or more of the above reasons, the dismissal is still "unfair" unless the employer acted reasonably in dismissing him: Employment Act 1980, s.6.

Certain persons are excluded from claiming "unfair dismissal", e.g. a person employed outside the UK, *or* if the employee is the spouse of the employer.

To qualify for a claim to unfair dismissal a person must:

1. Be under the normal retiring age.
2. Have been employed for at least 16 hours per week for 52 weeks (8 hours if employed for 5 years). If throughout the employment the employer had less than 20 employees, the qualifying period is extended to 102 weeks.

Dismissal of an employee for membership of an independent trade union is "unfair". An employee need not complete 52 weeks in employment to claim.

When a claim for "unfair dismissal" is successful the remedies available are compensation - within statutory limits - or an order for the employer to re-employ the employee.

Redundancy

An employer is bound to pay compensation to an employee who is dismissed for redundancy.

Definition of redundancy: dismissal of an employee because his job has ceased to exist: *Wynes* v. *Southrepps Hall Farm Ltd* (see page 88).

In order to obtain a redundancy payment the EPCA 1978 lays down qualifying provisions:

1. The employee is dismissed for redundancy.
2. He is under 65 (60 for a woman).
3. The redundancy brings to an end a contract of service in existence for 2 years or more at no less than 16 hours per week, not counting employment before age 18; if the hours are 8–16 per week, a contract of service for 5 years or more will entitle him to claim, not counting employment before the age of 18.
4. He is not excluded from claiming redundancy.
5. He is not covered by an agreement made between an employer and a trade union that has received approved exemption from the Act.

The amount of a redundancy payment is calculated by using three factors in accordance with Schedule 4 of the EPCA 1978 as amended:

1. The age of the redundant employee.
2. His length of service with his employer.
3. His weekly pay when made redundant.

Using these factors the redundancy pay is calculated on the following scale:

Employee's age at date of dismissal (inclusive)	A week's pay (maximum £130) for each year of continuous service (maximum 20 years)
18–21	$\frac{1}{2}$ week's pay
22–40	1 week's pay
41–64	$1\frac{1}{2}$ week's pay

The statutory maximum of £130 is adjusted from time to time.

Once a man has reached 64 (a woman 59) the payment is reduced by 1/12th for every month over 64 (or 59) so as to phase out completely by 65 (or 60).

E.g.: A 45-year-old employee is made redundant after continuous service with his employer from age 35 to 45. At the date of redundancy he was earning £120 per week.

His redundancy payment is calculated as follows:

Age	*Length of service*	£
35–40 (6 × 1 week's pay × £120)	6 years	= 720
41–44 (4 × $1\frac{1}{2}$ week's pay × £120)	4 years	= 720
He is entitled to a redundancy payment of:		£1440

A redundancy payment is made by the employer, who is entitled to claim a rebate (41 per cent) from a government-administered redundancy fund.

Unfairness by Reason of Redundancy

A redundant employee is a dismissed employee.

A dismissal for reasons of redundancy will only be "fair" if the employer acted reasonably in all the circumstances: Employment Act 1980, s.6.

The question of reasonableness may well be resolved in favour of a dismissed employee if the employer fails to comply with a collective agreement containing provisions for proper handling of redundancies.

TRADE UNIONS

Purpose of a Trade Union

See definition in the Trade Union and Labour Relations Act (TULRA) 1974, s.2 (see page 81). It is the duty of a trade union to represent the interests of its members.

Collective Bargaining

Collective bargaining is the process by which a trade union negotiates with an employer the terms of its members' contracts of employment and the procedures by which employment disputes are to be settled. A vast structure of bodies exists to promote and carry it out.

To be effective in the process of collective bargaining a trade union must be "certified" as "independent", i.e. separate from an employer – not merely a "staff association". The advantages of a trade union being independent include the right of union officials having time off work for trade union duties and an obligation imposed on an employer to consult with a trade union in the event of proposed redundancies.

Generally there is no national minimum wage (but see Wages Councils) as it is considered that there should be "free collective bargaining" or *caveat emptor*. However, depending on the economic or political climate the Government may, by law, determine the general level of pay rises for everyone.

Collective Agreements

These are the result of collective bargaining negotiations, usually forming part of an individual's contract of employment. See TULRA 1974, s.18.

Wages Councils

These are created by the Secretary of State for Employment (following representations being made to him by groups, e.g. trade unions) to create a national bargaining body, i.e. a wages council, for particular sections of industry where groups of workers are poorly organised or poorly paid, e.g. catering. (See Wages Councils Act 1979, page 85.)

Trade Disputes

A trade dispute is defined by law: see TULRA 1974, s.29, as amended. Persons engaged in a trade dispute may take a variety of actions to persuade the other party (to the dispute) to accept a particular point of view.

A trade union may go on strike to persuade an employer to agree to an increase of pay. A "strike" is action where a group of employees refuse to work, to compel an employer to agree to their demands, e.g. for more pay.

An employee who goes on strike is in breach of contract: *Secretary of State for Employment* v. *ASLEF* (see page 87). This breach of contract entitles the employer to end the contract and dismiss the employee. However, under the EPCA 1978 an employer who decides to dismiss "strikers" must dismiss all of them (i.e. he cannot "pick and choose"). Otherwise the dismissed employees can claim "unfair dismissal".

Under the common law it is a civil wrong (i.e. a tort) to induce another person to break a contract. But if a person or trade union does induce another to break a contract "in furtherance or contemplation of a trade dispute", statute law gives legal immunity (exemption) from liability: TULRA 1974, s.13. A trade union is further protected in certain circumstances, from all tort liability: TULRA 1974, s.14.

However, under s.13 of the Employment Act 1982, s.14 of the 1974 Act is inapplicable in certain cases (see pages 82-3).

The law restricts certain forms of behaviour by a trade union even if in furtherance of a trade dispute, e.g. in relation to "picketing". "Pickets" are persons who attend at or near a place of employment to persuade others not to work – see TULRA 1974, s.15 (page 82).

Generally, there is *never* exemption from *criminal liability* for matters connected with a trade dispute or trade union activities.

Conciliation and Arbitration

Industrial disputes are often resolved by the parties to the dispute (an employer and a trade union) being assisted in arriving at a settlement by the services of a "conciliator" or some third party adjudicating upon the outcome of a "trade dispute". Such resolutions of industrial disputes are carried out by an independent body called ACAS (Advisory, Conciliation and Arbitration Service): see Employment Protection Act 1975, s.1 (page 83).

Trade Union Membership

The rules of a trade union constitute a contract between that trade union and a member of it, and an employee cannot be penalised by his employer for being a member of an independent trade union. It is also *lawful* for a trade union and an employer to operate a "closed shop" arrangement, i.e. a union-membership agreement whereby no one may work in a particular job without holding a membership card from the union.

Nevertheless the Employment Act 1982 amends the law relating to "closed shops":

1. It is "unfair" to dismiss a person, (a) for membership or proposed membership of an independent trade union or participation in union activities once he is a member; or (b) for *not* being or refusing to be a member of *any* trade union.
2. Before a new union-membership agreement (a "closed shop") can be effective it must be approved by not less than 80 per cent of employees in a secret ballot (85 per cent in some circumstances).

Authorities on Employment Law

Employers' Liability (Compulsory Insurance) Act 1969

Every employer carrying on business in Great Britain must maintain an approved insurance policy covering injury to employees arising in the course of employment. Copies of the insurance certificate must be displayed at the place of business. Failure of an employer to comply with this duty is a criminal offence.

Equal Pay Act 1970

The purpose of this Act is to prevent discrimination between men and women in relation to the terms of employment.

Section 1 states that every contract of service must provide for equality of treatment between men and women by way of an "equality clause". A contract not expressly containing this clause shall be deemed (by implication) to contain it.

Note:

1. The Act is not restricted to equal pay but applies to all the terms of a contract of employment.
2. By Article 119 of the Treaty of Rome, men and women must receive equal pay for doing the same work.
3. Exceptionally, an "equality clause" shall not operate if the employer provides that the differences between the terms upon which a man and a woman are employed are genuinely due to a material difference (other than the difference in sex) between her case and his or vice-versa.

Health and Safety at Work Act 1974, Sections 2–8

It is the duty of every employer to ensure, so far as is reasonably practicable, the health, safety and welfare at work of his employers. In particular the employer must have regard to:

1. The provision and maintenance of plant and systems of work.
2. The use, handling, storage and transport of articles and substances.
3. The provision of information, instruction, training and supervision.

4. The maintenance of the place of work and the provision and maintenance of means of access to and exit from such places.
5. The provision and maintenance of a healthy and safe working environment and adequate welfare facilities and arrangements.

The Act imposes similar duties on the self-employed, upon persons who control premises and upon manufacturers and suppliers of goods.

Employees have a duty under the Act: to take reasonable care to avoid injury to themselves or to others by their work activities; to co-operate with employers and others in meeting statutory requirements; not to interfere or misuse anything provided to protect their health, safety or welfare in compliance with the Act.

Note:

1. The Act is concerned with criminal liability.
2. Health and Safety Inspectors have wide powers to compel persons to comply with the duties. In appropriate cases a person will be prosecuted for non-compliance.
3. Before the passing of the 1974 Act there was no legislation of general application; instead the law in relation to health and safety was based on different kinds of places of work, e.g. the Factories Act 1961, the Offices, Shops and Railway Premises Act 1963, and the Mines and Quarries Act 1954. This legislation is still effective but is being replaced by regulations made under the 1974 Act.
4. The Act gives the Secretary of State for Employment power to make regulations (by way of delegated legislation) acting on the advice of the Health and Safety at Work Commission. This power is used to repeal and modify existing statutory provisions; it enables the Minister to legislate upon a wide range of matters covered by the 1974 Act.

Trade Union and Labour Relations Act 1974

S2

A trade union is not a body corporate, but is nonetheless capable of making contracts, suing and being sued in its own name, and being prosecuted for an offence committed in its name.

S13

An act committed by a person (or trade union) in contemplation or furtherance of a trade dispute that induces another person to break a contract is not actionable in tort.

Note: By s.17 of the Employment Act 1980 the legal immunity in s.13 of the 1974 Act is restricted to the "primary" parties to a contract of employment that are involved in a "trade dispute"; i.e. this makes illegal an inducement to *another* employer.

S14

A tort caused by or on behalf of a trade union is immune (exempted) from legal liability. But a trade union may be liable for negligence, nuisance or breach of duty resulting in personal injury or breach of duty in connection with property if an act is not committed in contemplation or furtherance of a trade dispute (and see s.13 of the Employment Act 1982, below).

S15 (substituted by the Employment Act 1980)

Whilst it is lawful for a person in contemplation or furtherance of a trade dispute to attend at or near his own place of work for the purpose of peaceful picketing, he may be liable in tort for picketing at some location other than his own place of work.

Note: A recent Code of Practice says that pickets have only the right of peaceful persuasion when picketing; there is no right to stop vehicles or prevent persons going to work. The Code suggests that the number of pickets at any work entrance should not exceed six.

S18

A collective agreement is not intended by the parties to be a legally enforceable contract unless the agreement *(a)* is in writing and *(b)* contains a provision which states that the agreement shall be a legally enforceable contract.

S28 (Definition of a Trade Union)

A trade union is an organisation consisting of members of a certain description whose principal purpose is regulating their relationship with their employer(s).

S29 (Amended by the Employment Act 1982)

A "trade dispute" is a dispute between workers and their employer and relates wholly or mainly to the terms of employment. This includes matters relating to employment of members, discipline and membership of a trade union.

Employment Act 1982

S13

The "immunity" provisions of s.14 of the TULRA 1974 (see above) "shall cease to have effect" if a tort is committed by an authorised or responsible person of the trade union concerned, e.g. an employed official of that union.

Employment Protection Act 1975

S1

ACAS has a duty to promote the improvement of industrial relations and to encourage the extension and development of collective bargaining. In particular, ACAS will, when requested, assist in resolving and determining the outcome of a "trade dispute".

Sex Discrimination Act 1975

Under this Act discrimination is treating a person less favourably because of their sex in relation to employment opportunities, in education, in the provision of goods and services, and in the dispersal and management of services.

S6

It is unlawful for an employer to discriminate against a person on the grounds of sex in relation to selection, recruitment, training, transfer, promotion, dismissal or other facilities normally provided. (It is also unlawful to discriminate in employment against a person because that person is married.)

S7

Sex discrimination by an employer in recruitment, promotion, transfer or training for a job is not unlawful where a person's sex is a genuine occupational qualification.

Note:

1. The exception in s.7 of a "genuine occupational qualification" would apply where the employer could show that for reasons of authenticity or decency, discrimination was necessary; e.g. a male actor to play the part of "Tarzan", or a female attendant for a ladies' changing room.
2. Exemption from the Act is made where the employment is in a private household or in a small firm employing no more than five persons in total.
3. The Act does not apply to arrangements for special treatment of women in connection with pregnancy or childbirth or to arrangements relating to death, retirement or pension schemes.

Race Relations Act 1976

The Act is concerned with treating a person less favourably, i.e. discriminating, on "racial grounds" in the provision of employment, services, houses, etc.

S4

It is unlawful for an employer to discriminate against a person on the grounds of colour, race, nationality, or ethnic or national origins in relation to selection, recruitment, transfer, promotion, dismissal or other facilities.

S5

Racial discrimination by an employer is not unlawful where a person's race is a "genuine occupational qualification".

Note: The exception in s.5 would include a case where a person of a particular racial group was required for reasons of authenticity, e.g. an Indian for an Indian restaurant.

Employment Protection (Consolidation) Act 1978

S1

The employer, not later than 13 weeks after the start of the employment, must give to the employee a written statement containing the following particulars: the identity of the parties; the date the employment started; whether work with a previous employer is to be regarded as being continuous with the present employment; the rate of pay or the method of calculating it; the intervals at which payment is to be made, i.e. weekly, monthly or otherwise; arrangements relating to hours of work; the terms relating to holidays and holiday pay, to absence through sickness, sick pay (if any) and to pension schemes; the length of notice to be given by each side to terminate the employment; and the title of the job that the employee is to do.

Note:

1. Every written statement must give information upon any disciplinary rules or grievance procedures that apply.
2. The written statement need not be given to an employee: who works less than 16 hours per week; or who is a registered dock worker; or is a Crown employee; or is a merchant seaman; or is the husband or wife of the employer; or who normally works outside Great Britain.
3. Any dispute concerning the written statement can be referred to an industrial tribunal to resolve it.
4. The written statement is *evidence* of the contract of service; it is not necessarily the contract itself.
5. It is recognised by the Act that where the written statement is reasonably available to an employee from other documents, in the course of his employment, s.1 does not apply.

S29

An employer must permit an employee to have reasonable time off work for the purpose of performing his duties as: a justice of the peace; a member of a local authority; a member of a statutory tribunal; a member of a regional health authority; a member of the governing body of an educational establishment maintained by a local education authority; or a member of a water authority.

Note: An employee who is summoned to attend jury service must be given time off work for that purpose: Juries Act 1974.

S49

If an employer terminates a contract of employment by giving notice, the minimum period of notice to be given is determined by the employee's length of continuous employment in the employer's service as follows:

Employee's length of service	*Minimum notice to be given by the employer*
4 weeks – 2 years	1 week
2–12 years	1 week for each year of service
12 years and over	12 weeks

The minimum period of notice required to be given by *the employee* is one week, regardless of the length of service.

S55

An employee is treated as dismissed by his employer only if:

1. The contract of employment is terminated by the employer, either by notice or summarily (instantly) without notice; or
2. A fixed term contract of employment expires without being renewed under the same contract; or
3. The employee terminates the contract, with or without notice, in circumstances under which he is entitled to do so without notice by reason of the employer's conduct.

Wages Councils Act 1979

A Wages Council has the function of determining the minimum wages and other terms of employment in a particular trade or industry over which the council has jurisdiction. It may issue a wages order fixing the terms of employment of those members within its jurisdiction.

Failure to comply with such an order makes the employer liable to criminal prosecution. A wages order forms part of an employee's contract of service and a failure by the employer to honour the order will render him liable for breach of contract.

Employment Act 1980

S6

The question of a "fair" dismissal depends upon whether in the circumstances (including the size and administrative resources of the employer's undertaking) the employer acted reasonably in dismissing the employee; and that question shall be determined in accordance with equity and the substantial merits of the case.

Alidair Ltd v. *Taylor* (1976)

The court held that an airline pilot was "fairly" dismissed after landing an aircraft (full of passengers) in a manner giving rise to concern and resulting in an investigation being conducted. There are certain activities where the degree of professional skill and care required is so high, and the consequences of departing from these standards so serious, that even one departure constitutes a breach, and the employee's failure to perform the contract properly justifies dismissal.

The degree of skill and care expected from an airline pilot (or a surgeon, scientist, etc.) in performing his work properly would be much higher than that required from other persons performing less important jobs. Nevertheless, if an employee states, even by implication, that he can do a particular job, and he cannot, the employer may regard him as incompetent and unfit to do the job.

Cox v. *Phillips Industries Ltd* (1975)

The plaintiff was promoted in his work to the position of "product leader". His employers became dissatisfied with his performance in the job. They moved him to a position of lesser status; but his duties were vague, no one told him what to do and no further responsibilities were given to him. He became depressed, anxious, frustrated and ill; he accepted a redundancy payment but then brought an action for breach of contract.

It was claimed that there was an implied term of mutual respect required under the employment agreement, and the behaviour of the employer broke this term. The court agreed and awarded Cox damages; each party to a contract of employment should treat the other with such a degree of consideration and courtesy as would enable the contract to be carried on.

Hill v. *C. A. Parsons and Co. Ltd* (1971)

A senior professional engineer who had been employed for 35 years with the same firm was dismissed with 4 weeks' notice. He claimed that the termination was in breach of contract as 4 weeks was not a "reasonable" period of notice.

The court agreed and awarded Hill damages. In his case six months' notice would be reasonable. Generally, what is reasonable depends upon such factors as the status of the employee, salary, length of employment with that employer, age and so on.

Marrison v. *Bell* (1939)

In the absence of any contractual term, express or implied, to the contrary ". . . under a contract of service . . . wages continue to be payable through sickness and incapacity for work . . . until the contract is terminated . . . by the employer in accordance with the terms of the contract": Scott, L. J.

Pepper v. *Webb* (1969)

A head gardener had been in conflict with his employer for some time. There was a lengthy period when his attitude and behaviour were unsatisfactory. One day he decided to leave early instead of tending to his work as he was asked to do. He told his employer that he "couldn't care less about the bloody greenhouse and the sodding garden". He was instantly dismissed.

The court decided that the employer was justified in taking this action. The employee refused an order which was within the scope of his contract of employment and he was abusive in his refusal. The fact that there was a history of misconduct was also a relevant consideration.

Secretary of State for Employment v. *ASLEF* (1972)

It is an implied term of an employee's contract of service that he will carry out the agreement in good faith. Any conduct which is inconsistent with this obligation will amount to a breach of contract. Persistent lateness; incompetence; theft of employer's property; taking part in a strike, go-slow, work-to-rule or sit in – all these will justify dismissal.

Superflux v. *Plaisted* (1958)

The employee was in charge of a team of vacuum-cleaner salesmen. He was responsible for a van containing a large supply of vacuum-cleaners. Through his carelessness, fourteen were stolen from the van. The employer sued him for breach of contract, claiming repayment of the cost of the stolen vacuum-cleaners. The court *held* the employee in breach of contract. He owed a duty to take proper care of his employer's property and as he had not done so he was liable to reimburse his employer.

Western Excavating (ECC) Ltd v. *Sharp* (1977)

The Court of Appeal said that an employee would be "constructively dismissed" when his employer's conduct amounted to a breach of contract which entitled the employee to resign.

Such conduct on the part of an employer justifying the employee's resignation might include altering the employee's job, or significantly changing its location, in both cases, when there is no contractual right to do this.

Wilsons and Clyde Coal Co. Ltd v. *English* (1938) – see also page 51

The House of Lords laid down a general obligation upon an employer to provide a safe system of work for his employees. This can be classified as:

1. A duty to provide safe plant and machinery.
2. A duty to provide competent staff.
3. A duty to provide and maintain a safe system of work.

Note: Subsequent decisions have clarified that the individual employer's obligation is to take such care for the safety of his employees as a reasonable man would take in the circumstances of the case.

Wynes v. *Southrepps Hall Farm Ltd* (1968)

The purpose of redundancy payments is to compensate for loss of security and to encourage workers to accept redundancy without damaging industrial relations. A redundancy payment is compensation for loss of a right which a long-term employee had in his job, irrespective of whether that loss led to unemployment. It is to compensate him for loss of security, and for the anxiety caused by a change of job.

Note: Reasons for employers making employees redundant include the economic redeployment of skills, the need to reduce costs by cutting labour resources, or the ceasing of a business.

THE PROTECTION OF THE EMPLOYEE

There are a number of public bodies and offices which exist to further the protection of the employee. The principal ones are dealt with below.

Equal Opportunities Commission

The Equal Opportunities Commission (EOC) was established by the Sex Discrimination Act 1975 and comprises commissioners who are required to work towards the elimination of discrimination in employment, promote equality of opportunity between men and women, and keep under review the Equal Pay Act 1970 and the Sex Discrimination Act 1975.

The EOC may carry out investigations into alleged discrimination, bring proceedings in respect of discriminatory advertisements, and give assistance to "aggrieved" persons.

Commission for Racial Equality

The Commission for Racial Equality was established by the Race Relations Act 1976 and consists of full-time commissioners who have broadly the same powers and functions as the EOC.

Note: Complaints concerning discrimination may be taken to industrial tribunals by the Equal Opportunities Commission or the Commission for Racial Equality.

Industrial Tribunals

Industrial tribunals were established by the Industrial Training Act 1964. Since then they have developed, to hear complaints relating to unfair dismissal, redundancy payments, and a wide range of other grievances and applications. Industrial tribunals do not deal with issues of contract law (an action for breach of contract), except in so far as such behaviour is evidence of "unfair dismissal".

Each tribunal consists of a legally qualified chairman plus two other "lay" persons, often representing an employer and a trade union. An Appeal from an industrial tribunal will be heard by the Employment Appeal Tribunal.

Employment Appeal Tribunal

The Employment Appeal Tribunal was established in 1975 and consists of judges of the High Court and Court of Appeal and from a panel of persons having special knowledge or experience of industrial relations. Its main function is to hear appeals from industrial tribunals.

Health and Safety Commission and Executive

The Health and Safety Commission and the Health and Safety Executive were established by the Health and Safety at Work Act 1974. The

Commission has a chairman and commissioners having the general duty to promote and encourage the provisions of the 1974 Act. The Executive is responsible for the enforcement of the health and safety at work legislation. It has the power to inspect premises, issue warnings and instigate prosecutions.

Codes of Practice

A code of practice is a set of rules created for practical guidance. ACAS and other bodies connected with employment are authorised to produce such codes.

A code does not have the force of law: failure to observe it cannot give rise to legal liability. However, the provisions of a code of practice are admissible in evidence and can be taken into account in deciding a dispute. The Code of Practice on Disciplinary Practice and Procedure in employment suggests that an employee should not be dismissed for a first breach of disclipline except in a case of serious misconduct, and that a system of warnings ought to be used so that an employee can improve his conduct.

Certification Officer (CO)

The office of CO was created by the Employment Protection Act 1975. Its main function is to determine whether a trade union is entitled to a certificate of "independence".

5

Consumer Protection

The supply of goods and services is the nub of business activity. The range and complexity of goods and services have resulted in legislation and the assumption of responsibility by the Government to protect the interests of consumers.

GOVERNMENT RESPONSIBILITY

The Secretary of State (SOS) by way of the Department of Prices and Consumer Protection (DPCP) is the person chiefly responsible for consumer protection and "fair trading". This responsibility extends to overseeing the work of government-sponsored agencies existing to promote efficiency as well as to protect consumers, e.g. the British Standards Institution.

The responsibility in other areas of "consumerism" is given to different government departments, e.g. the Ministry of Agriculture, Fisheries and Food, for the safety and quality of food.

LEGISLATION AND CONSUMER PROTECTION

The influence of government in consumer matters has led to the following major Acts of Parliament, analysed as indicated below:

Fair Trading Act 1973: pages 97-8.

Trade Descriptions Act 1968 (and 1972): pages 99-101.

Unsolicited Goods and Services Acts 1971 and 1975: page 102.

Consumer Credit Act 1974: pages 102-9.

Consumer Safety Act 1978: pages 109-10.

Sale of Goods Act 1979: pages 117-8, 122-6.

Supply of Goods and Services Act 1982: pages 130-1.

Unfair Contract Terms Act 1977: pages 43-5.

The Laws of Consumer Protection

Sale of Goods Act 1979	Unsolicited Goods and Services Act 1971 and 1975	Fair Trading Act 1973
Unfair Contract Terms Act 1977	Supply of Goods and Services Act 1982	Trade Descriptions Act 1968
Part III of Hire Purchase Act 1964	Restrictive Trade Practices Act 1976	European Communities Act 1972
Consumer Credit Act 1974	Resale Price Act 1964	Weights and Measures Act 1963
Legal Aid and Assistance Act 1972	Consumer Safety Act 1978	Food and Drugs Act 1955
Misrepresentation Act 1967	Powers of the Criminal Courts Act 1973	The Theft Acts 1968 and 1978
and other Acts, plus hundreds of statutory rules, regulations, orders and codes of practice.		

Other important legislation on such matters as weights and measures, misrepresentation, insurance, banking and financial services, travel and holidays, and advertising supplement the above range of statutory laws existing to protect consumers. These laws can and often do add to the common laws (created, for example, by the law of contract and the law of torts).

Any Act of Parliament protecting a consumer (together with any Rules, Regulations and Orders made under it) imposes a *duty* on a supplier of goods and services. The extent of this duty depends on the particular Act in question. However, such a duty will give a

Consumer Protection

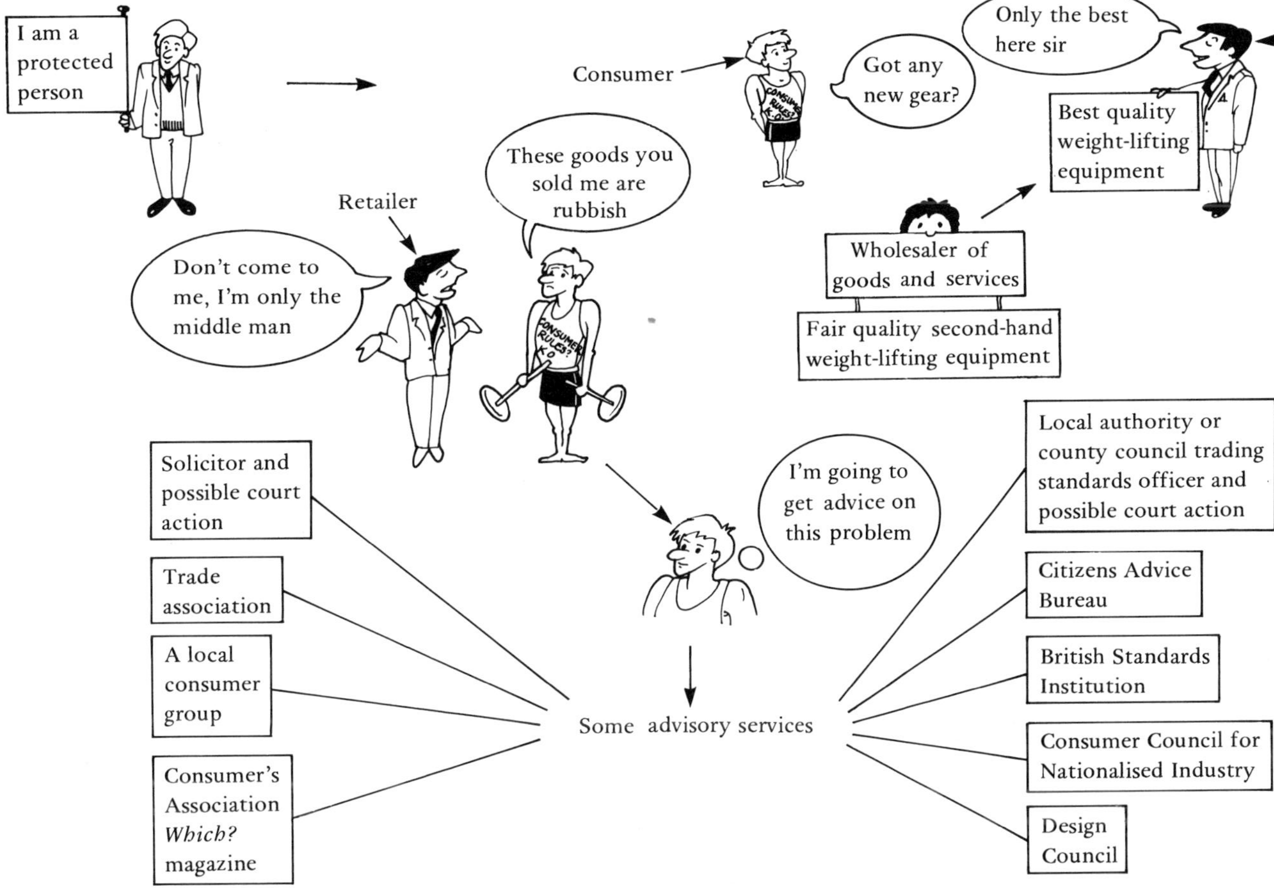

The Origins of Consumer Protection Laws

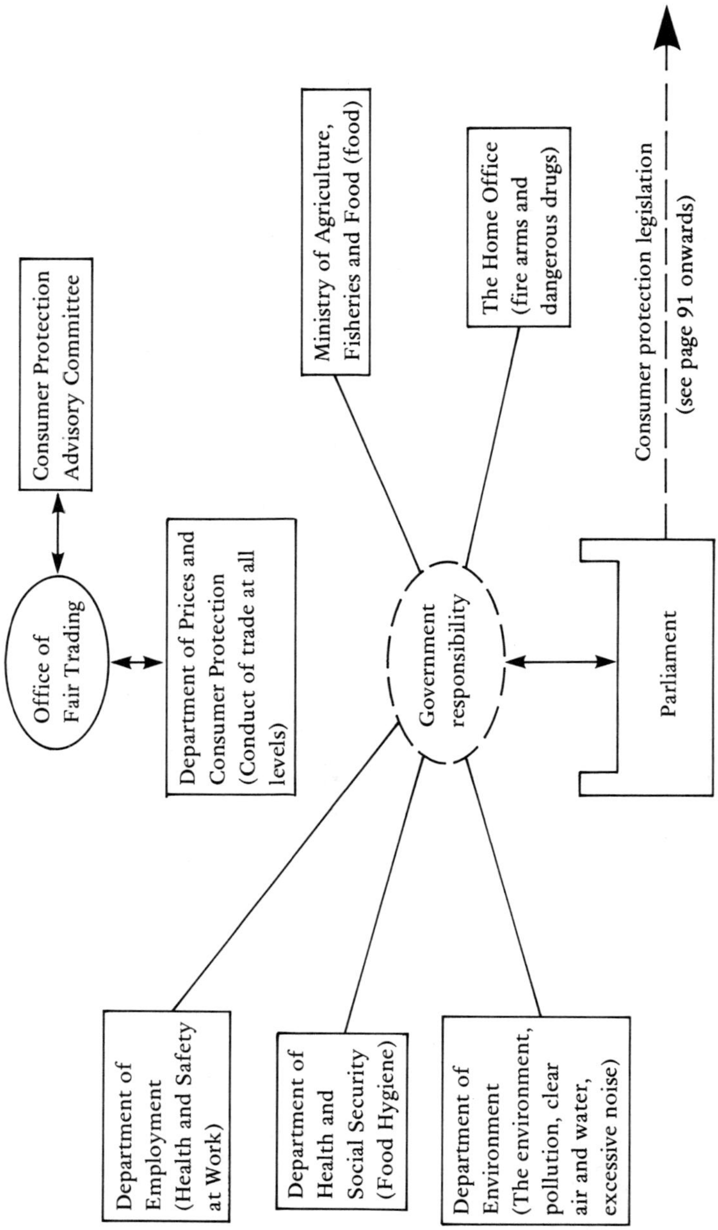

corresponding right to a consumer to pursue a claim against a supplier or manufacturer, or it will impose upon some other person or body the task of taking that action on behalf of the particular consumer, or on behalf of consumers generally (see, for example, the preamble to the Fair Trading Act 1974).

The action that can be taken is either of a civil or a criminal nature, or both. This, again, will depend upon examining the particular statute creating the *duty* to discover the *right(s)*.

E.g.:

	Sale of Goods Act 1979	*Trade Descriptions Act 1968*	*Consumer Safety Act 1978*
1.	A seller's duty to sell goods fit for their purpose	A seller's duty to describe goods correctly.	A duty to ensure that goods sold to consumers are safe.
2.	Giving a right to a buyer to claim damages for defective goods.	Giving a right to prosecute the seller for a false description.	Giving a right to a consumer to sue for breach of the duty and enabling a prosecution to be brought.
3.	This Act only gives rights in civil law.	This Act only gives rights in criminal law. (See Powers of Criminal Courts Act 1973 below.)	This Act gives rights in both civil law *and* criminal law.

LEGAL REDRESS

Consumer protection legislation imposing criminal liability is usually enforced by trading standards officers employed by local authorities; private individuals may in some cases carry out a prosecution if they so wish. In preference to a prosecution, a trading standards officer will often offer advice to suppliers and manufacturers in an attempt to prevent offences being committed. Warnings are given, some with a time limit attached to enable an offender to conform with the law.

Where, however, there is a prosecution which is successful, a criminal court may award compensation to a particular consumer as a result of an offence: Powers of Criminal Courts Act 1973.

Legislation imposing civil liability involves a consumer enforcing his own rights through either the County Court or the High Court; there exists in the County Court an informal, though binding, system for small claims: see "County Court Arbitration", page 194.

Legal advice and assistance can, of course, be obtained from a solicitor and a consumer with limited resources may be entitled to Legal Aid (see page 92).

CONSUMER INFORMATION, ADVICE AND HELP

Providing information, advice and help has become a function of government responsibility in consumer matters. This function is exercised through government departments and agencies and through local authorities. Independent from government are various organisations which also give assistance to consumers (see page 93).

An agency, whether government-sponsored or not, when carrying out its advisory role may well give not only advice but sometimes practical help to a particular consumer to help him resolve his problem. But in its advisory capacity the agency has no power in law to adjudicate (judge) on the dispute. This is a matter for the courts.

Nevertheless, many trade and professional associations, through voluntary codes of practice or, as appropriate, professional rules, operate systems (arbitration, conciliation, professional practices committees – which may have limited judicial powers) that can be effective in the settlement of individual consumer problems without recourse to the courts.

NATIONALISED INDUSTRIES AND THE CONSUMER

The consumer protection laws (both common law and statutory) apply to all forms of business activity. This liability normally extends to the actions of public bodies (nationalised industries – gas, electricity, transport, energy, postal, telephone services, etc.) Sometimes, however, a particular law gives exemption. For example, the Post Office is excluded from the provisions of the Fair Trading Act 1974 by s.29 of the Post Office Act 1969: "statutory immunity" is given for failures or omissions in relation to postal services.

However, connected to each nationalised industry there are representative consumers' or consultative councils acting as "watchdogs". The councils may consider complaints brought to them by individuals, or matters which they take up on their own initiative which affect consumers (of the goods and services of their industries). They may also advise both the boards of management of the particular industries, and the ministers concerned, from whom they sometimes hear referrals, and to whom they sometimes make recommendations. It should be emphasised that these councils only act as advisors, not "bloodhounds".

CONSUMERS AND COMPETITION LAWS

The common law recognises that an agreement in "restraint of trade" is generally against the public (consumer) interest and is therefore unenforceable (see pages 34-5).

Legislative measures have greatly increased this concept by way of the control and prohibition of commercial activities and agreements regarded as harmful to the public; see:

"Restrictive Trade Practices" (page 34);

"Resale Price Maintenance" (page 34);

"Monopolies, Mergers and Anti-Competitive Practices" (page 110).

CONSUMER PROTECTION LAWS

DEFINITION OF "A CONSUMER"

Definition: A consumer is a person who is, or is to be, supplied with goods and services from a business person. A business person who is supplied with goods and services from another business person is not a consumer.

E.g.:

1. A customer buys goods from a retailer. The customer is a consumer.
2. A retailer buys goods from a wholesaler. The retailer is not a consumer.

Fair Trading Act 1973

Preamble: An Act appointing the Director-General of Fair Trading (DGFT) and a Consumer Protection Advisory Committee, and to confer on them and on the Secretary of State (for Prices and Consumer Affairs) and the Restrictive Practices Court and certain other courts, new functions for the protection of consumers.

S2

It is the duty of the DGFT, as far as practical:

1. To keep under review consumer trade practices relating to goods and services supplied to consumers.

2. To collect evidence of consumer trade practices affecting the interests of consumers.
3. To keep under review and collect evidence relating to monopoly situations or anti-competitive practices.
4. To receive evidence of conduct of a person carrying on business appearing to be "unfair" to consumers, and to take action against that person (ss. 34–43).

S3

A Consumer Protection Advisory Committee (CPAC) shall be established consisting of independent specialists who are able to advise on goods and services supplied to consumers.

S13

"Consumer trade practice" means any activity carried on in connection with the supply of goods and services to consumers relating to: terms and conditions of supply, the manner of communicating the terms and conditions to consumers, the promotion of goods and services, selling methods, packaging, or methods of securing payment for such goods.

SS14–21

"Consumer Trade Practices" that adversely affect consumer interests may be referred by the DGFT to the CPAC who will investigate and *report* and make recommendations upon these practices to the Secretary of State.

If the DGFT considers that a trade practice is likely to mislead, confuse, unduly pressurise, or cause unequitable (unfair) terms to the consumer, the DGFT may recommend reform of the law.

Exclusion from "reference". Goods and services provided by many professions (doctors, dentists, accountants, architects, etc.) and by nationalised industries (gas, electricity, road and rail, postal services) cannot be the subject of a "reference".

SS22–26

If the CPAC in their report agree or substantially agree with the recommendations of the DGFT, the Secretary of State may make laws (by way of "orders") giving effect or substantially giving effect to the recommendations. They will impose criminal liability upon persons in contravention of the orders. Examples of such orders are given below.

Consumer Transaction (Restrictions on Statements) Order 1976

It is an offence by means of notices in shops, advertisements or statements or with goods to suggest that a consumer's statutory rights are excluded: Unfair Contract Terms Act 1977, s.6. Notices such as "No refunds" or "Sale goods non-returnable" are therefore illegal.

A manufacturer who supplies goods with a restriction on his obligations (perhaps by way of a "guarantee") must indicate on consumer goods that "statutory rights are unaffected".

The Business Advertisements (Disclosure) Order 1977

A person who is publishing an advertisement selling goods in the course of a business must make it clear that the goods are being sold in that way. For example, a car dealer who places an advertisement selling a car giving the impression he is a private seller commits an offence.

Price Marking (Bargain Offers) Order 1979

It is illegal for a retailer to indicate that the price of a particular item is lower than any other price for the same item offered by another retailer. A notice reading, "Normal price £25, our price £18", would be unlawful.

It is *not* unlawful for a retailer to compare a price with his own previous or future price, for example, by announcing an "introductory price". Nor is it unlawful for him to make comparison with a manufacturer's recommended price.

SS27-33

Trading Standards Officers are given the duty of enforcing the orders made under this Act and are given powers of inspecting, entry and seizure of goods and documents in relation to this duty.

SS34-43

The DGFT must take action against any business person who persists in a course of conduct which is unfair to consumers and their interests. Conduct will be "unfair" if it is a breach of the criminal law or a duty owed to consumers (other than a contractual duty). The DGFT must first attempt to secure an assurance that the conduct will cease and if it does not, a court order (civil) may be obtained.

The Trade Descriptions Act 1968

Preamble: An Act making it a criminal offence to misdescribe goods, services, accommodation and facilities provided in the course of a trade; or to give false or misleading indications as to the price of goods; or to wrongly suggest that devices or emblems have received royal awards.

S1

Any person who in the course of a trade or business applies a false trade description to any goods, or supplies or offers to supply any goods to which a false trade description is applied, shall be guilty of an offence.

Goods on display in a shop window will be regarded as "offers to supply". An oral statement may amount to a trade description.

E.g.: In 1974 a garage owner was convicted for telling a customer that a car was worth £2 in scrap and then buying the car for that amount and selling it for a large profit.

S2

A trade description includes: indications of quantity or other measurements; the method of manufacture, processing or reconditioning; composition; fitness for a particular purpose; various physical characteristics such as strength, performance, behaviour and accuracy; indications as to testing and the results; approval; place and date of manufacture; the manufacturer; and any other history of the goods, including previous ownership.

A description may be in advertisements, catalogues or circulars, or on the goods themselves, i.e. on the packaging.

E.g.: A car dealer states to a customer that a car has only done 12 000 miles when it has really done 24 000. That is a trade description which is false.

S3

A false trade description is one which is false to a material degree. This degree is a question of fact in the circumstances of each case.

If before the supply of goods or services takes place the supplier has "disclaimed" any misdescription, then under *this Act* such a disclaimer will be effective.

E.g.: "No responsibility is taken for any error, omission or misstatement which does not constitute an offer or contract."

S11

A person shall be guilty of an offence if he falsely indicates that the price at which goods are offered for sale is equal to or less than a recommended price or a price at which the goods were previously sold. It cannot be false if goods were offered for sale at the lower price for a period of at least 28 days within the previous 6 months.

E.g.: If a shop window indicates "Goods reduced by half", and the goods were so displayed for one month previously, then there is no offence.

S12

A person who in the course of a trade or business falsely indicates that goods or services are supplied to Her Majesty or any member of the Royal Family shall be guilty of an offence.

S14

A person who in the course of any trade or business makes a statement knowing it to be untrue in connection with any services, accommodation or facilities shall be guilty of an offence. Examples include travel firms falsely misstating holiday facilities abroad.

Section 14 covers all service businesses.

S24

A person charged under s.1 or s.14 is not guilty if he can show that the offence was: due to a mistake or reliance on information supplied to him, or to the act of "another person" or to an accident or some other cause beyond his control; *and* he took all reasonable precautions and exercised due diligence to avoid the offence being made by himself or by a person under his control.

In *Tesco Supermarkets Ltd* v. *Nattrass* (1972), the accused store was found not guilty when they showed that contrary to instructions their branch manager ("another person") had displayed a false "special offer" poster.

SS26–29

Local authorities are responsible for enforcing the Act. Usually each authority appoints an inspector who has wide powers to investigate, "test-purchase", seize goods and documents, and prosecute in appropriate cases. Annually, the number of successful prosecutions is between 1000 and 2000.

Because of the exclusively criminal nature of the Act there are no "civil" rights created under it. The criminal courts, however, do have powers to award compensation to specific "victims" of false trade descriptions.

Note: The Trade Descriptions Act 1972 requires that goods manufactured or produced outside Britain and carrying a British name or mark should (with some exceptions) be accompanied by a clear indication of their origin.

The Unsolicited Goods and Services Acts 1971 and 1975

Section references are to the 1971 Act.

The 1971 Act as amended by the Unsolicited Goods and Services (Amendment) Act 1975 makes "provisions for the greater protection of persons receiving unsolicited goods". Both Acts impose criminal liability.

This legislation was passed to prevent certain forms of "inertia" selling, where goods are delivered to a person who has not ordered them: he is informed that unless the goods are returned by a certain date it will be assumed that the goods are being purchased.

S6

"Unsolicited" means, in relation to goods sent to any person, that they are sent *without* any prior request made by him or on his behalf.

S1

A person who is sent goods in his private capacity (i.e. not for use in trade or business) without these goods being requested by him may treat the goods as a free gift if the following conditions are satisfied:

1. He does not agree to keep or return the goods.
2. After receipt of the goods he has kept them for 6 months *or* kept them for at least 30 days after notifying the sender in writing that he does not want them.
3. He has not unreasonably obstructed the sender in repossessing the goods.

S2

A person sending unsolicited goods who then demands payment or threatens certain other forms of action commits a criminal offence for which conviction carries a fine.

S3

A person who produces "trade directories" commits an offence if he demands payment from a business person for including his name in the directory without being requested to do so.

Consumer Credit Act 1974

Preamble: An Act to establish for the protection of consumers a new system, administered by the Director-General of Fair Trading, of licensing and controlling traders concerned with the provision of credit, or with the supply of goods on hire or hire-purchase, and their transactions, in place of the previous enactments regulating moneylenders and hire-purchase traders and their transactions, and for related matters.

S1

The Director-General of Fair Trading is responsible for the administration of the licensing system set up by this Act, for supervising the working and enforcement of it, and for keeping under review the social and commercial developments relating to the provision of credit.

S8

A consumer credit agreement is "regulated" by this Act when an individual ("the debtor") is provided with credit not exceeding £5000 by any other person ("the creditor"), unless exempt under s.16. "Credit" does not include any down-payment or interest charges: s.20.

E.g.: A consumer is to pay £7000 in total for goods supplied; £1000 is the down-payment and £1000 represents interest charges. The credit given is therefore £5000 and the agreement is "regulated".

S9

"Credit" includes a cash loan, and any other form of financial accommodation.

S12

A "debtor–creditor–supplier" agreement is regulated under the Act. Such an agreement is made by a creditor under pre-existing arrangements between himself and a supplier in the knowledge that credit is to be used to finance a transaction between the debtor and the supplier.

E.g.: A second-hand car dealer (supplier) negotiates with a customer (debtor) for him to purchase a vehicle on credit terms. The dealer has an arrangement with a finance company (creditor) who provide the finance for the customer to buy the car. This is a debtor–creditor–supplier agreement.

S13

A "debtor–creditor" agreement is regulated under the Act. Such an agreement arises where a creditor has no pre-existing arrangement with a supplier and the creditor is not the supplier.

E.g.: A bank agrees to loan a customer money to buy a car in the near future. The bank is not tied to any particular transaction, nor will the bank supply the car. It is a debtor–creditor agreement.

S14

A "credit token agreement" is an agreement by which a person promises that he or someone else will supply cash, goods or services on production of the card, is a regulated agreement. A credit token includes a credit card, check card, voucher, coupon, stamp, etc.

S15

A "consumer hire agreement" is an agreement to "hire" (bail) goods, which is not a hire-purchase agreement, which exists for more than 3 months, and which does not require the hirer (the person who takes the goods) to pay more than £5000. It is a regulated agreement.

S189

A "conditional sale agreement" is an agreement for the sale of goods where the purchase is payable by instalments and the property in the goods remains with the seller (even though the buyer is in possession) until such conditions as specified are fulfilled.

A "credit-sale agreement" is an agreement for the sale of goods, under which the purchase price is payable by instalments, but which is not a conditional sale agreement.

A "hire-purchase agreement" is an agreement *other than* a conditional sale agreement where:

1. goods are bailed (hired) in return for periodic payments by the person to whom they are hired; and
2. the property in the goods will pass to that person if the terms of the agreement are complied with *or* he exercises an option to purchase.

S16

A credit (or hire) agreement is *not* regulated (governed) by this Act where the "creditor" is either a local authority, building society, insurance company, friendly society, organisation of employers or members (e.g. a trade union), charity, land improvement company *or* a body corporate referred to in any public general Act.

S17

A "small agreement" is a regulated consumer credit or hire agreement which does not require the consumer to make, in total, payments exceeding £50.

Part III – Licensing of Credit and Hire Businesses (*ss.21–42*)

A licence is required to carry on a consumer credit or hire business regulated by the Act. Different licences are issued for the separate categories of business, e.g. consumer credit or consumer hire; and the

Director-General of Fair Trading (DGFT) must be satisfied that the applicant is a fit and proper person to hold a licence.

It is a criminal offence to carry on a business requiring a licence without having obtained one. The DGFT has powers to renew, suspend, vary or revoke a licence.

Part IV – Seeking Business

SS43-54

Advertising: Controls exist to restrict the content and form of advertising credit or hire arrangements. For example, an advertiser who conveys false or misleading information commits a criminal offence.

Canvassing: An individual who attempts to sell (canvass) certain forms of regulated credit, e.g. a cash loan (a debtor–creditor agreement) other than at his place of business ("off trade premises") and not at a consumer's request, can be liable to prosecution. It is also an offence to send a person under 18 a document inviting him to obtain credit, or to send *anybody* a credit token without invitation.

Part V – Entering a Regulated Agreement (ss. 55–74)

S60

Making the agreement: A regulated agreement must be in writing, clearly showing the rights and duties placed upon the consumer (i.e. the debtor or hirer), the total charge for credit, and the protection and remedies available to him under the Act.

S61

Both parties must sign the agreement.

SS62-63

The consumer is entitled to a copy of the agreement. If both parties sign at the same time, the consumer need only be given one copy; if the consumer has signed the agreement but it has to be signed by someone else (e.g. a debtor needs to send it to a creditor to sign), he must be given a second copy within seven days of that signature being obtained.

S64

If the agreement is "cancellable", this fact must be clearly stated on every copy. If the consumer is not entitled to a second copy of the agreement he is entitled to a separate notice of his right of cancellation within the (same) seven days following the making of the agreement.

Cancellation

S67

A regulated agreement may be cancelled by the consumer if:

1. there were oral statements (representatives) made to the consumer by the creditor or someone on his behalf concerning the terms of the "credit" or quality of the goods; and
2. the agreement is signed by the consumer elsewhere than at the place of business of the creditor or a person acting on his behalf.

E.g.: An agreement signed by a housewife after doorstep "salesmanship" can be cancelled, but an agreement signed on trade premises cannot be.

SS68–69

If within five days (the "cooling-off period") following the day he received notice of his cancellation rights the consumer serves notice of his intention to withdraw from the agreement, that notice will cancel the agreement. A notice sent by post is considered served at the time of posting.

E.g.: An agreement is made on 1 April. The consumer receives notice of his right of cancellation on 7 April. The agreement is "cancellable" until 12 April expires. A letter of cancellation posted on that day ends the agreement.

SS70–74

The broad effect of cancellation is to free both parties from any further commitment under the agreement. A consumer may recover any payments made and any goods supplied may be collected from him subject to a right (of lien) over the goods until he gets his money back.

S74

Exclusions from Part V: Certain agreements are excluded from this part of the Act, e.g. small agreements.

E.g.: A doorstep salesman sells a consumer a set of brushes for £25 — upon credit terms. This *is* a regulated agreement but it is not governed by the formalities of cancellation rights given in Part V.

Part VI — Matters Arising During the Agreement and Liability of Creditor for Breaches by Supplier (*ss.75–86*)

S75

A debtor under a debtor–creditor–supplier agreement (s.12) who has any claim against the supplier in respect of misrepresentation or breach of contract shall have a similar claim against the creditor.

E.g.: Following a misrepresentation made to him a consumer buys goods from a retailer, using his credit card (Access or Barclaycard). If he later has a claim for breach of contract or misrepresentation, he can bring an action against both the shop and the credit card company.

This *section* does not apply: to agreements not made in the course of a business or where the cash price of the goods is less than £30 or more than £10 000; or to cards issued before July 1, 1977.

Part VII – Default and Termination (*ss.87–104*)

SS87–89

If under the terms of the agreement a consumer is in breach of the agreement, the other party must serve him a "default notice". This must specify the breach alleged and the action required to remedy it, and it must give the consumer a period of not less than seven days to comply.

S90

If the consumer is in breach of a hire-purchase or conditional sale agreement and he has paid at least one third of the total price for the goods, they are called "protected goods" and can only be repossessed on an order of the court.

S92

Except under a court order a creditor or owner cannot take possession of goods located on private premises.

SS94–97

A consumer under a consumer credit agreement is entitled at any time to give notice that he intends to exercise his right to terminate it (by completing the payments ahead of time).

S98

If a regulated agreement so provides, a creditor or owner may terminate it for any reason after giving the consumer not less than seven days' notice of the termination.

SS99–101

A consumer under a hire-purchase or conditional sale agreement is entitled to terminate it any time on bringing his total payments to one half of that total.

Part IX – Judicial Control (*ss.127–144*)

The County Court is given wide powers to control regulated agreements where it "appears just" to the court to do so.

S129

To give a consumer more time to pay under the agreement: a "time order".

S131

To give a creditor or hirer protection from damage to goods: a "protection order".

S133

To order the return or transfer of goods in hire-purchase or conditional sale agreements: a "return order", or a "transfer order".

Extortionate Credit Bargains (*ss.137–140*)

If the court finds a credit bargain extortionate it may reopen the credit agreement to do justice between the parties; this power is not restricted to a £5000 limit; a credit bargain is extortionate if:

1. The consumer is required to make grossly exorbitant payments; or
2. The agreement is otherwise contrary to ordinary principles of fair dealing.

In deciding whether a credit bargain is extortionate the court shall take into account all relevant circumstances, including:

1. The interest rates prevailing at the time of the agreement.
2. The age, experience, business capacity and state of health of the consumer.
3. The nature and degree of financial pressure on the consumer at the time of the agreement.

Part X – Ancillary Credit Businesses (*ss.145–160*)

SS145–147

Generally, the provisions of Part III of the Act apply to ancillary credit businesses, such as credit-brokers (introducing consumers to loan companies), debt collectors and credit reference agencies.

Note: A "credit reference agency" is "a person" carrying on a business giving other persons information relevant to the financial standing of individuals.

E.g.: A person applies for a loan to a company. That company may ask a credit reference agency to investigate and report to them on the person's credit-worthiness.

The Consumer Credit (Credit Reference Agency) Regulations 1977 provide for the disclosure to a consumer of information held by them and for the correction of incorrect information.

Part XI – Enforcement and Liability under the Act (*ss.161–173*)

S161

The "enforcement authorities" are the Director and local authority trading standards officers.

S162

A trading standards officer duly authorised has the power at all reasonable hours to enter business premises and inspect books and documents used in connection with a consumer credit business. In certain circumstances he has powers of seizure over documents.

There are restrictions on a trading standards officer's powers under s.162 if the business is a bank, post office or credit reference agency: Consumer Credit (Entry and Inspection) Regulations 1977.

SS167–168

The provisions under the Act create, where defined, both civil and criminal liability. A person prosecuted may have a defence if he acted mistakenly and with all reasonable care.

Consumer Safety Act 1978

Preamble: An Act to make provision with respect to the safety of consumers and others.

S1

The Secretary of State for Prices and Consumer Affairs has the power to make regulations for the purpose of securing that goods are safe. These "safety regulations" may contain provisions concerning the manufacture, conformity, standard, testing, warning or instructions on or with goods, and the prohibiting of the supply of goods which are not safe.

S2

It is a criminal offence for either a manufacturer or supplier, or both, to contravene the regulations under s.1.

S3

Goods which are not safe will be banned by way of:

1. A "Prohibition Notice" on a particular person.
2. A "Prohibition Order" on business persons generally.
3. A "Notice to Warn" requiring a person to take steps to warn consumers about the dangers of goods he has already supplied.

Contravening 1–3 above is a criminal offence but it is a defence to prove that a person took all reasonable steps to avoid committing the offence.

The Act does not give legal power to recall unsafe goods, but a business may well attempt to do this.

S5

Local authorities have the obligation to appoint officers to enforce the criminal provisions under this Act.

S6

The duties imposed on business persons can be the subject of civil liability to *any other* person by a failure to perform that duty. In other words, a person who suffers damage as a result of unsafe goods (as defined by Regulations) may claim compensation in the civil courts direct from the supplier or manufacturer of the goods. The duty imposed is a statutory duty and there is no need to prove a contractual relationship or legal duty of care under common law.

MONOPOLIES, MERGERS AND ANTI-COMPETITIVE PRACTICES

A "monopoly" is the control of goods and services by one business (person). The DGFT has a duty to collect evidence relating to "monopoly situations": FTA 1973, s.2. A "monopoly situation" arises where at least a quarter of the supply of goods or services are controlled by one person. (See example, page 111.)

The DGFT refers "monopoly situations" to the Monopolies and Mergers Commission (a government advisory body) which investigates the evidence of a monopoly and reports to the SOS for Prices and Consumer Protection. The SOS has powers to ban or restrict a harmful monopoly. A business will incur civil liability for disobedience.

Note: Monopolies held by nationalised industries are, apparently, not regarded as harmful to the public interest. However, the SOS may at any time refer to the Monopolies Commission questions concerning the efficiency and costs of, or services provided by, or a possible abuse of a monopoly held by certain public and statutory bodies: Competition Act, 1980, s.11.

A "merger" is the acquisition by one firm (bus
so that only one unit remains. Proposed
when they create or strengthen a "monopo
"taken over" will exceed £5 million in value.

E.g.: Two large but separate companies, each having on
the supply of certain goods, propose a merger: a "monopoly situa

A practice which is anti-competitive is where a person engages in activities to restrict, distort or prevent competition for the supply of goods or services: Competition Act 1980.

E.g.: Dealers agree to restrict the supply of certain goods to keep prices up.

The DGFT is required to investigate and report on such practices to the SOS, who is empowered to control or prohibit them.

COMPETITION LAWS IN THE EUROPEAN COMMUNITY

It is the policy of the European Community that there is free and fair competition in trade between member states. By the European Communities Act 1972 the competition laws of the European Community became part of the law in Britain. Articles 85 and 86 of the Treaty of Rome, applying to trade between organisations of different member states, ban industrial or commercial practices that prevent, restrict or distort competition.

E.g.: In 1979 the European court heavily fined a large drug manufacturing and supply company for securing agreements with their European customers to buy goods only from them.

CONTRACTS FOR THE SALE OF GOODS

Introduction

A contract for the sale of goods is subject to the Sale of Goods Act (SGA) 1979 and such an agreement can be classified under the "umbrella" of Consumer Protection. Contracts for the sale of goods also form part of a much wider area of "laws", namely the *supply* of goods and services.

Contracts for the *supply* of *goods* can be distinguished as follows:

of Goods

A sale or an agreement to sell goods as part of a contract to transfer the *ownership* (property) in the goods from one person to another. Under this definition come the following agreements:

1. A sale of goods 2. An agreement to sell goods	Definition in SGA 1979, s.2(1)
3. A conditional sale of goods 4. A credit sale of goods	Definition in Consumer Credit Act 1974, s.189

A Hire of Goods

A contract for the *possession* of goods to be temporarily transferred from one person to another, i.e. a hire (of goods) contract.

A Hire-Purchase of Goods

A contract for the *possession* of goods to be transferred from one person to another. The hirer (the person in possession) has an option to eventually obtain the *ownership* (property) in the goods.

Note: Where any of the above contracts (1–4) are made on credit terms, i.e. a period of time given to make payment, then the contract *may* be governed by the laws relating to consumer credit.

The Sale of Goods Act 1979 *only* applies to contracts for the sale of goods. Sometimes it is a difficult question to determine whether a contract is for goods or services, e.g. in the case of a contract to paint a portrait, or to roof a house, which are both contracts for services.

Where the main purpose of a contract is the sale of services (and the supply of goods is incidental to it) then such a transaction is not subject to the 1979 Act. However, it is now governed by the Supply of Goods and Services Act 1982 (see pages 130-1).

TRANSFER OF PROPERTY

Definition of "transfer"	Passing the actual (physical) possession of goods from one person to another. **E.g.:** A shopkeeper lends (transfers) a radio (goods) to a customer.
Definition of "transfer of property" (ownership)	Passing the actual possession of goods *and* the *ownership* from one person to another. **E.g.:** A shopkeeper makes a gift (transfers the ownership) of a radio to a customer.

Definition of "contract of sale of goods"	The transfer or agreement to transfer property for a price: s.2(1). E.g.: A shopkeeper sells a radio to a customer.

Note: There is still a contract for the sale of goods if the "transfer of the property" is to take place at a later time, though the contract is then called an "agreement to sell": s.2(5).

E.g.: A shopkeeper agrees to sell a particular radio to a customer in a week's time, when the customer will pay the price.

But in such a case the ownership of the goods (s.17) and the risk (s.20) normally remain with the seller; if either party defaults on the agreement, the other can claim "breach of contract".

There is no "transfer of property" until goods are "ascertained" (identified): s.16.

E.g.: A shopkeeper sells "*that* type of radio" to a customer for collection in a week's time, when the price will be paid. There is a contract but there is no transfer of ownership until the subject-matter of the sale is identified.

Once the goods are "ascertained" the property (ownership) is transferred to the buyer when the parties to the contract intend it to be: s.17. In the example given above this will probably be after the customer has inspected the *actual* radio.

If it is impossible to determine the intention of the parties, then the Sale of Goods Act lays down guidelines for discovering the intention: s.18, rules 1–5, page 125.

E.g.: A shopkeeper sells (not agrees to sell) a *particular* radio to a customer in a week's time, when the radio will be collected and paid for. Without fault from either party the radio is destroyed before collection. It was the customer's radio that was destroyed: s.18, rules 1 and 2. If the shopkeeper had merely *agreed to sell* the radio, then by the Sale of Goods Act, s.7 (and see s.6) the agreement would be voided.

E.g.: A customer selects and buys a particular radio from a shopkeeper, who will send it to him by parcel post. The seller properly packages the radio and sends it as requested, but it is lost in transit. It is the buyer's property that is lost: s.18, rule 5; and see s.32.

A seller may (by the terms of the contract) retain the "ownership" (property) in the goods (called reserving a right of disposal) even though the goods are delivered to the buyer: s.19; and see *The Romalpa Case*, page 126.

E.g.: A shopkeeper sells a radio to a customer and gives him possession of it. It is agreed that he will pay for the radio by monthly payments *and* that until these payments are complete the radio belongs to the seller.

The risk (of loss) in goods depends upon the agreement of the parties to the contract; if there is no agreement, the risk passes from seller to buyer when the property is transferred: s.20.

E.g.: A customer buys a radio and will collect and pay for it in one week. He asks the shopkeeper to "look after the radio" for him until collection. Because of this request the risk remains with the seller (but see s.7).

TERMS IMPLIED BY STATUTE IN A CONTRACT FOR THE SALE OF GOODS

(see pages 123–5)

"Title"

1. A *condition* that a seller has a right to sell the goods when the property passes to the buyer: s.12(1).

   E.g.: A store sells stereo equipment to a customer, who later discovers the goods were stolen and must be returned to the rightful owner. (See the *nemo dat* rule.) The customer can treat his contract with the seller as at an end and sue for damages (i.e. the price he paid).

2. A *warranty* that, unless otherwise agreed, a buyer's title to goods will remain free from any restriction: s.12(2) and (3).

   E.g.: The seller has the right to sell but the goods are subject to a mortgage (see page 168).

"Description"

A *condition* that where goods are sold by description, the goods correspond with that description: s.13(1).

E.g.: A mail order company advertises in a catalogue the sale of garden sheds "9 foot high". A customer orders one but on delivery discovers the shed is only 6 foot high. He can end the contract and claim damages.

Description includes any aspect of the goods: specifications, quantity, measurement, size, quality, packing, labelling, etc.

"A ton does not mean about a ton": *Arcos Ltd* v. *Ronaason & Son* (see pages 126-7); *Beale* v. *Taylor* (see page 127).

Goods displayed in a shop window are "sold by description": *Grant* v. *Australian Knitting Mills* (see pages 128-9).

"Merchantable Quality"

A *condition* on a seller that goods *supplied* in the course of *a business* are of merchantable quality: s.14(2).

E.g.: A baker is in breach of this condition if he sells to a customer a loaf of bread containing a foreign substance, e.g. a ring. He cannot claim the *bread* was all right, since the condition applies to *all* goods *supplied.*

"Course of a business" includes a sale by a retailer to a customer, but not a "private sale", e.g. an individual selling his car to a neighbour.

A "business" includes a profession and the activities of any government department or local or public authority: s.61.

"Merchantable quality": goods, including second-hand ones, being fit for their normal purpose, taking into account the price paid, age of goods and all other relevant circumstances: s.14(6). See also *Godley* v. *Perry* (page 128); *Cehave N.V.* v. *Bremer* (page 127).

The implied condition of merchantable quality does *not* apply if:

1. Defects in the goods are specifically drawn to the buyer's attention before the contract is made: s.14(2)(a); or,
2. A buyer examines the goods and his examination ought to reveal the defects: s.14(2)(b). For example, a purchaser examines a second-hand car which he later decides to buy. If the buyer does *not* examine the car, his rights under s.14(2) are unaffected (see *Grant* v. *Australian Knitting Mills*).

"Fitness for Purpose"

A *condition* that goods sold *in the course of business* (see above) are reasonably fit for their purpose: s.14(3).

E.g.: After examining a second-hand car a customer buys it from a dealer. The following day he discovers defects rendering the vehicle unroadworthy. These defects were not disclosed by the seller. He is in breach of this condition. A car that will not go is not a car at all.

See (at the end of this chapter): *Crowther* v. *Shannon Motor Co.*; *Griffiths* v. *Peter Conway Ltd*; *Godley* v. *Perry*; *Priest* v. *Last*.

The implied condition of "fitness for purpose" will not apply if the buyer does not rely, *or* it is unreasonable for him to rely, on the seller's "skill or judgement": s.14(3).

E.g.: An expert mountaineer who buys a pair of climbing boots from a self-service store, cannot later claim he relied on the seller's expertise.

"Sample"

A condition that in the case of a sale by sample the bulk (total) of the goods correspond with the sample: s.15(1) and (2).

E.g.: A customer agrees to buy a large quantity of "dark green" carpet on the basis of a sample seen at a store. When the bulk is delivered it is light green. (See also *Godley* v. *Perry*.)

"NO FAULT" LIABILITY

A seller cannot claim that a breach of one of the implied terms was "not his fault". He is strictly liable: *Frost* v. *Aylesbury Dairy Co.* (see page 128).

TRANSFER OF TITLE: SELLING "PROPERTY" WITHOUT OWNERSHIP

A person cannot transfer the "ownership" in "property" without owning it. (*Nemo dat quod non habet* – No one can give what he has not.)

E.g.: X is the owner of a dozen typewriters, Y *hires* the typewriters and, in breach of the agreement, sells them to Z, who is then in possession of goods that do not belong to him, and which he must return to the owner.

The *nemo dat* rule developed from the common law and is embodied in the Sale of Goods Act 1979, s.21: "Subject to this Act, where goods are sold by a person who is not their owner, the buyer acquires no better title to the goods than the seller . . .".

Exceptions to the *Nemo Dat* Rule

The *nemo dat* rule does not apply in all cases where goods are sold and the seller is not the owner. If in the example above the buyer (Z) had come within one of the exceptions to the rule that follow [a)–h)] , he would have become the owner, entitled to retain the goods.

In each and all of these exceptions the buyer (third party) only obtains ownership (title) if he buys honestly (in good faith), believing in the seller's apparent right to sell.

Sale of Goods Act 1979

a) *S21*

A sale of goods where some positive conduct of an *owner* prevents him denying the seller's authority to sell.

E.g.: The owner of a menswear shop is present when a salesman sells a suit to a customer; the owner (because he was present at the sale) cannot later claim *nemo dat*; the customer is the owner of the suit.

Where this exception applies the owner is said to be stopped (estopped) from denying the third party his title.

b) *S21*

A sale by a mercantile agent (an agent having in the usual course of his business the authority to buy or sell goods) who is in possession of the goods, with the owner's consent.

E.g.: A motor dealer agrees to sell an owner's car for "not less than £1000"; the dealer takes possession of the car and sells it in the course of his business for £750 to a customer; the buyer becomes the owner.

c) *S21*

A sale by order of the court: courts have special common law or statutory powers to order goods to be sold.

E.g.: In certain circumstances a court can order the sale of goods that were used to commit a crime.

d) *S22*

A sale in "market overt" – a recognised public market or any shop in the City of London where goods are sold by the shopkeeper in the normal way.

E.g.: If a person innocently buys stolen goods in a market he becomes the owner.

e) *S23*

A sale by a seller with "voidable" title – i.e. a title which is valid but can be made void. See *Phillips* v. *Brooks* (page 29), where a third party obtained a goods title before an agreement was voided.

f) *S24*

Resale by a seller in possession of the goods after a "sale".

E.g.: A shopkeeper sells a fridge to a customer who will collect it the following week. Before collection the shopkeeper sells the fridge to a different customer who takes collection immediately. That customer gets title, i.e. ownership of the fridge.

g) *S25*

Resale by a buyer "in possession" before ownership has passed.

E.g.: A buyer is given possession of goods, the ownership of which is to be transferred to him upon signing a document; before he signs he sells the goods to a third party, who becomes the owner.

A buyer under a conditional sale agreement (see Consumer Credit Act 1974, s.189) is excluded from this exception: s.25(2).

h) Hire-Purchase Act 1964, Part III

The sale of a motor vehicle acquired under a hire-purchase agreement. Usually under a hire-purchase agreement the hirer cannot sell the goods and pass title until all the payments are made; but this exception only arises where a motor vehicle is the subject-matter under a hire-purchase agreement *and* the sale is to a private buyer and not a car dealer.

Performing a Sale of Goods Contract: Acceptance, Delivery, Payment

(The effect of s.8 and ss.27–37 of the Sale of Goods Act 1979.)

S27

A seller must deliver the goods and the buyer accept and pay for them in accordance with the terms of the contract. "Delivery" means voluntarily transferring the possession of the goods: s.61.

E.g.: A customer goes into a shop, selects clothing and tenders payment. The seller takes the buyer's money, wraps the clothing and gives it to the customer.

Unless otherwise agreed: (these three words are vital):

S28

Payment is due at the same time as delivery.

E.g.: A customer who does not agree on credit terms must pay the full price for goods when he gets them.

S29

The place of delivery is the seller's place of business.

E.g.: A shopkeeper is not obliged to deliver goods to a customer's home.

S30

When a seller delivers the wrong quantity or type of goods, the buyer may reject all the goods; if he accepts any of them he must pay for the goods accepted at the contract price (i.e. *pro rata*).

E.g.: A shopkeeper buys 100 pairs of gloves from a wholesaler at £3 per pair; when the goods are delivered there are only ninety pairs, which the buyer decides to accept. He must pay £270.

S31

A buyer is not obliged to accept delivery by instalments, but if he does accept instalments and agrees to pay for them separately, a defective delivery of one instalment will not necessarily give him a right to end the contract. It will depend on the circumstances of each case.

E.g.: A large company orders 12 000 pens to be delivered in monthly instalments of 1000 and paid for monthly over 12 months. The first ten instalments are of good quality, but there are fifty unusable pens in the next instalment. The buyer can claim damages but *not* a right to end the contract.

SS32–33

Delivery of goods to a carrier (e.g. a post office) with a buyer's assent is regarded as delivery to that buyer unless the seller's contract with the carrier is unreasonable.

E.g.: It would probably be regarded as unreasonable for a seller to send valuable jewellery by ordinary post. If such goods were lost, the buyer could decline to treat the goods as being delivered.

S34

A buyer who has not previously examined goods does not "accept" them until he has had a reasonable opportunity to do so.

E.g.: A buyer who orders goods from a mail-order catalogue must be given a chance to examine those goods.

S35

A buyer "accepts" goods when he does something to show he has accepted them, e.g. by keeping them for a long time without telling the seller he has rejected the goods. Acceptance of the goods usually means that a buyer can only treat a breach of a condition as a breach of warranty: s.11(4), (page 123); (page 127).

E.g.: A customer buys a coat in October; an attempt to "reject" the coat the following March would be unsuccessful. See *The Algemene Case* (page 126) and *The J. B. Ashley Case* (page 127).

S36

When a buyer rightfully refuses to accept goods and he tells the seller this, the buyer is under no duty to return them.

E.g.: A customer orders, through a newspaper advertisement, some weight-lifting equipment. When the goods arrive he finds them unsatisfactory. Providing he informs the seller that he does not "accept" the goods, and there was nothing in the agreement to the contrary, the buyer is not obliged to return them.

S37

If a seller is ready and willing to deliver goods but the buyer wrongly refuses to accept them, the buyer is liable for any loss caused by his wrongful refusal.

E.g.: A company orders a quantity of flowers from a flower shop. When the sellers attempt delivery the company say they do not now want the goods; they are in breach of contract.

S8

The price of goods can be fixed by the contract, or *to be* fixed by the contract, or may be determined by a course of dealings between the parties. Otherwise, the buyer must pay a "reasonable" price.

REMEDIES FOR BREACH OF A SALE OF GOODS CONTRACT

The rules of the common law apply to sale of goods unless inconsistent with the 1979 Act.

Sellers' Remedies

1. To bring an *Action for the price*. This is appropriate: where the goods are delivered and not paid for *or* payment is due on a certain day irrespective of delivery, s.49.

2. To claim *Damages for non-acceptance*: assessed on the basis of loss directly and naturally arising, and the buyer may recover any damage the seller ought to have known would result: ss.50, 54. If there is an available market for goods, the damages will be the difference between the market value and the price of the goods at the time when they ought to have been accepted or were refused, unless this would lead to an unjust result (see common law principle, page 68).
3. *Rights of unpaid seller*: in some circumstances the seller may retain the goods until the price is paid: ss.39, 41.

Buyers' Remedies

1. To claim *Damages for non-delivery*: assessed in accordance with the common law principle: s.51. Where there is a breach of a warranty by the seller or where the buyer elects (or is compelled) to treat any breach of condition as a breach of warranty, the buyer is not entitled to reject the goods but may:
   a) Set up the breach of warranty as a reduction or extinction of the price; or
   b) Bring an action for breach of warranty: s.53.
2. To bring an *Action for specific performance*: A court may, if it thinks fit, order the contract to be performed: s.52.

A MANUFACTURER'S LIABILITY TO A CONSUMER

Negligence

A manufacturer is liable to a consumer in the tort of negligence if that negligence results in loss or damage to the consumer (see page 49). A manufacturer is a person who makes articles or materials for sale, e.g. the owner of a factory. (Negligence can, of course, be claimed against others, including sub-contractors, assemblers, packers, wholesalers, distributors and sometimes retailers.) A manufacturer owes a *duty* of care to a consumer. A consumer is anyone whom the manufacturer ought to have considered when carrying out the manufacturing activity.

Standard of Care

A manufacturer must take reasonable care to prevent any harm which he can foresee, but he is entitled to expect reasonable and proper use of his product. He is not liable if injury is caused to an abnormally sensitive person, as in *Griffiths* v. *Peter Conway* (see page 129).

The common law suggests that if a product is capable of causing damage if wrongly used, a manufacturer must place a warning on the product; otherwise he will be liable in negligence; (e.g. in the case of dangerous chemicals).

A manufacturer will escape liability for dangerous products unless it is proved he was at fault. If an accident occurs with a product and it is no one's fault, the manufacturer will not be liable.

Contract

A consumer when buying goods makes a contract with a retailer. It is possible that there is also a contract with a manufacturer *when* a consumer fills in a manufacturer's "guarantee" (or "warranty") form, which usually contains promises or undertakings by the manufacturer.

The consumer submits to the manufacturer's terms (of contract) in exchange for buying the goods.

The consumer's rights against the manufacturer are much greater in contract than in tort because the consumer – in the event of a breach of contract – need not prove fault: *Frost* v. *Aylesbury Dairy Co.*

In a consumer transaction the duties in tort and the obligations in contract are governed by the Unfair Contract Terms Act 1977 (see pages 43-5).

"Products Liability"

Definition by European Convention of "Products Liability in Regard to Personal Injury and Death," 1977: "A producer shall be liable to pay compensation for death or personal injuries caused by a defect in the product". i.e. it is unnecessary to prove fault.

"Products Liability" does *not* apply in Britain.

The Royal Commission on Civil Liability for Personal Injuries (1978) said there was no justification for "no fault" liability for defective products.

Authorities on Sale of Goods

The Sale of Goods Act 1979

S2(1)

A contract of sale of goods is a contract by which the seller transfers or agrees to transfer the property in goods to the buyer for a monetary "consideration" called the price.

S2(5)

Where under a contract of sale the transfer of the goods is to take place at a future time or subject to some condition to be fulfilled, the contract is called an "agreement to sell".

S4(1)

A contract of sale may be made in writing, or by word of mouth, or partly in writing and partly by word of mouth, or may be implied from the conduct of the parties.

S6

Where there is a contract for the sale of specific goods, and the goods without the knowledge of the seller have perished at the time when the contract is made, the contract is void.

S7

Where there is an agreement to sell specific goods and subsequently the goods, without any fault on the part of the seller or buyer, perish before the risk passes to the buyer, the agreement is voided.

S11(2)

Where a contract of sale of goods is subject to a condition to be fulfilled by the seller, the buyer may waive the condition or elect to treat the breach of the condition as a breach of warranty.

S11(3)

Whether a term is a condition or a warranty depends on the construction (interpretation) of the contract, and a term may be a condition though called a warranty in the contract.

S11(4)

Where a contract is not severable and a buyer has accepted the goods, or part of them, the breach of a condition by the seller can only be treated as a breach of warranty, *unless* there is an express or implied term in the contract to say otherwise.

S12(1)

In a contract of sale there is an implied condition upon a seller that he has a right to sell the goods, and in the case of an agreement to sell he will have such a right at the time when the property is to pass.

S12(2)

There is an implied warranty on a seller, unless agreed otherwise, that the title to the goods will be free from any restriction or limitation (charge, encumbrance or disturbance to quiet enjoyment).

S13(1)

Where there is a contract for the sale of goods by description, there is an implied condition that the goods will correspond to the description.

S14(1)

Except as provided by ss.14 and 15 of this Act and subject to any other Act, there is no implied condition or warranty in law about the quality or fitness for any particular purpose of goods supplied under a contract of sale (of goods).

S14(2)

Where a seller sells goods in the course of business there is an implied condition that the goods supplied are of merchantable quality. There is no such condition as regards defects specifically drawn to the buyer's attention before the contract is made. Nor is there any such condition if the buyer examines the goods before the contract is made, as regards defects which the examination ought to reveal.

S14(3)

Where a seller sells goods in the course of a business and the buyer, expressly or by implication, makes known to the seller any particular purpose for which the goods are being bought, there is an implied condition that the goods are reasonably fit for that purpose, whether or not that is a purpose for which such goods are commonly supplied, except where the circumstances show that the buyer does not rely, or it is unreasonable for him to rely, on the skill or judgement of the seller.

S14(6)

Goods are of "merchantable quality" if they are as fit for the purpose(s) for which goods of that kind are commonly bought as it is reasonable to expect having regard to any description applied to them, the price (if relevant) and all other relevant circumstances.

S15(1)

A contract of sale is a contract of sale by sample where there is an express or implied term in the contract to that effect.

S15(2)

In a contract of sale by sample there is an implied condition that:

1. the bulk corresponds to the sample; and
2. the buyer will have a reasonable opportunity of comparing the bulk with the sample; and

3. the goods will be free from any defect rendering them unmerchantable which would not be apparent on reasonable examination of the sample.

S16

Where there is a contract for the sale of unascertained goods, no property in the goods is transferred to the buyer unless and until they are ascertained.

S17

Property in ascertained goods is transferred to the buyer when the parties intend it to be transferred. This intention is discovered from all the circumstances of the case.

S18

Unless there is a different intention, the property in specific (identified) goods will be transferred to the buyer according to one of the following rules:

Rule 1: When the contract is made, even if payment or delivery, or both, be postponed;

Rule 2: When some action is required from the seller to make the goods "deliverable", and this has been done and the buyer informed;

Rule 3: Where the goods are "deliverable" but need to be tested (weighed, measured, etc.) by the seller, and this has been done and the buyer informed;

Rule 4: Where the goods are sent to the buyer "on approval" or on "sale or return" or by some similar arrangement, and the buyer has signified his acceptance of the goods in some way or retained the goods beyond the agreed time, or a reasonable time;

Rule 5: When the goods are unconditionally allocated (appropriated) to the buyer and the buyer assents to this allocation.

S19

By the terms of the contract, even if the goods are delivered, the seller may reserve (keep) the right of disposal (ownership) in the goods.

S20

Unless otherwise agreed, the goods remain at the seller's risk (of loss) until the property is transferred to the buyer.

S55

Where a right, duty or liability would arise under a contract of sale of goods by implication of law, i.e. terms implied by the courts, it may (subject to the Unfair Contract Terms Act 1977) be negatived, i.e. cancelled, or varied by express agreement of the parties to the contract, or by such usage (custom) as binds both parties to the contract.

S61

Interpretation: "goods" includes all personal chattels (things) other than things in action and money; "business" includes a profession and the activities of any government department or local or public authority.

S62(2)

The rules of the common law, unless inconsistent with this Act, apply to contracts for the sale of goods.

The Algemene Case (1978)

The buyers ordered a commodity called "crude maize oil"; when the oil was delivered the buyers considered that the commodity might not be crude oil at all but semi-refined oil. They waited seventeen days before deciding to reject the oil but the court *held* this length of time was too long and the buyers were deemed to have accepted the goods (s.35). They could only claim a breach of warranty: s.11(4).

Aluminium Industrie Vaassen BV v. *Romalpa Aluminium Ltd* (1976)

A clause in a sale of goods contract said that property (ownership) in certain goods would only pass to the buyer when he had paid the agreed price (s.17 and s.19) although the agreement said that the "risk" passed when the goods were delivered (s.20). A dispute later arose as to the ownership of the unpaid for goods and the court *held* the clause valid. The seller had retained *ownership* of the goods by the terms of the contract.

Arcos Ltd v. *Ronaasen & Son* (1933)

There were contracts for the sale of staves "half an inch thick". When the goods were delivered, one per cent of the staves were more than five-eighths of an inch thick, and the remainder were between half an inch and five-eighths of an inch thick. The buyer claimed he was entitled to reject the consignment for breach of the implied condition as to correspondence with description.

The court upheld the buyer's claim. The contract specified half an inch, and any deviation from that gave the buyer a right to reject the whole. "A ton" does not mean "about a ton"; likewise "half an inch" does not mean "about half an inch".

Note: Under the *de minimus* principle ("the law does not concern itself with trifles") a very minor deviation will be ignored by the court; e.g. a buyer of 4950 tons of wheat could not reject the consignment when the seller delivered 4950 tons, 55lb: *Shipton, Anderson* v. *Weil Bros.* (1912).

The J. B. Ashley Case (1979)

English buyers ordered cloth from Italian sellers. The goods arrived in lots, most of which went direct to a warehouse, a small amount coming direct to the buyers for inspection. The goods in the warehouse were sold to sub-buyers, and in May, complaints started coming in from these sub-buyers about the quality of the cloth.

The buyers contacted the sellers, who claimed there was nothing wrong with the goods. In July, after lengthy negotiations, the buyers "rejected" the cloth; the court had to decide whether they were entitled to do so under s.35.

Held: In the circumstances of this case the buyers had not "accepted" the goods and were entitled to reject them for the breach of a condition: s.11(4).

Beale v. *Taylor* (1967)

Taylor advertised a car for sale: "Herald convertible, white, 1961 . . .". Beale read the advertisement, contacted Taylor and was given a test-drive. Beale agreed to buy the car. Unknown to both parties the car was made up of two parts: the rear part was from a 1961 model, and the front part from an earlier model, the two parts being welded together. Beale claimed breach of s.13 – goods failing to comply with the description.

The court *held* this was a sale by description and the seller was in breach of the implied condition. The argument by the seller that this was not a sale by description failed.

Cehave N. V. v. *Bremer* (1976)

The Court of Appeal considered the meaning of "merchantable quality". It ruled that even though goods are damaged and lose their value that is not conclusive evidence the goods are not "fit for the purpose". If the goods can still be used for the purpose intended, there will be no breach of the condition in s.14, though there may be a breach of a warranty.

Crowther v. *Shannon Motor Co.* (1975)

A buyer purchased an 8-year-old Jaguar car from a dealer. The car had 82 000 miles on the clock. At the time of the sale the dealer said the engine was "hardly run in". Three weeks later, after the car had been used for a further 2300 miles, the engine "seized up". The buyer claimed the car was not fit for its purpose: s.14(3). The court heard evidence that the previous owner of the car (who sold it to the dealer) regarded the engine as "clapped out".

Held: The buyer had, by implication, made known the purpose he wanted the car for; he had relied on the seller's skill and judgement; as a matter of fact and degree the condition of fitness for purpose had been broken. Judgment to the buyer.

Frost v. *Aylesbury Dairy Co. Ltd* (1905)

A dairy company supplied milk to the plaintiff for consumption by him and his family. The milk supplied was infected with typhoid and the plaintiff's wife died as a result of drinking some of the milk. He sued the company for breach of the implied condition: s.14(3).

The court *held* that the defendants knew by implication the purpose for which the plaintiff bought the milk; further, it was no defence that they had exercised all reasonable care and skill in purifying the milk. They were still liable even though not at fault, i.e. strictly liable.

Godley v. *Perry & Others* (1960)

A six-year-old boy, Godley, purchased a cheap catapult from a stationer, Perry. When the boy used the catapult to fire a stone, the plastic snapped and caused Godley to lose an eye. Godley sued Perry for:

1. Breach of the condition of description: s.13.
2. Breach of the condition of merchantable quality: s.14(2).
3. Breach of the condition of fitness for purpose: s.14(3).

The court *held* that Godley had relied on Perry's skill and judgement and the catapult was not reasonably fit for its purpose; the sale was by description and the catapult was not of merchantable quality. Perry was, therefore, in breach of all the implied conditions as alleged. Perry, in turn, sued the wholesaler who sold him the catapult as it had been purchased in a sale by sample, tested by pulling the elastic. The court held the wholesaler liable in damages to Perry under s.15.

Grant v. *Australian Knitting Mills Ltd* (1935)

Grant bought a pair of underpants from a retailer. He became seriously ill after catching a disease caused by wearing the underpants. The retailer had purchased the garment from the Australian Knitting Mills. Grant sued the retailer for breach of s.14 and sued the manufacturer in the tort of negligence.

Held: The goods were not fit for their purpose nor of merchantable quality and the retailer was liable. The claim that Grant had not relied on the seller's judgement under s.14(3) was rejected. Such reliance can be inferred from most retail transactions.

The court also said that there will be a sale by description when goods are displayed in the normal way by shops: s.13. The action against the manufacturer in tort succeeded. (See also: *Donoghue* v. *Stevenson*, page 49.)

Griffiths v. *Peter Conway Ltd* (1939)

The defendant company made (to measure) a Harris Tweed coat for the plaintiff buyer Mrs. Griffiths. The wearing of the coat caused her to suffer from dermatitis (a skin disease) and she brought an action claiming the coat was not "fit for its purpose": s.14(3).

Held: The coat caused her dermatitis because *her* skin was particularly sensitive. She failed to reveal this fact at the time the contract to make the coat was made. The goods were fit for the purposes of a person with a "normal" skin and she failed in her action.

Priest v. *Last* (1903)

A customer went into a shop and purchased a hot water bottle. The buyer's wife used the bottle for its usual purposes but was badly injured when the bottle burst. The buyer sued the sellers for breach of s.14(2); they claimed he had not told them the purpose he wanted the bottle for.

The court said the purpose of the sale of a hot water bottle is self-evident: the buyers were liable. The same goes for food, cars, under-clothing, catapults, etc.

TERMS IMPLIED BY STATUTE IN A HIRE-PURCHASE AGREEMENT

By the Supply of Goods (Implied Terms) Act 1973, ss.8–11, substantially the same terms are implied in a hire-purchase agreement (i.e. implied conditions and warranties relating to "title", "description", "merchantable quality", "fitness for purpose" and "sample") as in a sale of goods contract.

The Unfair Contract Terms Act 1977, s.6, imposes the same restrictions on "contracting out" of implied terms by "exclusion clauses".

THE SUPPLY OF GOODS AND SERVICES ACT 1982

This new Act implies terms:

1. in those contracts for the supply of goods which are not subject to the Sale of Goods Act 1979 and the Supply of Goods (Implied Terms) Act 1973, and
2. in contracts for the supply of services.

Supply of Goods: Contracts for the Transfer of Property in Goods and Contracts for the Hire of Goods (Part I, ss. 1–11)

The terms implied in these contracts are identical, with appropriate modifications, to the implied terms in the Sale of Goods Act 1979 relating to transfer of title (or possession), description, merchantable quality or fitness, and sample.

E.g.:

1. A consumer transfers his motor vehicle in exchange for a car from a motor dealer.
2. A consumer hires a carpet cleaner from a shop.

The 1982 Act implies terms in both examples. A supplier impliedly promises that he has a right to transfer the ownership or possession of the goods and, where relevant, that the goods are as described, of merchantable quality, fit their purpose and conform with any sample.

Supply of Services (Part III, ss. 24–28)

Section 24 defines a contract for the supply of a service as a contract under which a person ("the supplier") agrees to carry out a service. Excluded from this definition is a contract of service (i.e. employment) or apprenticeship, a contract of sale of goods, or a hire-purchase agreement.

Section 25 says that in a contract for the supply of a service where the supplier is acting in the course of a business, there is an implied term that the supplier will carry out the service with reasonable care and skill.

Section 26(1) says that where, under a contract for the supply of a service by a supplier acting in the course of a business, the time for the service to be carried out is not fixed by the contract, left to be fixed in a manner agreed by the contract or determined by the course of dealing between the parties, there is an implied term that the supplier will carry out the service within a reasonable time.

Section 26(2) says that what is a reasonable time is a question of fact.

Section 27(1) says that where, under a contract for the supply of a service, the consideration for the service is not determined by the contract, left to be determined in a manner agreed by the contract or determined by a course of dealing between the parties, there is an implied term that the party contracting with the supplier will pay a reasonable charge.

Section 27(2) says that what is a reasonable charge is a question of fact.

Exclusion of Liability

The 1982 Act confirms that both contracts for the supply of goods and contracts for the supply of services are subject to the provisions of the Unfair Contract Terms Act 1977 (see pages 43-5).

6

Company Law

THE PRIVATE ENTERPRISE BUSINESS COMPANY

A partnership is governed by the Partnership Act 1890.

A registered company is governed by the Companies Acts 1948, 1967, 1976, 1980 and 1981.

A Registered Limited Company must have a minimum of two shareholders and is either:

1. A Public Limited Company (PLC), registered as public, having an authorised share capital of at least £50 000 and a minimum of 2 directors.
2. A Private Limited Company is a company not registered as public, having at least 1 director.

Only a public limited company can invite members of the public to buy shares or debentures in it.

Company Laws control the formation of companies, the trading of companies, their financing and their ending.

A company may be registered as limited by guarantee; this is for non-profit-making organisations, e.g. educational, trade or professional bodies. An "unlimited" company can be registered, but then the liability of its members is unlimited.

PARTNERSHIP FIRMS

Doctors, solicitors, accountants, bankers and vets are examples of partnership firms.

A partnership is an unincorporated association; the firm will be given legal status (see page 8) but the members of the partnership have unlimited liability. It is possible to form a limited partnership, but there must still be one partner with unlimited liability; this kind of partnership is very rare: Limited Partnership Act 1907.

The Partnership Act 1890

S1

A partnership is "the relationship which subsists between persons carrying on a business in common with a view to profit". The definition is often used to decide whether an individual is an employee or a partner.

"Business in common": persons carrying on different businesses together are *not* partners.

"To profit": a charity is not a partnership.

S2

Persons who are jointly owning property or sharing profits are not automatically in partnership. But it may be evidence of a partnership.

A partnership can be created in the same way as a contract: orally, in writing or by conduct.

Usually a written agreement is made called "Articles of Partnership", which confirms who are the partners and what are the rights, obligations and duties of each partner. The Articles can be in a "standard form" modified to suit a particular business.

A partnership is known as a "firm" and may be called a "company" but may not be called a "limited company". The maximum number of partners is 20 but many professional firms are exempt from this requirement.

A Partner Dealing with Persons Outside the Partnership

S5

"The act of every partner, who does any act for carrying on in the usual way business carried on by the firm, binds the firm and the partners." The meaning of "usual . . . business" depends upon the kind of firm; it is usual for all partnerships to hire staff, sell their own goods or services, and purchase items for use in the business. It is within the usual business of a trading firm to borrow money.

Partners are jointly liable for a firm's debts: liability can be shared equally. A creditor can bring an action against the partnership firm or an individual partner, but in either case the partners are personally liable. The authority of a partner to bind the firm and his responsibility for the debts of a firm continues after a partnership ends.

Rights, Obligations and Duties of a Partner to Another Partner

The partnership contract (e.g. the Articles) usually governs the relationship, but the 1890 Act imposes implied terms subject to any express agreement:

SS24, 28-30

A partner is entitled to:

1. Share equally in profits (but must contribute equally to losses).
2. Take part in the management of the business.
3. Be reimbursed for expenses incurred in the course of the business.
4. Prevent a new partner being taken into the firm.
5. Examine the "books" of the firm.
6. Be dealt with honestly (with the utmost good faith) by his other partners.

Failure to comply with a term of the partnership agreement is a breach of contract.

Ending the Partnership

A partnership that comes to an end is said to be "dissolved". A dissolution can occur in a variety of ways in accordance with the agreement. The bankruptcy or death of a partner, or an order of the court, will bring the partnership to an end.

PROMOTING A COMPANY

A "promoter" is a person who undertakes to form a company with reference to a given project and to set it going, and who takes the necessary steps to accomplish that purpose: *Twycross* v. *Grant* (1877). He is under a duty to disclose any profits he makes from promoting a company, i.e. he is in a fiduciary (trusted) position: *Erlanger* v. *New Sombrero Phosphate Co.* (1878).

A promoter (or other person) who makes a contract before a company is incorporated can be held personally liable on that contract: *Kelner* v. *Baxter* (1866).

REGISTRATION OF A LIMITED COMPANY

The Registrar of Companies is the person legally responsible for bringing a company into existence. A company (public or private) must obtain registration before it commences business. In order to do this it must present the following completed documents to the Registrar of Companies (and pay fees):

1. The Memorandum of Association.
2. The Articles of Association.
3. A Statement of the First Directors.
4. A Statutory Declaration.
5. A Statement of Capital.

If the documents are approved, the Registrar issues a Certificate of Incorporation. A private company may then commence business, but a public company may not commence business until it has been issued with a trading certificate, which will be issued when it has satisfied the Registrar that the authorised share capital is £50 000.

Incorporating a Limited Company

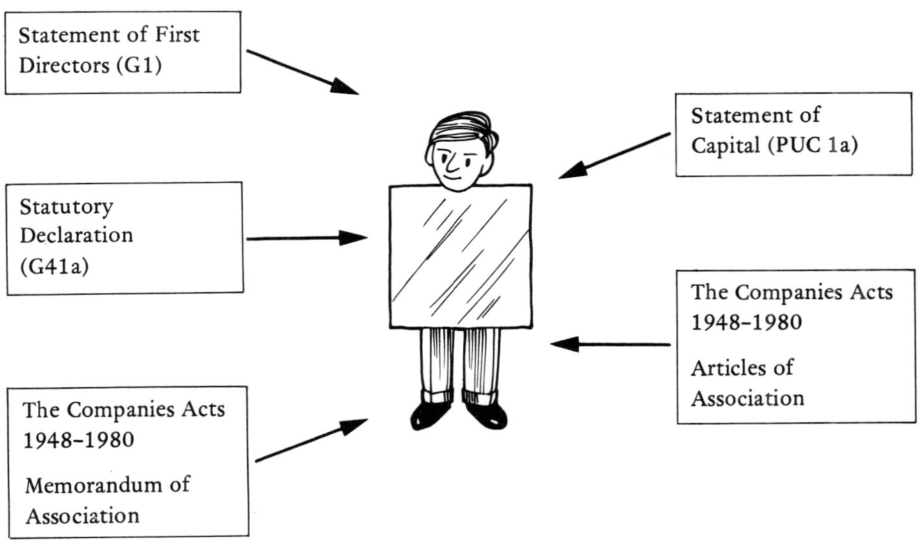

Forming a Legal Person

Form No. 1

G

THE COMPANIES ACTS 1948 TO 1980

Statement of first directors and secretary and intended situation of registered office

1

Please do not write in this binding margin

Pursuant to sections 21 and 23(2) of the Companies Act 1976

Please complete legibly, preferably in black type, or bold black lettering

*delete if inappropriate

Company number

Name of Company

Limited*

The intended situation of the registered office of the company on incorporation is as stated below

If the memorandum is delivered by an agent for the subscribers of the memorandum, please mark 'X' in the box opposite and insert the agent's name and address below

If the spaces provided on page 2 are insufficient and use has been made of continuation sheets (see note 1), please enter in the box opposite the number of continuation sheets which form part of this statement

Presentor's reference (if any):

For official use

General section

Post room

The name(s) and particulars of the person who is, or the persons who are, to be the first director or directors of the company are as follows:

Please do not write in this binding margin

Important
The particulars to be given are those referred to in section 21(2)(a) of the Companies Act 1976 and section 200(2) of the Companies Act 1948. Please read the notes on page 4 before completing this part of the form.

Name (note 2) | Business occupation

Former name(s) (note 3) | Nationality

Address (note 4)

Date of birth (where applicable) (note 6)

Particulars of other directorships (note 5)

I hereby consent to act as director of the company named on page 1

Signature | Date

Name (note 2) | Business occupation

Former name(s) (note 3) | Nationality

Address (note 4)

Date of birth (where applicable) (note 6)

Particulars of other directorships (note 5)

I hereby consent to act as director of the company named on page 1

Signature | Date

Name (note 2) | Business occupation

Former name(s) (note 3) | Nationality

Address (note 4)

Date of birth (where applicable) (note 6)

Particulars of other directorships (note 5)

I hereby consent to act as director of the company named on page 1

Signature | Date

Please do not write in this binding margin

Important
The particulars to ge given are those referred to in section 21(2)(b) of the Companies Act 1976 and section 200(3) of the Companies Act 1948. Please read the notes on page 4 before completing this part of the form.

The name(s) and particulars of the person who is, or the persons who are, to be the first secretary, or joint secretaries, of the company are as follows:

Name (notes 2 & 7)
Former name(s) (note 3)
Address (notes 4 & 7)
I hereby consent to act as secretary of the company named on page 1 Signature Date

Name (notes 2 & 7)
Former name(s) (note 3)
Address (notes 4 & 7)
I hereby consent to act as secretary of the company named on page 1 Signature Date

*as required by section 21(3) of the Companies Act 1976

Signed by or on behalf of the subscribers of the memorandum*

† delete as appropriate

Signature [Subscriber] [Agent] † Date

Signature [Subscriber] [Agent] † Date

Notes

1 If the spaces on page 2 provide insufficient space the names and particulars must be entered on the prescribed continuation sheet(s).

2 Full names must be given. In the case of an individual, his present Christian name or names and surname must be given. 'Christian name' includes a forename, and 'surname' in the case of a peer or person usually known by a title different from his surname means that title. In the case of a corporation, its corporate name must be given.

3 In the case of an individual, any former Christian names and surname must be given in addition. The expression 'Christian name' includes a forename.

'Former Christian name' and 'former surname' do not include:

a in the case of a peer or a person usually known by a British title different from his surname, the name by which he was known previous to the adoption of or succession to the title; or

b in the case of any person, a former Christian name or surname where that name or surname was changed or disused before the person bearing the name attained the age of eighteen years or has been changed or disused for a period of not less than twenty years; or

c in the case of a married woman, the name or surname by which she was known previous to the marriage.

4 Usual residential address must be given or, in the case of a corporation, the registered or principal office.

5 The names of all bodies corporate incorporated in Great Britain of which the director is also a director must be given, except bodies corporate of which the company making the return is the wholly-owned subsidiary or bodies corporate which are the wholly-owned subsidiaries either of the company or of another company of which the company is the wholly-owned subsidiary. A body corporate is deemed to be the wholly-owned subsidiary of another if it has no members except that other and that other's wholly-owned subsidiaries and its or their nominees. 'Director' includes any person who occupies the position of a director by whatsoever name called, and any person in accordance with whose directions or instructions the directors are accustomed to act.

6 Dates of birth need only be given in the case of directors of a company which is subject to section 185 of the Companies Act, 1948, namely a company which is not a private company or which, being a private company, is the subsidiary of a body corporate incorporated in the United Kingdom which is neither a private company nor a company registered under the law relating to companies for the time being in force in Northern Ireland and having provisions in its constitution which would, if it had been registered in Great Britain, entitle it to rank as a private company.

7 Where the secretary or one of the joint secretaries is a Scottish firm the details required are the firm name and its principal office address. Where all the partners in a firm are joint secretaries the name and principal office address of the firm alone may be stated.

THE COMPANIES ACTS 1948 to 1980 Form No. 41a

G **41a**

Declaration of compliance with the requirements on application for registration of a company

Pursuant to section 3(5) of the Companies Act 1980

Please do not write in this binding margin

Please complete legibly, preferably in black type, or bold black lettering

For official use **Company number**

*Insert full name of Company

Name of Company ________________________ Limited*

I, ________________________

of ________________________

____

____

† Please indicate whether you are a Solicitor of the Supreme Court (or in Scotland 'a Solicitor') engaged in the formation of the company, or a person named as director or secretary of the company in the statement delivered under section 21 of the Companies Act 1976

do solemnly and sincerely declare that I am † ________________________

____

of* ________________________

________________________ Limited*

and that all the requirements of the Companies Acts 1948 to 1980 in respect of the registration of the said company and of matters precedent and incidental thereto have been complied with. And I make this solemn Declaration conscientiously believing the same to be true and by virtue of the provisions of the Statutory Declarations Act 1835

Declared at ________________________ Signature of Declarant

____

____

the ____________ day of ____________

One thousand nine hundred and ____________

before me ________________________

A Commissioner for Oaths or Notary Public or Justice of the Peace or Solicitor having the powers conferred on a Commissioner for Oaths

Presentor's name, address and reference (if any):

For official use New companies section	Post room

Form No. PUC1 (revised)

G

Statement on formation of a company to be incorporated with limited liability under the Companies Act 1948

PUC1

Pursuant to Part V of the Finance Act 1973

Please do not write in this binding margin

Please do not write in the space below. For Inland Revenue use only

Please complete legibly, preferably in black type, or bold block lettering

For official use | Company number

Name of company

Limited*

*delete if inappropriate

†Distinguish between ordinary, preference, etc.

A Nominal Capital	£		
Description of shares†			
B Nominal value of each share	£	£	£
C Number of shares taken on incorporation			
D Total amount payable on each (including premium if any)	£	£	£
E Amount paid or due and payable on each	£	£	£
F Total amount paid or due and payable in respect of C	£		
G Capital duty payable on F at £1 per £100 or part of £100	£		

Notes

This form must be delivered to the Registrar of Companies when applying for incorporation of the company.

If amounts are contributed otherwise than in cash, that fact with full particulars must be stated and attached to this form. ☐ Please tick box if attached

I hereby certify that the above particulars are correct in all respects

‡delete as appropriate

Signed______________[Director] [Secretary]‡ Date________

Presentor's name, address and reference (if any):

For official use

Capital section | Post room

THE MEMORANDUM OF ASSOCIATION
(see e.g. on page 214)

The Name of the Company

A company limited by shares or guarantee must end its name with the word "Limited" if a private company, and with the words "Public Limited Company" (PLC) if a public company. A charitable or other non-profit-making limited company must get permission to omit "limited" from its name. An undesirable name will not be registered, e.g.: "Fred's Royal Fruit and Veg".

The name of the company and other details must be shown on all the company's business documents. "Goodwill" is attached to a company name and it will be protected by the tort of "passing off" (see page 62).

The Registered Office

This fixes the nationality of the company, which cannot be altered; legal documents are served on a company at its registered office; the register of directors is kept at the registered office.

The Objectives of a Limited Company

The "Objects Clause" in the Memorandum of Association protects persons dealing with a limited company, enabling potential and actual members (shareholders) and creditors to be aware of the activities for which their money, goods or services will be used by the company.

A company can only engage in activities expressly or impliedly stated in the "Objects Clause"; a company has implied power to buy goods, employ staff and own premises.

The "Objects Clause" defines the contractual capacity of a company and it cannot give to its agents (directors) the power to do what the company itself cannot do. A transaction entered into by a company which is outside its objects clause is at common law *ultra vires* and so is void and of no effect. *Ultra vires* is defined as "beyond the powers"; in regard to a company, *vires* refers to the powers given to a company, expressly or impliedly, by the objects clause.

If the directors of a company decide to enter a contract which is *ultra vires* in relation to the objects of the company, and the other person to such a contract is unaware of this, then under statute law that person is entitled to enforce the contract *against* the company:

European Communities Act 1972

S9(1)

"In favour of a person dealing with a company in good faith, any transaction decided on by the directors shall be deemed to be one which is within the capacity of the company to enter into, and the powers of the company shall be deemed to be free of any limitation under the memorandum or articles of association; and a party to a transaction so decided on shall not be bound to enquire as to the contractual capacity of the company to enter into it or as to any such limitation on the powers of the directors, and shall be presumed to have acted in good faith unless the contrary is proved."

A person is unaware of the contract being *ultra vires* if he does *not* know of the limits imposed by the objects clause.

A company cannot itself enforce an *ultra vires* contract; it may however, sue the directors or other officers of the company to recover for the company any loss it has suffered as a result of their breach of duty.

Alteration of objects: A company cannot change its objects to confirm (ratify) an *ultra vires* act, but it may decide to alter its objects clause so as to carry on the business more economically or more efficiently.

A company can construct (draft) an objects clause in such a way as to give it the powers to engage in every kind of transaction it may wish to undertake.

Bell Houses Ltd v. *City Wall Properties Ltd* (1966)

A company carried on a business as property developers. The objects clause gave them the power to do this and "to carry on any other trade or business whatsoever which can, in the opinion of the board of directors, be advantageously carried out by the company in connection with or as ancillary to . . . the general business of the company".

The company entered into a contract only partially connected with property development and the other party refused to pay the agreed fee claiming that the agreement to do so was *ultra vires* in relation to the company, and therefore void.

The court *held* that the disputed object was valid. A company can engage in any business which the directors honestly believe (*bona fide*) can be carried on for the benefit of the main object of the company.

A modern objects clause will usually contain a long list of alternative main objects with the power to interpret each object as a main object. This is legal.

Limited Liability Clause

This simply states that the limitation of the members is limited.

The Share Capital Clause

A company limited by shares must state the amount of the share capital and how it is divided.

E.g.: The share capital of the company is £100 divided into 200 shares at 50p each.

The authorised share capital is the maximum amount in shares that a company can issue.

After the compulsory clauses *additional* clauses may be added; a public limited company must add a sixth clause stating it is a public limited company.

Subscribers to the Memorandum

This part is signed by the first shareholders (subscribers) and witnessed. The subscribers must also sign the articles and the form giving particulars of directors, etc. The first directors are often the subscribers.

THE ARTICLES OF ASSOCIATION

(see e.g. on page 218)

This document shows the internal management regulations of the company and the relationship of the company to its members and the rights of one member (shareholder) to another.

The articles will include the following provisions:

1. The issue and transfer of shares.
2. The appointment and duties of the directors and the company secretary.
3. Details about company meetings.
4. Payment of dividends and presentation of company accounts.

A company limited by shares may either have its own special articles or it may adopt the statutory model articles (in Table A of the 1948 Companies Act) with or without modifications.

A company may in certain circumstances alter or add to its articles if the alteration is in the interests of the company as a whole.

THE LEGAL EFFECT OF THE MEMORANDUM AND ARTICLES

The memorandum and the articles constitute the terms of a contract (subject to the provisions of the Companies Act):

1. Between a company and a member of it; or
2. Between one member of a company and another member of that company.

After registration of a company the failure of either party to comply with the terms of the agreement can amount to a breach of contract.

PUBLICITY

A company is under a duty to make detailed information about itself available to the public. This is to protect shareholders (members), creditors and other persons dealing with a company.

The formation documents (e.g. Memorandum and Articles) are available for public inspection at the Companies Registry in Cardiff or at Companies House (on microfilm) in London.

A company must deliver an "annual return" to the Registrar.

A COMPANY AND ITS CONTRACTS

A company enters contracts through its agents, i.e. directors and persons acting under their authority. Its contracts are subject to the general law of contract (see page 17).

The capacity of a company to make contracts is defined by its objects clause (in the Memorandum) and restricted by the *ultra vires* rule.

THE PROSPECTUS

A prospectus is defined as "any prospectus, notice, circular, advertisement or other invitation offering to the public for subscription or purchase, any shares or debentures of a company": Companies Act 1948, s.455. Only a public company may offer shares or debentures to the public; a private company is prohibited from doing so.

Strict rules are laid down as to the issue and form of a prospectus; e.g. it must give details of its profits and losses for the previous five (sometimes ten) years. A copy of the prospectus must be signed on behalf of the company and delivered to the Registrar before it is issued, and a company failing to comply with the requirements for a prospectus may be liable in civil and criminal law.

CAPITAL

The "capital" (assets less liabilities) of a company may come from money provided by "share capital" (below) or from money borrowed, or from credit agreements, e.g. buying goods on credit.

SHARE CAPITAL

The share capital is the total amount which a company's shareholders have contributed or are liable to contribute as payment for their shares.

A company need not obtain the full amount due on shares when they are issued to shareholders, i.e. "partly paid" shares.

By s.42 of the Companies Act 1981 a limited company is prohibited from providing financial assistance for the purchase of its own shares except where such provision is an incidental part of some larger purpose of the company and given in good faith in the company's interest. There are also rules prohibiting a company from reducing its share capital.

SHAREHOLDERS

A shareholder (member) is a person owning a share (shares) in a company; a share is a form of property which can be transferred and carries rights and obligations (see page 165). The rights attached to shares are defined in a company's articles.

A shareholder is entitled to receive dividends and usually has a right to attend and vote at general meetings. Different rights can attach to different shares, e.g. preference and ordinary shares.

A share certificate is issued to a person buying shares; it is evidence of ownership of shares.

Shares are "property" which can be transferred subject to:

1. Any restrictions on transfer imposed by the articles; and
2. The statutory rule in s.75 of the Companies Act 1948 that a company may only register a transfer of its shares if a written document (instrument) of transfer is delivered to the company (so as to enforce payment of stamp duty, i.e. a tax on the transfer).

The articles of a private company usually provide that the directors *may* refuse to register the transfer of any share; the directors must act honestly in the interests of the company in reaching their decision to refuse to register the transfer. The articles may restrict the right to transfer shares by giving existing members the right of first refusal on shares to be sold (a right of pre-emption).

Unless shares are "fully paid" the shareholder is liable to pay the balance on shares when "called" on to do so.

There are rules that sometimes prohibit a person connected with a company (e.g. a director) dealing in "quoted securities", i.e. shares bought and sold on the stock exchange; this is called "insider dealing" and Part V of the Companies Act 1980 imposes criminal liability for it.

LOAN CAPITAL AND CHARGES

The objects of a company usually express a power to borrow money; the money borrowed is termed *loan capital*.

Any document which states that a company has borrowed money is called a *debenture*: a debenture may create a "charge" on a company's assets as security for a loan, i.e. a *legal right* to be paid money; "Security for a loan" refers to something pledged (promised) to ensure the fulfilment of an obligation.

Usually a debenture is sealed in a mortgage created by deed (a formal document) and this gives the creditor power to enforce his security.

A charge over assets gives to one creditor a prior claim (over other creditors) to the payment of his debt out of those assets (see pages 154-5).

A charge can be either:

1. A fixed (or specific) charge: a right attaching to *an asset* as soon as the charge is created; or,

2. A floating charge: a right over present and future assets, but not attaching to any assets until the charge "crystallises".

A charge "crystallises" (i.e. turns into a fixed charge) when the company ceases business or the company is "wound-up" (see page 151), or the security is enforced, or the terms of the trust deed come into force.

A fixed charge gives greater security to a creditor since he has a claim to be paid out of an identified asset, the value of which he can estimate; and the company cannot dispose of the asset so as to deprive him of his right.

The advantage to a company of a floating charge is that it can use its current assets as security for loans and yet be free to trade normally.

If a company creates a charge, fixed or floating, it must be registered with the Registrar within 21 days. Failure to register a charge makes it void and the loan secured by it becomes immediately repayable.

A floating charge created within twelve months of the "winding-up" (see page 151) of a company shall be invalid unless it is proved that a company was solvent (i.e. able to pay its debts) immediately after the creation of the charge: Companies Act 1948, s.322.

MEETINGS

There are two kinds of general meetings for members of a company:

1. The annual general meeting (AGM);
2. An extraordinary general meeting (EGM).

Usually at least two members must be present at a meeting.

A company must hold an AGM in each calendar year, but the directors may convene an EGM when they consider it fit to do so – and sometimes they can be compelled to do so.

A meeting reaches a decision by passing a resolution; there are three kinds of resolutions:

1. An Ordinary Resolution: carried by a simple majority of votes cast.
2. An Extraordinary Resolution: needing a three-quarters majority of votes cast.
3. A Special Resolution: needing a three-quarters majority *and* a special notice given to shareholders in advance that such a resolution is being proposed, e.g. to dissolve the company without reason needs a special resolution (see page 151).

At a meeting, one share normally carries one vote.

A shareholder, having a right to attend and vote at a meeting, may appoint a "proxy", i.e. another individual to attend and vote for him.

MAJORITY RULE AND MINORITY PROTECTION

The directors of a company are responsible for the internal management of it, but the ultimate control is with the majority shareholder(s), who can remove the directors at an annual general meeting.

The basic principle is, therefore, that a company's shareholders exercise control of it through the general meeting: "Majority rule", known as the rule in *Foss* v. *Harbottle* (1843).

The common law and statute (the Companies Act 1980) gives a minority shareholder protection from "unfair prejudicial" conduct to the interests of minority shareholders, and the court has made powers to order a company to do or refrain from doing something.

In *Scottish Co-operative Wholesale Society* v. *Meyer* (1959), the parties to the case formed a *separate* company to carry out a joint venture. The majority of the shares in this new company were owned and controlled by SCWS. After a time SCWS used its control of the company to prevent it carrying on business so as to enable SCWS (as a competitor) to expand its *own* interests. It was *held* that this was "unfairly prejudicial" conduct to the minority shareholder, Meyer.

DIRECTORS

Every company must have at least one director; a public company must have at least two. A "director" includes every person occupying the position of director whatever name the position is given; e.g. "member of the board of management". An employee called, for example, a "sales director" is not a "director" in the legal sense unless he is also a member of the board of directors.

THE DUTIES OF A COMPANY DIRECTOR

A board of directors is appointed in accordance with the articles of association of a company, and is responsible for the management of the company.

Directors are agents of the company and *not* of the shareholders, and the company is responsible for the actions of a director who is properly exercising his powers.

The duties of a director include the following:

1. To exercise his powers honestly in what he considers to be the interests of the company.
2. To exercise his powers for proper purposes only, i.e. as given by the articles.
3. Not to allow his personal interest to conflict with the interests of the company.
4. Only to benefit from his position as the company consents.
5. To show reasonable competence.
6. To have regard to the interests of the company's employees as well as the shareholders.

A director in breach of duty (or negligent in performance of the duty) can be sued by the company; a member may sue if minority protection (see page 148) applies.

ACCOUNTS AND REPORTS

The directors of a company are required to prepare for the shareholders at the AGM:

1. A Profit and Loss Account.
2. A Balance Sheet.
3. A Directors' Report.
4. An Auditor's Report (an auditor is a qualified accountant).

There are different accounting requirements depending upon whether a company is small, medium or large: Companies Act 1981.

A company having share capital must make an annual return to the Registrar of Companies giving information to include matters as to issued capital, directors, members and charges.

DIVIDEND

The dividend is the amount paid to a shareholder as a return on his investment.

The Companies Act 1980 lays down detailed rules for the payment of dividends. A company may not make a payment of a dividend unless it is made from profits and not capital.

A declared dividend becomes a debt to shareholders if it is not paid and in the liquidation of a company it is a deferred debt payable only when ordinary debts have been paid.

COMPANY TAKEOVERS: RECONSTRUCTION AND MERGER

A company may transfer itself and its property to a new company whereby the shareholders of the old company are entitled to receive shares in the new company: a *reconstruction.*

Where a company amalgamates with one or more other companies there is said to be a *merger*.

ENDING A COMPANY

A sole trader or partner (subject to the Partnership Act 1890) may make a decision to end his business at any time. Sometimes this decision is forced upon a businessman when he is in financial difficulties.

An inability of any individual to pay his debts causes the possibility that he will be made bankrupt under procedures laid down in the Bankruptcy Acts of 1914 and 1926, the related rules and the Insolvency Act 1976.

In defined circumstances, a creditor may present a petition to a court to have a person, i.e. a debtor, declared "bankrupt".

The process of bankruptcy is the administration of the estate (property) of an insolvent person (bankrupt) by the court for the benefit of his creditors.

The objects of bankruptcy are to enquire into the reasons for a debtor's insolvency and to secure a fair distribution of his property among creditors.

After the presentation of the petition there may be a public examination; then there will be a creditors' meeting, a court order of bankruptcy (adjudication) and eventually a discharge (freeing) from bankruptcy.

In the case of a registered company, it comes to an end by "dissolution", after a process called "winding-up" (or liquidation). The "winding-up" involves realising, i.e. selling the assets, paying the debts, and returning the surplus (if any) to the members of the company; it is then "dissolved". A "winding-up" may be either voluntary or compulsory.

Voluntary "Winding-Up"

A company must pass a resolution (see page 148) to wind up, as follows:

1. An ordinary resolution – if the company was incorporated only for a specified time or specified event and the time or event has occurred.
2. A special resolution – giving no reason for the dissolution.
3. An extraordinary resolution – when a company cannot meet its liabilities.

The winding-up commences on the passing of the resolution; a signed copy of the resolution must be delivered to the Registrar, who publishes notice of the winding-up in the *London Gazette.*

A "liquidator" is a person responsible for realising the assets and paying the company's liabilities. He is appointed at the time of the resolution.

A voluntary winding-up may be either a members' winding-up or a creditors' winding-up.

A members' winding-up occurs when the directors – before the resolution to "wind up" – make a *declaration of solvency*, stating that the directors have enquired into the affairs of the company and are of the opinion it will be able to pay its debts in full within 12 months.

A creditors' winding-up occurs when there is no declaration of solvency.

The type of voluntary winding-up normally determines who (i.e. members *or* creditors) shall decide the person to be the liquidator, and he has greater powers of investigation in a creditors' winding-up.

The directors would "much prefer" a members' winding-up as their nominee (e.g. the company secretary or accountant) is likely to be appointed liquidator, "and he will probably not investigate their past conduct too closely": Gowers, *Principles of Modern Company Law*, page 723, 4th edn. The court does have power to take over the supervision of a voluntary winding-up but this rarely occurs.

Compulsory "Winding-Up"

A "petition" may be presented to a court (High Court or County Court) to order the compulsory winding-up of a company. Normally, a creditor (owed a minimum of £200) or a member (having held shares for 6 months), will present the petition for winding-up.

The petition must state one of the following grounds for compulsory winding-up:

1. The company has not commenced business within a year of incorporation or has suspended business for a year.
2. The company has less than the minimum number of members, i.e. less than two.
3. The company has failed to submit the Annual Report or hold the Annual Meeting.
4. The company is unable to pay its debts.
5. The court considers it is "just and equitable" to wind up the company.

It will be "just and equitable" to wind up a company when:

1. The main object of the company can no longer be achieved; or,
2. The mutual respect between directors no longer exists; or,
3. The directors of the company are unable to work together.

In *Re Yenidje Tobacco Co.* (1946). Two directors of a company, who were also the only shareholders, argued repeatedly and eventually one sued the other for alleged fraud; they refused to speak to each other and conducted board meetings by passing notes through the hands of the secretary. The court *held* that in the circumstances it was "just and equitable" to wind up the company.

When the court grants a petition to wind up a company it will then appoint a liquidator (Official Receiver) who will usually be an official of the Department of Trade.

THE LIQUIDATOR

A liquidator, who is responsible for the winding-up of a company, is obliged to carry out the liquidation process as quickly as possible. He assumes the position of the directors and is regarded as the agent of the company. He must bring into his control all the property of the company (including "calls" or shares) and must satisfy himself that a creditor's claim is genuine by a procedure known as "proof of debts".

If a company is solvent when being wound up, all debts and claims against it can be paid in any order of priority. It is, however, more complex when the company is insolvent, i.e. in a position that its liabilities exceeds its assets. The payment of such a company's liabilities will be in the following order:

1. Creditor Secured by Fixed Charge

A creditor with a valid fixed charge secured by a trust deed (a formal document) is entitled to take assets secured by that charge in priority to *all* other creditors.

E.g.: A bank holds a debenture for £20 000 secured by a mortgage on an insolvent company's factory premises; the factory premises are valued at £18 000 and the bank will then claim ownership and sell the premises and claim for the balance of £2000 under "unsecured creditors".

A secured creditor will often appoint a representative to enforce his security called a "receiver".

2. Liquidators' Expenses and Fees

These include the petitioner's costs, the fees in disposing of the available assets, and the expenses of those employed by the liquidator in the winding-up.

3. The Payment of Preferential Debts

1. One year's taxes: corporation tax, PAYE income tax deducted, local rates, VAT unpaid.
2. Wages and salaries for the services of an employee (for definition of employee see page 72) rendered during the 4 months prior to the date of the resolution to liquidate.
3. Holiday pay that is owed to an individual employee.

By the Insolvency Act 1976 an individual employee can claim a maximum of £800; (2 and 3 combined).

The debts under 1–3 rank equally among themselves and if they cannot be paid in full, payment is made in equal proportions.

A preferential debt has priority over debentures secured by a floating charge and may be paid out of any property subject to such a charge. The priority is lost if the floating charge crystallises before the winding up (see page 147).

Note: By s.320 of the 1948 Act, the disposing of any property by a company (e.g. by way of sale) or other act relating to property such as the creation of a charge, fixed or floating, on the property, is void as a "fraudulent preference" if:

1. It is made within the 6 months *before* the commencement of liquidation; and,
2. It is done voluntarily; and,
3. It is done with the intention of preferring one creditor over another.

Payment of an ordinary debt made without the intention of giving an advantage to a creditor is not a fraudulent preference; nor is the payment of a debt following the threat of legal proceedings – it is not then a voluntary payment.

The purpose of s.320 is to stop a company that is heading for liquidation from deliberately giving a preferential position to one or more creditors; this section enables the liquidator to recover cash or property transferred by the company.

By s.332, when a company is carried on to defraud creditors or for a fraudulent purpose and a person knowingly is a party to such a fraud, he can be made personally liable for debts of the company.

4. The Payment of Debts Secured by a Floating Charge

A creditor who has obtained a fixed charge *after* the creation of a floating charge has priority because his charge attaches to property as soon as it is registered. He will *not* obtain priority if the floating charge prohibits the creation of a fixed charge with priority *and* the holder of the fixed charge *knows* of this prohibition.

5. Unsecured Creditors

All other debts outstanding, including debenture holders without security.

6. Deferred Debts

If the debts are paid in full, the liquidator will apply what remains (if any) in repayment of capital, i.e., the members will be entitled to a share of what is left. All shares rank equally but the articles often provide that preference shares are to be paid in priority.

After repayment of debts the winding-up is then complete and the company is dissolved.

There is a procedure for dissolving a company without winding up when the Registrar is satisfied that the company has ceased to function (a "defunct" company); but in such a case there is provision for the liability of directors and members of the company to continue after dissolution.

The process of bankruptcy (e.g. on sole trader or partner) has some similarity to a winding-up, though the person responsible is not called a liquidator but a "trustee in bankruptcy".

7

The Law of Property

INTRODUCTION

"Laws" govern the relationship of persons:

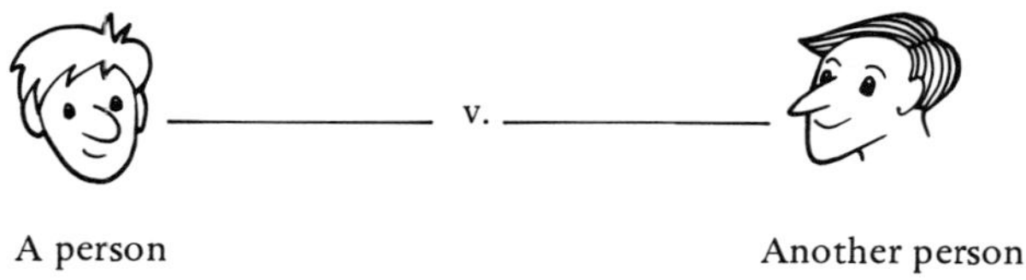

From this personal relationship come *rights*
- in contract law
- in the law of torts
- in employment law

"Laws" also recognise and govern the "subject-matter" arising from a personal relationship.

E.g.: Contract for the sale of a car.

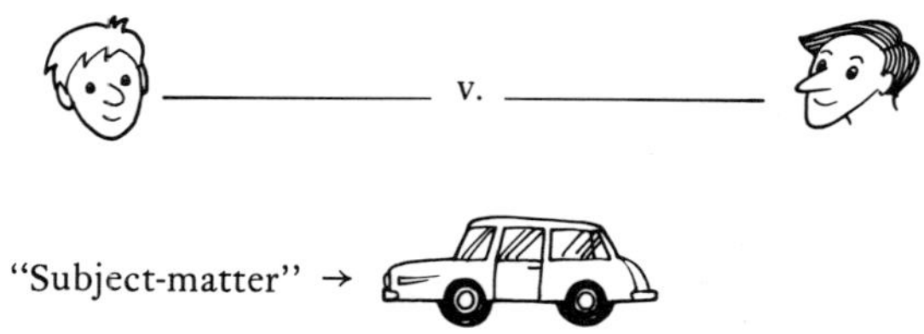

The "subject-matter" of a personal relationship is something that is recognised by laws as attracting *rights*. Therefore:

1.	"Subject-matter"	=	any "thing" which is recognised as attracting rights;
2.	"Things" having rights in law	=	any "thing" which can be owned: i.e. property.

3. Property = *a)* Immovable property: land

b) Movable property: Tangible things (Choses in possession)

c) Intangible abstract property: things (Choses in action)

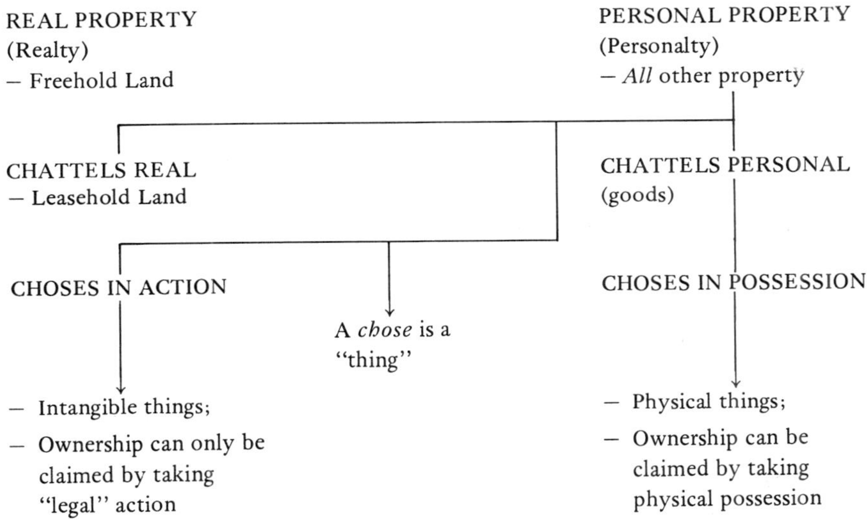

Property capable of ownership includes:

Land:	A house; a shop; a factory; a building.
Tangible things:	A car; a piece of office furniture; a book; a carpet; a typewriter; a telephone.
Abstract things:	*The rights in*: The "goodwill" of a business; a debt; a copyright; a patent; a registered design; a trade mark; a trade name; shares in a company; debentures in a company; a cheque.

PROPERTY = OWNERSHIP

The word "property" can be used to refer to one of the types of "property" (i.e. land, goods, or intangibles) or *alternatively* to the right of ownership in each type.

THE RIGHT OF OWNERSHIP

Ownership is the exclusive right to something (one of the types of property) based upon rightful "title": the evidence of the ownership right.

Ownership disputes arise where there is a conflict based on a personal relationship:

For the methods of transferring rights in ownership see pages 165-8.

LEGAL AND EQUITABLE OWNERSHIP

The development of English Law has resulted in the recognition of two sorts of ownership in the *same* thing:

1. *Legal ownership*: the absolute and exclusive right to something.
2. *Equitable* (*or beneficial*) *ownership*: the right to something which may only be denied by the *legal* owner.

This right of dual ownership in "property" has proved a useful device for transferring it.

E.g.: The legal ownership of a house (land) can be transferred to an adult (a trustee) to hold until a child (beneficial) owner reaches the age of majority.

The fact that there are two sorts of ownership in the same "property" is particularly relevant in the laws relating to land, in that there are only two ways to hold *legal* ownership: freehold or leasehold (see page 159); any other form of ownership is beneficial.

Legal ownership of land or other "property" entitles the owner to possession, but possession like ownership can be transferred. Property "laws" recognise interests (rights or claims) held by third parties against the "property" of the owner. These interests may themselves be legal or equitable, an interest will if *legal*, or may, if *equitable*, restrict an owner's right to deal with the "property".

OWNERSHIP COMPARED WITH POSSESSION

Possession is the physical control of some "thing"; it is "nine points of the law" and evidence of ownership, but not conclusive evidence.

The law protects a person in possession of "property" and in the case of intangible things (choses in action) – because they cannot be physically possessed – the right to ownership can only be obtained by a court order.

LAND

Definition of land: any ground, soil, earth, meadows, pastures, woods, waters, castles, houses and other buildings.

"Land Law" is governed by statute, specifically the Law of Property Act 1925.

The Right of Ownership in Land

There are two ways to hold *legal* ownership in land:

Freehold: (technically called "fee simple absolute in possession")	The freeholder owns (holds) the land *free* from any restriction of time.
Leasehold: ("term of years absolute")	The leaseholder owns (holds) the land for a certain length of time, e.g. a 99-year lease.

The owner of land (freehold or leasehold) is said to hold the legal estate: Law of Property Act 1925, s.1.

The freehold owner of land may create leasehold ownership by granting a lease in all or part of his land.

E.g.:

1. A property development company buys the freehold ownership of a large empty house.

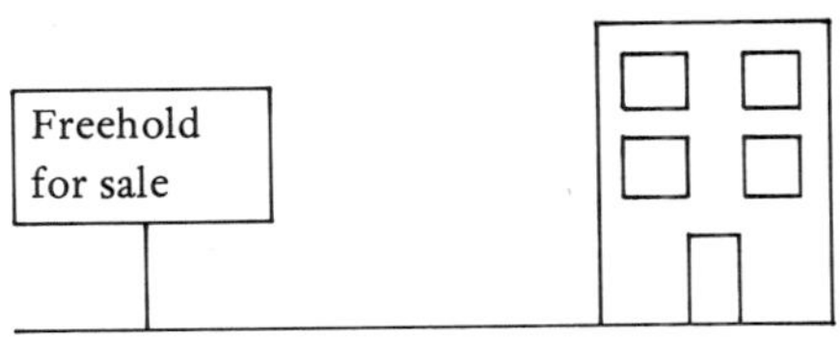

2. They convert the house into separate dwellings, i.e. flats, and sell 99-year leases to four individual purchasers.

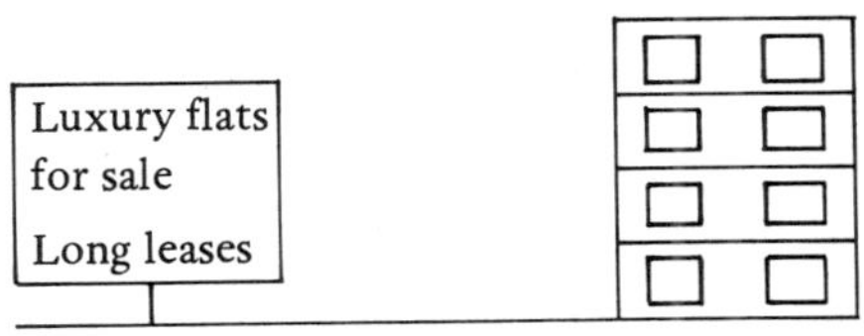

During the duration of the lease there is both freehold and leasehold ownership which are *both* capable of sale.

A leaseholder is entitled to possession of the flat; the right of ownership terminates at the end of the "term".

The method of transferring ownership of lands is by a process of conveyancing (see page 165) and a person gets evidence that he owns land by "title" documents.

The phrase "Landlord and Tenant" refers to a freeholder (lessor) who grants a lease to a leaseholder (lessee), but it is often understood to refer to an owner of land, e.g. a house or flat, who gives possession of the land to another in return for rent.

BUSINESS PREMISES

Most businesses carry out their trading activities on or from business premises, e.g. in a factory or shop, and a businessman or organisation will often be in the position of a business tenant.

A business tenant will usually occupy land under a "leasehold" agreement, and the owner of the "freehold" in the premises or building, i.e. the landlord, is likewise often a business organisation.

RIGHTS AND RESTRICTIONS UPON BUSINESS TENANTS

A business lease is similar to any other contract and is often in "standard form"; it will contain clauses (terms) concerning the amount of the rent, the intervals at which it is paid, the duration of the tenancy, and the rights and obligations of the parties to do repairs and pay rates.

The agreement will usually carry restrictions called "covenants": the tenant agrees that he will not conduct certain types of activities on the premises, e.g. in an agreement for the lease of a clothing shop a clause might read "not to permit the premises to be used for the purpose of carrying out any other trade or business without the landlord's consent in writing".

A tenant trading from business premises will invariably have made improvements and alterations to the premises and developed "goodwill" (see page 163) in the business; at the end of the tenancy agreement a landlord may be inclined to refuse renewal of the lease, or to demand a much higher rent from the tenant for a new lease.

The Landlord and Tenant Act 1954, as amended, gives statutory protection to a tenant, and he may apply to a court for the creation of a new tenancy at a rent and for a period to be fixed by the court.

A tenant is entitled to the grant of a new tenancy *unless* the landlord can show that his grounds for opposing a renewal come within one of the following grounds specified by the 1954 Act:

1. The tenant is in breach of an obligation to repair and this has led to a serious deterioration in the condition of the premises.
2. The tenant has persistently delayed paying the rent.

3. The tenant has committed other substantial breaches of obligations under the lease.
4. The landlord has offered and is willing to provide suitable alternative accommodation for the tenant on reasonable terms.
5. The landlord requires the whole of the premises to let or re-let as a whole.
6. The landlord intends to demolish or reconstruct the premises, and cannot reasonably be expected to do so without the whole of the premises.
7. The landlord intends to occupy the premises himself for the purpose of his own business or residential use.

If a landlord is successful in proving one of the above grounds then the court may not grant a new tenancy, but if the grounds specified are within 5–7 (above) the court can award compensation to the outgoing tenant.

If a new tenancy is granted by the court it will be for a maximum of 14 years, but there is no limit on the number of applications that a tenant can make under the Act.

STATUTORY CONTROLS ON LAND

Planning Permission

Under the Town and Country Planning Acts 1947–1977 a person must obtain planning permission from a local authority to "develop" land.

The Town and Country Planning Act 1971, s.22 defines development of land as "the carrying out of building, engineering, mining or other operations in, on, or over land, or the making of any material change in the use of any buildings or other lands".

Unless it alters the use of a building an internal alteration does not require planning permission, though it may be subject to other controls, e.g. Building Regulations (see page 162).

Permission must be obtained for a change in the external appearance of a building and this would include putting a luminous sign on the outside walls of premises.

The 1971 Act divides business activities into different types ("use-classes"): e.g. an office is in one class but a shop is in another; it would be a "material change of use" to change office premises into a shop (and so require planning permission), but replacing a bank with a building society would not need permission as both are in the same class, i.e. office.

A variety of other controls exist under the Planning Acts, including: Tree Preservation Orders (preventing the cutting down of trees); regulations restricting advertising on land; and "listing" buildings of special or historic interest, preventing their alteration or demolition.

Public Health

Building regulations control the safety of buildings; new buildings and the alteration of existing ones must comply with standards of structure and a local authority has power to prohibit or modify proposed changes.

Business premises must have adequate fire escapes and exits and under the Fire Precautions Act 1971 many organisations are compelled to obtain a fire certificate giving its approval to the fire system used on its premises.

Under the Water Act 1973 a local authority must ensure that a "wholesome" supply of water is available to all premises. Further, a local authority has a duty to collect household waste and industrial or commercial waste – but an organisation can be charged for the latter service; firms who amass large quantities of potentially harmful waste must place it in suitably safe receptacles.

Under the Control of Pollution Act 1974 each local authority has enforcement powers to prevent pollution of streams, noise nuisance and the emission of smells and fumes; and the Clean Air Acts control the "emission of pollutants" into the atmosphere.

OTHER RESTRICTIONS ON LAND

A person can be restricted in his use of land by a right that *another person* has over it.

Easements

An "easement" is a right that attaches *to the land* of one person and is exercisable over the land of another person.

Examples of easements include: a right of way; the right to have a building supported by the land of a neighbour; a right of light; a right to prevent an adjoining owner from obstructing the flow of light to a particular window or windows of a house or building.

Restrictive Covenants

A "restrictive covenant" is a restriction upon the use of a person's land, being so restricted for the benefit of *the adjoining land*.

E.g.: A restriction "not to build a factory" on land.

The significance of both easements and restrictive covenants is that they "travel *with the land*". A new owner of land, e.g. a businessman, who does not properly investigate the ownership and interests in the land *before* purchasing may *afterwards* discover that a neighbour has a right to use or restrict the use of the businessman's land.

E.g.: A "right of light" may prevent a new owner constructing a storey on top of an existing building.

Easements and restriction covenants originate from agreements between owners of adjoining land.

RESTRICTIONS BY TORT

A business organisation is, of course, subject to the duties created by the Law of Torts (see page 49) especially as regards Occupiers' Liability and Nuisance.

INTANGIBLE PROPERTY

Goodwill

An intangible "asset" resulting from a right to the advantages of a business gained from its past reputation; i.e. the trade connections (customers) of a business.

A Debt

A sum (e.g. of money) that one person is bound to pay to another. The word "debt" normally has one or the other of two meanings:

1. An obligation to pay money.
2. A sum of money owed.

A Copyright

The ownership of an original work, i.e. an "invention" that is of either a literary, dramatic, musical or artistic nature; e.g. the right in a musical composition.

A copyright holder has the "exclusive right" to authorise another person to reproduce or publish the work. Copyright usually lasts for fifty years from the origination of the work, or from the death of the originator, whichever is later. (A book, for example, may be published *after* the author's death.)

In *Performing Rights Society* v. *Harlequin Record Shops* (1979) a copyright was infringed when a record shop played music to the public without permission (licence) of the owner.

A Patent

The exclusive right to make, use, or sell an invention, which is conferred on a person who produces an original process or machine.

A patent must be registered at the Patents Office and the grant of a patent will only arise if it is:

1. new;
2. involves an inventive step;
3. capable of industrial application;
4. not offensive;
5. does not consist of a scientific theory, computer programme, or aesthetic creation (e.g. a mental act): Patents Act 1977.

The purpose of patent law is to encourage the full disclosure of a new invention whilst allowing the inventor a monopoly of exploitation, usually for twenty years.

An invention by an employee in the normal course of his duties is "owned" by his employer; if the employer patents it he may be obliged to pay compensation to his employee.

A Registered Design

A "design" is the artistic shape or pattern applied to an article, e.g. the pattern on wallpaper.

A "design" can be a protected property: Registered Designs Acts 1949–1961.

A Trade Mark

A mark used in relation to goods to indicate a connection between the goods and the owner of them: Trade Marks Act 1938.

E.g.: A stork on a margarine packet.

The exclusive right to use a trade mark arises by registration of it at the Patents Office.

A Trade Name

The name of a well-known product can be protected at common law by the tort of "passing off" (see page 62); the registered name of a business is protected by law.

Shares and Debentures

A share is the interest of a shareholder in a company, measured by a sum of money; shares form part of the capital of a company; a shareholder is a member of a company.

A debenture is *not* part of a company's capital and is the name given to a document acknowledging a debt owed by a company; debentures are usually secured by a charge on a company's assets (see page 147); a debenture-holder is a creditor of a company.

TRANSFER OF OWNERSHIP RIGHTS IN PROPERTY

The effective transfer of ownership differs between the three types (land, tangibles and intangibles) of "property".

In the case of sale of goods (tangibles) the transfer depends upon the intention of the parties: Sale of Goods Act 1979 (see page 113).

Conveyance

The transfer of the *ownership* or *other interest* in "property": Law of Property Act 1925, s.205.

A conveyancing deed is normally used to transfer freehold or leasehold ownership in land; for example, a solicitor will be employed to *convey* ownership of land rights.

Gift

All forms of property (land, goods, intangibles) may be transferred by gift (defined as the gratuitous transfer of property).

The right of ownership in a gift will only be effectively transferred if there is an intention on the part of the giver to give and deliver the gift to the recipient.

Choses in action are only "delivered" when the giver has done all that is necessary to transfer the ownership; e.g. shares must be validly transferred to the recipient by registration of the transfer to be an effective gift.

Assignment

The voluntary transfer of intangible "rights" between persons.

Under the Law of Property Act 1925, s.136, "a debt" or other legal chose in action can be assigned if it is:

1. In writing; and
2. Signed by the assignor (i.e. the person transferring the property); and
3. Absolute, i.e. not conditional or partial; and
4. Written notice is given to the debtor.

E.g.:

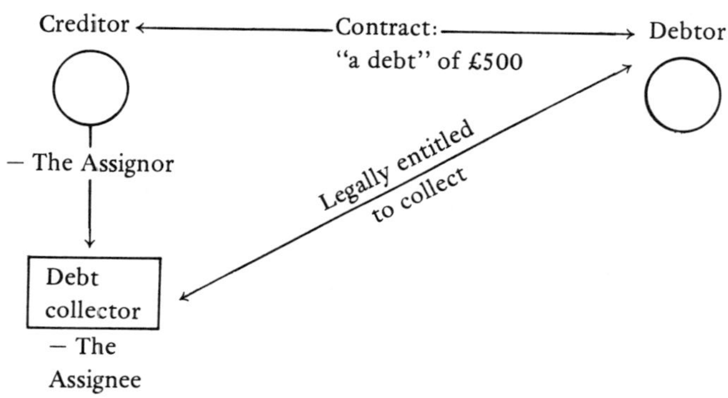

A creditor, after numerous unsuccessful attempts to collect "a debt" of £500, "sells" it to a debt collection company: they are entitled to collect the full amount and if it is not paid, sue in their own name for recovery from the debtor.

An assignment created under s.136 is called a "legal" assignment; the courts *may* still regard an assignment as valid even though the formalities under s.136 are not completed properly; it is then called an "equitable" assignment.

Whatever type of assignment is created, the assignee takes "subject to equities", i.e. subject to any defects in the assignor's title and claims which the debtor has against the assignor, whether or not he knew of their existence; in the example (above) if the creditor assigned the debt *and then* committed a breach of his contract with the debtor, this could be used as a defence by the debtor against the assignee's action to recover the money.

Note: The rights under *a contract* can be assigned by operation of law, e.g. on bankruptcy or death.

Negotiation

Negotiation is a method of *transferring a right* to be paid money, e.g. a debt:

E.g.:

A ———————— (Debt) ————————→ B ———————— (Debt) ———————— C

A owes money to B and B transfers the right to be paid money to C.

The transfer of such a *right* is evidenced and contained in a document called a "negotiable instrument"; the document embodies a promise to pay the money, e.g. bank notes (paper cash).

Apart from bank notes, statute law and commercial custom recognise that certain documents are capable of being "negotiable", e.g. a cheque. Once a document has acquired "negotiability" it will be treated as a "*right*" to money.

A document will only give a *right* to *transfer money* when the document itself is properly created and is delivered to entitle the holder of the document to enforce the original debt.

E.g.: A owes £100 to B who in turn owes £100 to C; A gives B a properly "drawn" and freely negotiable cheque in payment. B – to settle his debt – gives the cheque to C who is then legally entitled to obtain payment from A.

The main characteristics of a negotiable instrument are:

1. The "title" document (evidence of *the right* of payment) passes on "delivery"; and,
2. The holder of the document may, if necessary, sue the debtor who originally created *the debt*; and,
3. Notice of assignment (see page 166) need not be given to the debtor; and,
4. A person who obtains a negotiable instrument honestly and by giving consideration takes the *right* to be paid, *free* from any defect in the title of an earlier party – unlike the position under assignment.

Only certain types of choses in action (intangibles) are recognised as being negotiable, including bills of exchange, cheques and promissory notes: Bills of Exchange Act 1882.

The transferability of a right to money (e.g. by way of a cheque) is made "certain" by the principle of negotiability, in contrast to the uncertainty of assignment.

MORTGAGE SECURITY

A businessman or organisation will often need to borrow money to finance business activities. A person who lends money usually requires the borrower to provide "security" for the loan - some "thing" deposited or promised (pledged) to ensure the fulfilling of an obligation.

Rights in "property" enable "security" for a loan to be given.

E.g.: An individual needs £10 000 to finance a proposed business venture; he owns a house, and a lender, perhaps a bank, is prepared to lend him the money on the "security" of his house. The borrower may transfer his right of ownership in the house to the bank in order to "secure" the debt of £10 000, the individual remaining in possession of the house.

Security is usually given by creating a "mortgage" (charge) - a transfer of an estate or interest in land or other "property" to secure the payment of a debt or some other obligation.

Borrower (Debtor) = Mortgagor

Lender (Creditor) = Mortgagee

A mortgage may be either a "legal" or an "equitable" mortgage.

A "legal" mortgage is a formal transaction created by a deed by which the creditor is given legal rights over the "security", and these rights cannot be defeated.

E.g.: The borrower (mortgagor) who has secured his house for a loan will transfer the right of ownership to the lender (mortgagee) until the debt and interest payments are discharged.

An "equitable" mortgage is a less formal transaction, perhaps because a loan is only required for a short period of time; the lender takes possession of the "title" documents, e.g. deeds to land or share certificates, without having the *ownership* transferred to him.

A legal mortgagee has a legal right to the property but an equitable mortgagee has no such right, though his retention of the title documents effectively prevents the mortgagor selling the property.

MORTGAGE OBLIGATIONS

All forms of "property" can be mortgaged and the obligations of the parties to a mortgage contract differ, depending upon the type of mortgage (legal or equitable) and the subject-matter under it.

A mortgagor as part of the mortgage transaction will agree to repay the loan plus interest, and if he fails to do so, the mortgagee can sue him for the contract "debt", i.e. breach of contract.

TYPES OF MORTGAGE

Land

Subject to the mortgage contract, if a mortgagor breaks the terms of the agreement, a legal mortgagee is entitled to a court order to end the mortgage and give him ownership (foreclosure), to sell the land, to take possession of it, or to appoint a person, called a "receiver", to hold any rents and profits from the land for the mortgagee. An equitable mortgagee has similar rights.

The law is reluctant to enforce the above rights except when the borrower has defaulted badly on the agreement.

Once a mortgagor has repaid the debt he is entitled to recover unconditionally the right of ownership to his land (called "redemption") and even if the mortgagor does not repay the debt on the agreed date, a mortgage contract cannot restrict the mortgagor's right to his ownership of land after repayment of the debt: the "equity of redemption".

Note: Mortgages of land are exempt from the Consumer Credit Act 1974.

Goods

Goods can be mortgaged by registering a "bill of sale" at the High Court, but a more common form of mortgaging goods is by "pledge".

A pledge of goods is the delivery of them to a lender (pledgee, e.g. a pawnbroker who must be licensed under the Consumer Credit Act 1974). The ownership of the goods remains with the debtor, who is entitled to the return of the goods on repayment of the loan and interest.

A pledgee *and* certain persons who have possession of goods (e.g. a hotelier) have a "lien" (a right of retention) over goods until a debt is paid; sometimes the law gives the power to sell goods, e.g. to an unpaid seller of goods, but this power is only exercisable in defined circumstances.

Intangibles

A lender who takes a right to intangible property as "security" may have the right transferred by assignment (legal or equitable) or by negotiation in the case of a cheque.

THE LAW RELATING TO CHEQUES

A cheque is evidence of a *right* to money, i.e. a right in property (see page 157).

A cheque properly completed and transferred by negotiation to another person (a holder) who takes the cheque for consideration (value) gives *him* an unconditional *right* to be paid the face value shown on the cheque (see page 172).

A cheque is *one type* of bill of exchange.

Bills of Exchange and Cheques

A bill of exchange is "an unconditional order in writing, addressed by one person to another, signed by the person giving it, requiring the person to whom it is addressed to pay on demand at a fixed or . . . future time, a sum certain in money or to the order of a specified person or bearer": Bill of Exchange Act 1882, s.3(1).

E.g.: A Bill of Exchange.

	London 2 June 1982
To: C	
Pay: B, £1000, or order, 3 months after date.	
Signed: A	

There are three parties to a Bill of Exchange:

1. A is the *drawer* – the person who draws (creates the bill).
2. B is the *payee* – the person to whom or to whose order the sum is to be paid.
3. C is the *drawee* – the person who is to pay the order.

A cheque is far more commonly used for domestic (as opposed to international) business transactions than a bill of exchange. However, the definition and law relating to a bill of exchange apply in modified form to a cheque and Part III of the Bills of Exchange Act 1882 applies exclusively to a cheque.

A cheque is defined by s.73 of the Act: "A cheque is a bill of exchange drawn (created) on (by) a banker payable on demand."

E.g.: A cheque.

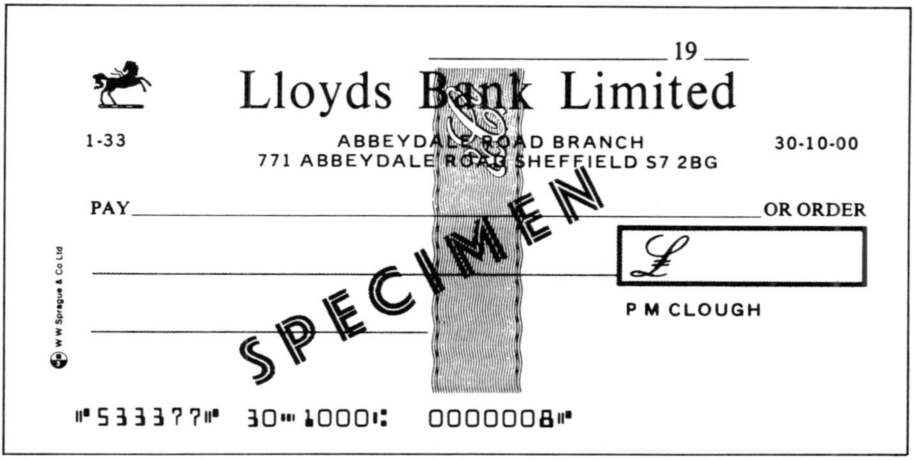
_________________ 19 ___

Lloyds Bank Limited

1-33 ABBEYDALE ROAD BRANCH 30-10-00
771 ABBEYDALE ROAD SHEFFIELD S7 2BG

PAY ________________________________ OR ORDER

£

P M CLOUGH

SPECIMEN

W W Sprague & Co Ltd

⑈533377⑈ 30⑆1000⑆ 0000008⑈

E.g.:, and see below.

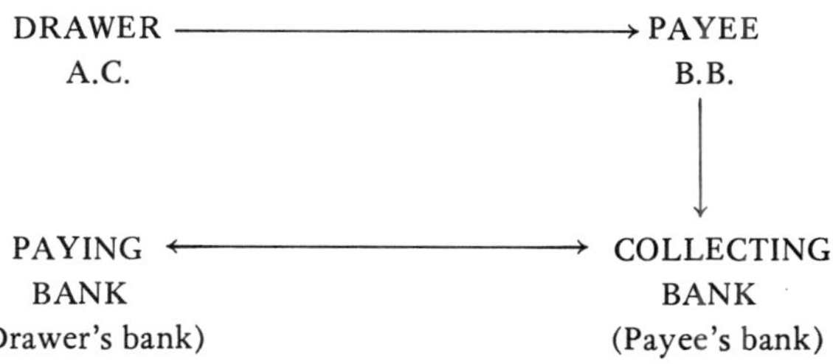

The combined effect of s.3 and s.73 is to require a cheque to be drafted in a particular way to be valid.

A cheque must be:

1. "An unconditional order"—e.g. "pay BB if he passes his driving test" is conditional.
2. "In writing"—on *any* material.
3. "Addressed by one person to another"—only two parties to a cheque.
4. "Signed by the person giving it"—this instructs a bank to pay.
5. "Drawn on a banker"—the paying bank.
6. "Payable on demand"—providing there is sufficient money in the drawer's account.

Points to Note

An undated cheque is not invalid; the holder of the cheque may fill in the date.

A post-dated cheque cannot be paid by a bank until the date on the cheque.

Liability to pay a cheque is avoided when the cheque is materially altered; changes in the date and sum payable are material alterations.

A person may agree or authorise an alteration (e.g. by initialling a correction), in which case the cheque is valid.

Types of Cheques and Crossing

A cheque is either:

1. Payable to the bearer: the person presenting a cheque to the drawer's bank, i.e. the paying bank; or
2. Payable to order: payable to a particular person: — "or order".

A person in possession of an "or order" cheque may convert it to a bearer cheque by "endorsement" (signing the reverse of the cheque).

A cheque is paid to the presenter (i.e. cash given "over the counter") unless the cheque is *crossed*, thus instructing a paying bank that the amount on the cheque must be paid only to another banker: s.79.

General crossing (two parallel lines with or without "& Co") makes the money payable only to another bank, i.e. a collecting bank.

Special crossing (indicates name of banker) requires the paying bank only to pay to the banker named for collection.

A drawer or any holder of a cheque may add to the cheque: "Account Payee": this indicates that the collecting bank must collect *only* for the payee named.

S8

"Not Negotiable"; "Not Transferable": Either of these phrases on a cheque prevents it being negotiable.

Negotiation of a Cheque

S31

A cheque is negotiated when a right to be paid money is transferred from one person to another in such a manner as to constitute the other person (the transferee) the holder of the cheque.

"Negotiation" is delivery of the cheque; an "order" cheque must be endorsed (signed) on the reverse by the person transferring it; a bearer cheque need not be endorsed.

Note: The drawer of a cheque does *not* negotiate it when he gives it to a payee.

A person who himself gives value (consideration) for a cheque is called a "holder in due course", and is entitled to claim payment from the drawer. If the cheque is then not paid, he can claim from *anyone* else who signed the cheque, i.e. an endorser.

E.g.:

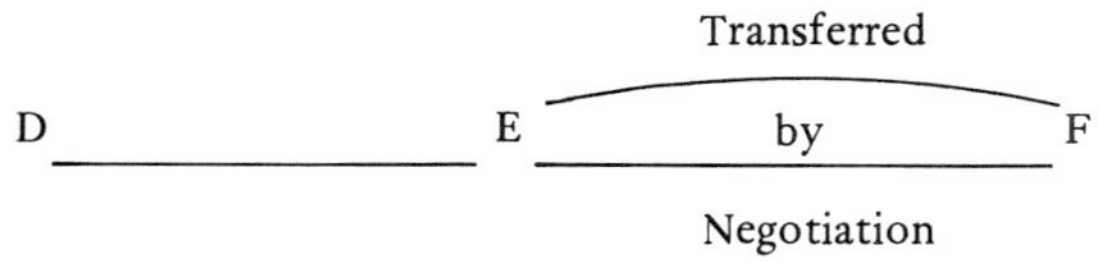

D owes E £1000.

D signs an order cheque, post-dates it, and gives it to E.

E signs the back of the cheque (endorses it) and sells (negotiates) it to F (a holder) for £900.

F's banker presents the cheque on the due date for payment to D's banker who collects the £1000 for F.

If F (a holder in due course) is not paid by D, he is entitled to claim payment of the £1000 from E.

Note: A person who obtains a negotiated cheque without himself giving consideration is called a "holder for value" (i.e. value at some time given); he has limited rights to claim payment on the cheque, but does not take free from defects in title (see page 16).

A Promissory Note

A promissory note may be used to transfer a right to money.

S83

"A promissory note is an unconditional promise in writing made by one person to another signed by the maker, engaging to pay, on demand or at a fixed or . . . future date, a sum certain in money to the order to a specified person or bearer."

A = Maker

B = The Payee

> London, 2 June 1982
>
> £1000
>
> One month after date I promise to pay B, or order,
> one thousand pounds Signed A

The 1882 Act applies, as appropriate, to a promissory note; a bank note is a bearer promissory note. An IOU is *not* a promissory note: it is an acknowledgement of a debt.

BANKERS AND CUSTOMERS

A banker who opens an account for a customer creates a contractual relationship.

Duty to Honour Cheques

A banker is obliged to honour a customer's cheques as long as the cheques are properly "drawn" and there is sufficient money in the customer's account (or an overdraft facility is agreed).

If a banker wrongly refuses payment of a customer's cheque, the banker is in breach of contract and may also be liable for the tort of defamation.

E.g.: A banker, by mistake, returns a business customer's cheque marked "insufficient funds" – as a consequence, the business customer loses a sale. The customer has a right of action (contract or tort or both) against the bank.

A banker's obligation to pay a cheque terminates upon notice of the death of the customer, or, in the case of a company customer, upon receiving notification of a petition for compulsory winding up or a resolution for voluntary winding up of the company.

The obligation of the banker to pay cheques terminates in other ways, primarily by the instruction (countermand) of the customer; a bank will require written authority from the customer.

Payment of a Cheque Without the Customer's Authority

A bank has no authority to pay a customer's cheque if:

1. The obligation of the bank is terminated, e.g. by countermand.
2. The signature of the customer (i.e. the drawer of the cheque) is forged.
3. The cheque is void for "material alteration" (see page 172).

A bank paying a cheque without authority cannot debit a customer's account; but a bank may be able to do so if a customer is careless or breaks his duty to the bank.

A Customer's Duty to a Bank

A customer owes a duty to take care when drawing cheques.

E.g.: *London Joint Stock Bank Ltd* v. *Macmillan* (1918): A clerk obtained a signed cheque from his employers for £2, but without any amount written on the cheque and a space left between the digit; the clerk put a 1 and a 0 either side of the digit, to make £120, and inserted that amount in words. He then cashed the cheque at the bank. The court decided the bank were entitled to debit the employers' account because the employers had failed to take care.

A customer who becomes aware that his signature is being forged on cheques must notify the bank as soon as possible; otherwise the customer may be unable to deny that the bank is entitled to debit his account.

E.g.: *Greenwood* v. *Martins Bank* (1933): A husband discovered that his wife was forging his signature on cheques to obtain cash from his bank account. He did not tell his bank. They eventually were made aware of the forgeries because (his wife having committed suicide) the husband was claiming the amount of the forged cheques debited to his account. The court *held* that the customer by his non-disclosure of the forgeries represented to the bank that the signatures were genuine.

Note: It is only in exceptional cases — like this one — that a **forged** or **unauthorised** signature of a *drawer* on a cheque gives a bank any rights.

A Banker's Duty of Secrecy

A bank owes a duty to keep confidential all information about a customer unless compelled by law, public interest or the consent of the customer to do otherwise.

E.g.: A customer may request a bank to give him a "reference", and so authorise the bank to give confidential information.

TRANSFERRING MONEY AND BANKERS' PROTECTION

Banks are the main medium used for the transfer by cheques of rights to money between individuals and business persons. Because of the enormous turnover in cheques by banks, the law gives them special protection in certain circumstances.

A Paying Bank

On receiving a cheque for payment a bank must satisfy itself that there is authority to pay, that the drawer's signature is correct, and, if the cheque is crossed, the money is paid in accordance with the crossing (general or special);

By the Bills of Exchange Act 1882, s.80, a bank paying a crossed cheque is protected from liability, even if the value of the cheque is not paid to the "true owner", if it pays:

1. In accordance with the crossing; and,
2. In good faith (i.e. honestly) and,
3. Without negligence (see page 177).

E.g. 1: A drawer signs a cheque failing to fill in the payee's name and sends it to him; the cheque is intercepted by a thief who fills in his own name and obtains payment. Providing the bank complies with s.80, it cannot be held liable to the "true owner".

By the combined effect of the Bills of Exchange Act 1882, s.60, and the Cheques Act 1957, s.1, a bank is protected from liability in spite of any forged, unauthorised or irregular *endorsement* on a cheque, providing it is paid in good faith and in the ordinary course of business.

E.g. 2: A thief steals a properly signed and completed cheque (a negotiable document). He forges the payee's endorsement and obtains payment. The paying bank is protected. A bank usually has no means of knowing whether an endorsement is genuine or authorised.

Note: When a cheque is "open" (i.e. paid over the counter) it is normal banking practice to require the person presenting the cheque to sign the reverse of the cheque.

A Collecting Bank

By s.4 of the Cheques Act 1957, a bank is protected from liability if it receives payment for a customer in good faith and without negligence.

E.g. 3: A bank credits the account of a customer with cheques (unknown to them) obtained by fraudulent methods. The customer (thief) withdraws the money from his account and absconds. Providing the bank complies with s.4 it cannot be held liable to the "true owner".

Liability of a Banker

A bank that cannot avail itself of the statutory protection (above) may be liable:

1. To a drawer; e.g. a paying bank cannot debit his account; or
2. To a payee or other "true owner"; either the paying or collecting bank may be liable in the tort of conversion (see pages 57-8).

Negligence of a Banker

The decisions of the courts suggest that a banker may be negligent in any of the following circumstances:

1. Opening an account for a customer without making proper enquiries, e.g. not taking references.
2. Obtaining payment for a customer on a cheque endorsed to him when the drawer or payee is his employer.

   E.g.: A local authority official credits his private account with cheques originally payable to the local authority.

3. Paying a cheque in suspicious circumstances or circumstances that ought to put a bank "on enquiry".

   E.g.: Paying several open cheques over the counter to an individual carrying a mail bag.

8

Constitutional Law

The Rule of Law: "Government is based upon the general acceptance of the law . . . the law predominates over and excludes the arbitrary (uncontrolled) exercise of power by the government . . . all people are equally subject to the law administered by the ordinary courts and that law is derived from individuals' rights as declared by the courts." (Dicey, *Law of the Constitution*, 1885.)

The constitutional process in the UK is based upon statute, common law and accepted parliamentary practices (called conventions); there is no written constitution as in some countries, e.g. the United States of America.

The constitutional process is protected from abuse by the "separation of powers"; meaning that the function of government, parliament and the judges are separate and "check and balance" each other (see below).

A more fundamental constitutional doctrine is the principle of the "rule of law", explained by Dicey and just as relevant nowadays as in 1885. The practical effect of the "rule of law" is twofold: firstly, all persons legal and artificial (including government bodies) must conduct themselves in accordance with the law; secondly, no person can be successfully prosecuted or sued unless they have committed a breach of the law.

Judges in the courts of law are the *only* persons who have the power to decide whether someone has broken the law. The judiciary are independent from government and parliament and are regarded as upholders of individual rights (freedoms) that have been declared by the common law over a long period of time.

Examples of Individual Freedoms: Freedom of Speech; Freedom of Religion; Freedom of Assembly and Procession; Freedom from Unlawful Arrest; Right to a Fair Trial; Freedom from Race or Sex Discrimination.

These "basic freedoms", as they are sometimes called, derive from the individual's personal freedom to think and say what he wants, and go where he wishes without hindrance from other persons; looking at the existing laws, e.g. defamation and trespass to land, it might seem at first glance that they impinge upon the basic freedoms. But another view is that such laws are necessary to protect these freedoms.

To an individual the basic freedoms are of very great importance and, at the least, provide a remedy against the unlawful exercise of power from the executive, or indeed, from lower courts, whose decisions are always open to appeal to the higher courts (see pages 189–90).

To a larger organisation or body, whether private or nationalised, the individual freedoms are equally relevant; the business community is contained within the legal system, *not* the other way around.

Hence, some of the legal conflicts reaching the courts focus upon a conflict between, on the one side, an individual and on the other, a corporation; and any attempt to deny an individual his basic freedoms will usually be overturned by the judges.

The Constitutional Process

The Separation of Powers

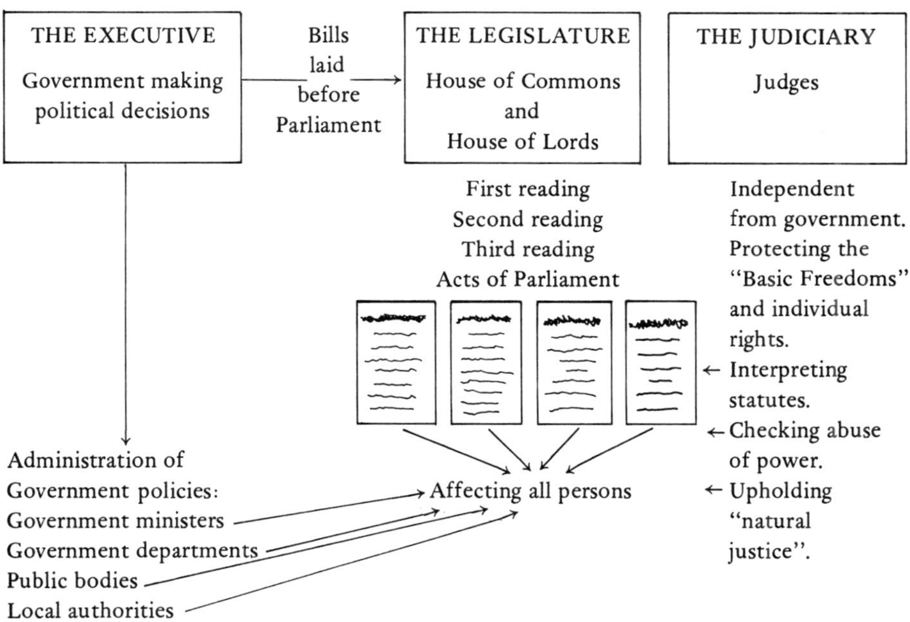

However, it does not follow that every constitutional (basic freedom) dispute will be between an individual and a large organisation, or vice-versa. Neither does it follow that a legal dispute will involve any constitutional element; most conflicts reaching the courts relate to arguments over "substantive" law rights, e.g. contract, tort, consumer, employment, property and company laws, and a judge is not usually required or expected to consider any "constitutional" issue.

EXECUTIVE POWER

Chief Executive

The prime minister, who appoints the cabinet, i.e. government ministers.

The Government Executive Power

Ministers in charge of government departments. Historically the Executive is identified with the Sovereign in whose name executive acts are performed by the prime minister, the cabinet and other ministers: "Her Majesty's Government" – responsible for the administration of the nation's affairs.

The Executive is answerable to, and dependent on, Parliament.

The Executive Function

Initiates legislation; maintains order; promotes social and economic welfare; conducts external (overseas) affairs.

Part of "central government administration" includes the Civil Service.

The Police and the Armed Forces are part of the responsibility of the executive.

Local authorities perform executive functions regionally, i.e. local government.

Public corporations are *not* part of the Executive but must answer to government ministers who themselves are subject to Parliament.

The Executive receives advice from government advisory bodies including Royal Commissions, Consultative Committees (e.g. consumer affairs), the Council on Tribunals.

Executive power is subject to the Rule of Law:

In *Congreve* v. *The Home Office* (1976) The Home Office (a government department) had threatened certain holders of TV licences that their licences would be revoked by the Home Secretary if they did not pay an extra £6. An aggrieved licence-holder challenged this executive decision.

The Court of Appeal *held* the Executive had acted improperly and abused its power; Parliament had given the Home Office no authority (by way of legislation) to demand the extra money and so they could not recover it.

LEGISLATIVE POWER

The Legislative

Parliamentary sovereignty – "the very keystone of the constitution" (Dicey).

Parliament

The House of Commons; The House of Lords; The Queen – Parliament *is* the Sovereign.

Act of Parliament

A law made by Parliament.

Parliament Controls the Government

The continuance of the Government (Executive) depends upon the confidence of Parliament – "Parliament should control the operations of Government" (John Stuart Mill).

The Legislative Function

1. To regulate the conduct of individuals and organisations.
2. To enact the structure and powers of public authorities.
3. There are certain legislative powers conferred on other persons or bodies: government ministers, government departments, local authorities, public corporations.
4. The power given to others to make "laws", e.g. rules, regulations or orders, is only possible when an Act of Parliament (an enabling act) delegates legislative powers to them.
5. Generally the courts of law have *no* delegated function, their task is to interpret statutory law; *nor* can the courts examine Parliamentary proceedings.

In *Pickin* v. *British Railways Board* (1974) The owner of a piece of land claimed that the B.R.B. had misled Parliament when persuading them to pass an Act in 1968 abolishing a right to give landowners parts of adjoining land when railway lines were discontinued.

The House of Lords *held* that the courts have no power to disregard an Act of Parliament, nor had they any power to examine proceedings in Parliament to determine whether an Act had been passed by irregularity or fraud.

JUDICIAL POWER

The Judiciary

The term applied to persons who judge (adjudicate) upon disputes between persons.

The Judicial Power

The ability to determine questions of rights, duties and obligations.

A Judicial Decision

Presupposes an existing dispute between two or more parties.

Judicial Independence

Judges are separate from Parliament and immune from legal liability when acting judicially.

A Judge

A person with the power to decide a dispute and determine the appropriate penalty.

The Judicial Function

To declare a person's rights; e.g. in contract, tort, property, etc.

To interpret statutory laws.

The Scope of Judicial Power

The judges are not responsible for the efficiency of government administration nor the merits of official decisions. See *Pickin* v. *B.R.B.* (above). However, at common law a High Court judge does have the ability to ensure that:

1. Executive decisions are not without power – see *Congreve* v. *Home Office* (above).
2. Executive decisions are not *ultra vires*, i.e. beyond the powers conferred by statute.

   In *Bromley Council* v. *GLC* (1982) the (judicial) House of Lords held that the GLC had exceeded its powers in ordering London Transport to reduce fares by 25 per cent.

In *Attorney General* v. *Fulham Corporation* (1921), a local council installed a laundry, manned by council employees for the benefit of residents. Under the Baths and Wash-houses Acts 1846 and 1847 the council had power to establish a wash-house where people could *wash their own* clothes.

A ratepayer sought an injunction restraining the council from conducting the laundry as a business. The court granted the injunction as the statutory power given to the council was confined to a "wash-house" for residents to do their *own* washing and it was *ultra vires* for the council to establish something different.

But an Act of Parliament may expressly give to an executive body the unqualified discretion to carry out a statutory power or duty; and a nationalised corporation may have a special statutory power which, if exercised properly, is unchallengeable in the courts, e.g. to enter private property for the purpose of reading gas or electricity meters.

3. Executive decisions containing a judicial power must be exercised according to the rules of "natural justice"; i.e. many decisions of the Executive, e.g. granting or refusing planning permission, assessing tax liability or social security benefits, involve elements of deciding personal rights.

   Such decisions should be considered "judicially"; i.e. by the two main rules of natural justice:

   a) *The rule against bias*: no person should be a judge in his own cause. In *Metropolitan Properties Ltd* v. *Lannon* (1969), the court "quashed", i.e. made void, the decision of a Rent Assessment Committee when the chairman of the committee was also a tenant in the block of flats where the rent was assessed.

   b) *The right to a hearing*: no person is to be condemned unheard. In *Cooper* v. *Wandsworth Board of Works* (1863), Cooper failed to notify the Board (as he was legally bound to do) that he was building a house on his land. The Board had a statutory power to demolish his house and this is what they did.

      Even though there were no express words in the relevant Act of Parliament requiring Cooper to have the chance to object to the demolition, the court said it was only "just", i.e. in accordance with natural justice, that he have the opportunity to do so. He was therefore entitled to damages in the tort of trespass from the Board.

      If he had been afforded the right to a hearing and the Board had *then* decided to destroy his house, the demolition would have been lawful.

Important Note

1. The rules of natural justice do not apply to purely executive decisions where there is no judicial function: e.g. a government minister may have the power to reduce grants to local authorities; this is an exclusively political decision, probably based on economic grounds.

2. The principle and rule of natural justice is prominent amongst and originates from the power of High Court judges to control powers exercised in lower courts or tribunals.

9

The Courts of Law and the Legal Process

The chart below shows the hierarchy of separate courts in the legal process. They are described in detail in the pages that follow.

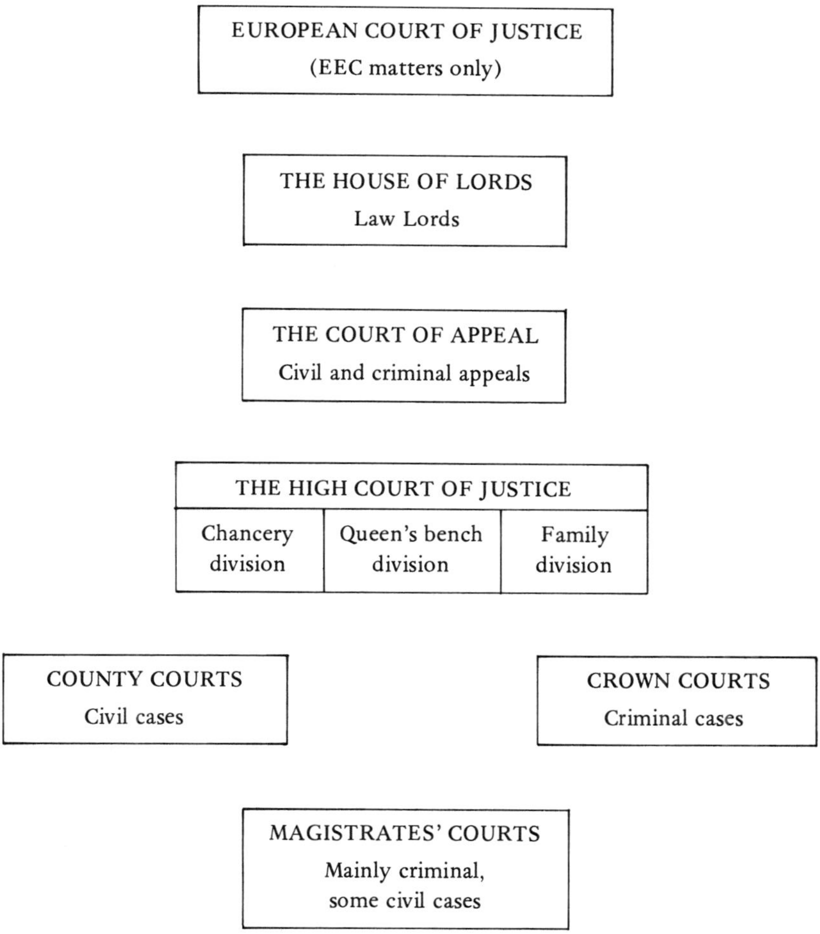

CIVIL COURTS

County Courts

Over 400 in England and Wales.

Handle cases in their areas.

Claims in contract and tort up to £5000.

Claims for possession of land or houses.

Family matters: undefended divorces, adoption, guardianship, cases involving domestic violence.

Cases heard by a circuit judge (called County Court judge), no jury.

Claims for less than £500 heard by a Registrar of the County Court. Appeals go to the Court of Appeal.

The High Court

Three divisions of the High Court:

Queen's Bench Division (Q.B.D.);

Chancery Division (Ch.D.);

Family Division (F.D.).

Cases heard by one High Court judge, no jury.

High Court based in London may hear a case in towns outside London.

Q.B.D.: Breach of contract, claims for damages in tort.

Ch.D.: Mortgages, trusts, disputed wills, company matters, taxation.

F.D.: Defended divorces, complicated matrimonial cases including disputes about the ownership of property between spouses.

Note: Within the Queen's Bench Division is the Commercial Court which specialises in commercial cases, e.g. insurance claims.

Each division of the High Court can act as an appeal court; appeals heard by two or three judges of the court, acting as a "divisional court".

The "divisional court" of the Q.B.D. supervise the lower courts, tribunals and various public bodies or officials when application is made for:

1. *Writ of Habeas Corpus*: to compel anyone to justify detention of a person.
2. *Order of Certiorari*: claim of misuse of power or breach of "natural justice".
3. *Order of Mandamus*: claim for a lower court or tribunal to try a case, or for an order that a public body carry out its legal duty.
4. *Order of Prohibition*: to stop a lower court or tribunal exceeding its powers.

Appeals from the High Court go to the Court of Appeal, and then can go to the House of Lords. Where a point of law of public importance is involved an appeal may "leapfrog" the Court of Appeal and go straight to the House of Lords.

Note: In certain cases, e.g. defamation, a jury may be used if the parties to the case so request.

The "divisional court" of the Q.B.D. also hears appeals on points of law from the Magistrates' Courts.

CRIMINAL COURTS

Magistrates' Courts

Over 900 Magistrates' Courts in England and Wales.

Cases heard by magistrates (Justices of the Peace – JPs), unpaid, part-time, non-lawyers.

Usually three (sometimes two) magistrates sit together to hear cases.

In large towns, legally qualified full-time stipendiary magistrates are appointed to hear cases; each sits alone.

Juvenile Courts: magistrates sit in private to hear cases concerning young persons under 17 years of age.

Crown Courts

Cases tried by judge and jury.

Crown courts in all the major towns and cities, the best known being the Central Criminal Court in London, the Old Bailey.

Judges are either circuit judges, recorders (senior lawyers acting judicially) or High Court judges.

Crown courts try the most serious criminal cases.

Classification of Criminal Offences:

1. *By summary trial*: Triable *only* in Magistrates' Courts and relate to "minor" offences, such as road traffic, theft of property under £500.
2. *On indictment** (pronounced "inditement"): May only be tried in a Crown Court and relate to serious offences including murder, manslaughter, causing grievous bodily harm, and rape.
3. *Triable in either court*: Certain offences may be heard in either a Magistrates' Court or by a Crown Court. In these cases the magistrates may state whether they will hear the case or not, *or* the accused person may choose whether to be tried summarily by the magistrates, or elect trial by judge and jury at a Crown Court. If he elects to be tried summarily and is found guilty, he can still be sent to the Crown Court for sentencing.

*A person charged with an indictable offence will first of all have to appear before a Magistrates' Court for "committal proceedings" where the prosecution evidence is revealed. If the evidence is weak the magistrates may decide that there is "no case to answer" and stop the case going any further; if there is a *prima facie* case to answer, the accused is committed to the Crown Court for trial. In practice, by agreement between the prosecution and defence, most "commital proceedings" are now conducted in such a way that the prosecution produces its evidence in the form of statements, exhibits, etc. by "handing" them in to the court, and on their strength the accused is or is not committed to stand his trial.

Sentencing Powers

Magistrates' sentencing powers are limited to a maximum of six months' imprisonment and/or a fine of £1000. Both Magistrates' and Crown Courts may, however, have their sentencing powers restricted by statute for certain offences.

Appeals

From the Magistrates' Courts, appeals against sentence or conviction, or both, go to the Crown Court. Further, either the defendant or the prosecution can appeal to a divisional court (Q.B.D.) by "case stated" on a point of law, i.e. whether the law was applied correctly by the magistrates to the facts of the case. Crown Court appeals against conviction or sentence and by "case stated" go to the Court of Appeal (Criminal Division).

COURTS OF APPEAL

The Court of Appeal

Cases heard by three Lord Justices of Appeal (L.J.s).

Hears appeals from County Courts, Crown Courts and the High Court.

This court hears cases either as the Court of Appeal (Civil Division) or Court of Appeal (Criminal Division) depending on the nature of the case.

Leave to appeal to the House of Lords may be given.

The House of Lords

The highest court in the land.

Cases heard by Lords of Appeal – specially appointed and legally qualified life peers, separate from the Parliamentary House of Lords.

Five "Law Lords" normally hear appeals.

Disputes over interpretation of European Community legislation are referred to the European Court of Justice.

European Court of Justice

The European Court is the final authority on the interpretation of community legislation. Problems concerning interpretation can be referred to it by any court of the EEC. It has *no* jurisdiction over cases which affect only the United Kingdom, i.e. domestic disputes concerning contract, tort, employment, property, etc. It is mainly concerned with matters such as restrictive practices by one member state against another and with company laws.

OTHER COURTS

Restrictive Practices Court

A court created by the Restrictive Practices Act 1956, presided over by a High Court judge and consisting of judges of the High Court and lay members. Cases are referred to it by the Director-General of Fair Trading or parties to a restrictive agreement who have been ordered to give particulars to the Restrictive Practices Court.

The task of the court is to declare whether a restriction is contrary to the public interest and, if so, to declare it void.

Tribunals

These are bodies outside the hierarchy of the courts with administrative and judicial functions (see page 182). Examples include rent tribunals and industrial tribunals (see page 89).

Tribunals are often referred to as "specialised" courts, and are ultimately controlled by the High Court.

THE PARLIAMENTARY COMMISSIONER FOR ADMINISTRATION: "THE OMBUDSMAN"

The Parliamentary Commissioner Act 1967 created the position of Parliamentary Commissioner for Administration, usually called "The Ombudsman". It is the function of the Commissioner to investigate complaints about maladministration by executive bodies, primarily government bodies and certain public bodies.

E.g.: There is a very long delay between the time that an unemployed person applies for and then receives his entitlement to supplementary benefits. The delay appears due to the administrative slowness of a Department of Health and Social Security office. This would be an appropriate case for investigation by the Ombudsman.

An individual who claims to have suffered injustice in consequence of maladministration must make a written complaint to a member of the House of Commons who will refer the complaint to the Commissioner. The Commissioner has no power to investigate complaints where there is a possible right of appeal to a court or tribunal or, indeed, a remedy exists through legal action in the courts.

E.g.: An unemployed person applies for, but is refused, any entitlement to supplementary benefits by a Department of Health and Social Security office. He has a right to appeal against this decision to a tribunal. It is not a matter for the Ombudsman.

The powers of the Ombudsman, in cases that are within his jurisdiction, are purely investigatory, but he can make recommendations to the appropriate executive body. The Commissioner also makes an annual report to Parliament which is subject to review by a Parliamentary Committee.

LOCAL COMMISSIONERS FOR ADMINISTRATION: "LOCAL OMBUDSMEN"

The Local Government Act 1974 established Commissioners for local administration who are given powers to investigate complaints by individuals who claim maladministration by local and other authorities, including police and water boards.

A Local Ombudsman is given responsibility for a particular area and he hears complaints channelled through a local authority councillor. The powers of the Local Ombudsman are restricted to investigation and recommendation of complaints in the same way as the Parliamentary Commissioner.

CIVIL LAWS

Civil laws are created by statute and the common law to protect a person from the wrongful conduct of another person.

Civil Wrongs

These include breach of contract and tort.

Civil Liability

In the law of contracts a person is liable for breach of contract irrespective of "fault".

Under the law of torts a person is only liable if it is proved that he was at "fault". Certain torts, such as breach of statutory duty, create "strict liability"; a person is held liable even though not at fault.

An employer (master) may be vicariously liable for a tort committed by his employee (servant), e.g. *Rose* v. *Plenty* (page 64).

Purpose of Civil Law

To award compensation for loss, injury or damage.

CRIMINAL LAWS

Criminal laws are created by statute and the common law to protect persons from injurious or offensive conduct.

Crimes

Offences against the people or the state (such as obtaining a state benefit by deception, a fraud).

Criminal Liability

No person will be found "guilty" of a criminal offence unless it is proved by evidence in a court of law that he intended to commit the crime (he had *mens rea*, i.e. a guilty mind) at *the time* of the offence. Certain statutory laws create offences of "strict liability" – a person is guilty whether or not he had the intention.

An employer (master) may be vicariously liable for offences committed by an employee (servant), for example under the Trade Descriptions Act 1968.

Purpose of Criminal Law

To punish offenders for crimes, e.g. by way of fines, compensation orders, or imprisonment.

THE INTERPRETATION OF STATUTES

The words in an Act of Parliament, or delegated legislation, will sometimes be unclear or uncertain. When this leads to a court case the judges will be obliged to interpret the words in dispute.

In the interpretation of a statute a judge is concerned with what the statute *itself* says and he is not required to consider anything said in Parliament whilst a bill is becoming an Act.

The importance of interpreting statutes lies in the fact that a judge in defining the extent or limits of statute law is himself making law. For example, in *Bourne (Inspector of Taxes)* v. *Norwich Crematorium Ltd* (1967) the dispute concerned whether the cremation of humans is "the subjection of goods or materials to any process".

The basic task of a judge is to discover the intention of Parliament and the approach used by the judiciary is that words will be interpreted in their original sense unless this produces an unintended or absurd result: the *literal* rule.

Other rules and presumptions exist and a judge will read the statute as a whole, obtaining guidance from any preamble or interpretation section in the statute. In so doing, the *ejusdem generis* rule applies, i.e. general words following particular words must be confined to a meaning of the same kind (*ejusdem generis*) as the particular words.

E.g.: An Act of Parliament might refer to "cats, dogs and other animals", and a judicial interpretation of "other animals" would restrict the animals to domestic ones: *Evans* v. *Cross* (1938), pages 4-5.

Certain words and phrases that are often encountered in Acts of Parliament are defined in the Interpretation Act 1978 and a judge may seek guidance from it; e.g., s.6 of the Act says that unless the contrary intention appears, words "importing the masculine include the feminine", i.e. *he* includes *she* (and vice-versa), and the same Act says that a "person" includes a body corporate.

ARBITRATION

Arbitration is the settlement of a dispute by an arbitrator. Many commercial contracts make provision that a dispute is to be settled by arbitration and this is governed by the Arbitration Act 1950 as amended by the Arbitration Act 1979.

In an agreement the parties may name the arbitrator or provide some other means to appoint him. There may be a right of appeal from the decision of an arbitrator on a point of law to the High Court, but it is possible for the parties to agree in writing that the arbitrator's award is final, and so there is no right of appeal.

An arbitration is held in private and the arbitrator is often an expert and experienced in a particular commercial area.

County Court Arbitration

Where a disputed claim involving less than £500 is commenced in the County Court, this "small claim" may, if the amount involved does not exceed £500 or if the parties agree, be referred to arbitration. The arbitrator is usually the Registrar (a court official) of the County Court, who hears the dispute privately in an informal atmosphere. Whoever "wins" the arbitration is unable to claim costs (e.g. of paying a lawyer, see page 196). The arbitrator's decision, called an "award" is treated as a County Court judgment and is open to appeal.

LEGAL ADVICE AND LEGAL ACTION

The main method of obtaining legal advice is by consulting a lawyer. The legal profession is divided into solicitors and barristers: the former are the "general practitioners"; the latter specialise in advocacy in the courts. A senior barrister is known as a Queen's Counsel (QC), which denotes that he is particularly experienced or capable at his job.

The practical significance of the division of the legal profession is that a person seeking legal help will sometimes require the services of both types of laywer for the *same* dispute. This is because only solicitors are entitled to deal directly with the public whilst only barristers have the right to represent a client in the higher courts. Hence, solicitors "instruct" barristers to conduct such cases.

Lawyers are mostly "self-employed" and are independent and separate from the Executive.

A lawyer "earns his living" by receiving payment by way of fees from clients that he has advised or represented in court. Persons of limited resources may be entitled to legal aid to meet the cost of work done by a lawyer. Legal aid is paid from a government-granted fund.

When a decision is taken to proceed with court action various legal documents will be issued, notably a summons, or writ of summons. (See the example opposite.)

THE LITIGATION DECISION

Legal disputes in civil matters will often be negotiated by an "out of court" settlement. Where this is not possible or is unlikely to result, then a decision must be made whether to take a court action, i.e. litigation. A number of factors will influence this decision. Some of these considerations are relevant to the criminal law since the *initial* decision to start the *criminal* process may be left to the businessman, e.g. the apprehension (and so prosecution) of "shoplifters".

Writ of Summons

IN THE HIGH COURT OF JUSTICE 19 . , No.

DIVISION

[Group]

DISTRICT REGISTRY

Between

Plaintiff

and

Defendant

To the Defendant*

of†

THIS WRIT OF SUMMONS has been issued against you by the above-named Plaintiff in respect of the claim set out on the back.

Within [14 days] after service of this Writ on you, counting the day of service, you must either satisfy the claim or return to the Court Office mentioned below the accompanying ACKNOWLEDGMENT OF SERVICE stating therein whether you intend to contest these proceedings.

Acknowledgment of Service

ACKNOWLEDGMENT OF SERVICE OF WRIT OF SUMMONS

Directions for Acknowledgment of service

1. The accompanying form of *Acknowledgment of Service* should be detached and completed by a Solicitor acting on behalf of the Defendant or by the Defendant if acting in person.
   After completion if must be delivered or sent by post to the District Registrar,
   (address)

The Need for Compensation

Especially in commercial contracts there are regularly large sums of money resting upon the fulfilment of an agreement. In the event of a breach of contract one party's business prospects could be ruined without there being recourse to the courts for an award of damages. Although punishment of offenders is the primary purpose of criminal law, the criminal courts do have power to award compensation. Further, a conviction in a criminal court can be used as evidence in a subsequent civil case against the criminal.

Punishment, Principle or Policy

This factor – although mainly relevant to criminal law – is certainly not unheard of in the civil courts. Litigants may sometimes wish to publicise the wrongdoings of others; the chief drawback to this is the legal expense involved.

Fees for Legal Representation

Merely to consult a solicitor for an hour can cost between £20 and £50, and if the solicitor is instructed to take legal proceedings on behalf of a client the latter amount is about the sum payable for every hour spent on the case.

When both solicitor and a barrister are employed, both must be paid, and it would not be incorrect to estimate that the costs of a case proceeding in, for example, the High Court for five days will run into several thousands of pounds.

Costs in a Case

The total costs for legal representation of *both* parties to a court case will usually (except where the dispute is for less than £500) be paid by the loser of the dispute. In other words, someone who "risks" taking civil action may be liable not only for his own costs but also the costs of his opponent (should the latter win the case), *plus* the amount of damage compensation awarded.

The Task of Proving a Case

The crucial factor of success in litigation is "evidence"; anyone with insufficient evidence would be ill-advised to proceed to court. Evidence can be by way of oral testimony or documents or exhibits acceptable to a court. Many day-to-day negotiations in business would be regarded as inadmissible evidence; even where evidence is acceptable it is open to very close scrutiny in court, particularly by cross-examination.

Many conflicts in court succeed or fail by the availability of documentary evidence and this is one reason why a businessman ought to keep proper records: accounts, receipts, invoices, etc.

A competent lawyer is useful, for assessing and advising on the question of evidence. Nevertheless, even he cannot guarantee the eventual outcome of a case and the burden of proving a case rests firmly on the party bringing it.

Time Factor

Most particularly in civil law the time it takes for a case to eventually be heard at a court and then the time actually spent on the case in court will influence the decision to litigate.

Whether the businessman is in sole-tradership or an executive in a large organisation, he inevitably must spend time concentrating on the case and so, perhaps, lose business. It might therefore be beneficial to him to end a dispute by accepting a sum in settlement rather than to risk gaining nothing, except considerable costs.

Solvency of Opponent

Although not relevant in criminal law (except perhaps when it comes to the question of punishment, e.g. fine or compensation order, the financial standing of an opponent may be decisive in civil litigation. A debtor without resources is a "man of straw" and even with a judgment against him there is little that can then be done if he has no money. Before taking proceedings in such circumstances, a litigant may well decide to assess the prospects of an improvement in the debtor's financial status or accept a sum in settlement or just write off the debt as "bad".

Assignment 1

"So You Think *You've* Got Problems"

Frank Spencer is a shopkeeper who has a number of difficulties involving "laws". He wants you to tell him the areas of law most appropriate to his problems.

Here are the problems

a) He is being accused of tax evasion.

b) He plans to sell his business premises.

c) He owes £5000 and wants to exchange his second-hand car for the debt, and needs to know whether such a transaction would be valid.

d) He hopes to start a new business selling donkeys and wishes to convert part of his house into a stable.

e) His brother has asked to join him in partnership.

f) His wife is divorcing him and has accused him – in public – of being "an idiot".

g) He wants to know whether he must pay VAT on donkeys.

h) He has accidentally ridden a donkey into the property of a limited company causing extensive damage.

Here are the "source" areas

Revenue laws	
The laws of contract	
The laws of real property	
Criminal laws	
Family laws	
Law of torts	
Planning law	
Company laws	

Instructions

1. Select the "source" area most appropriate to each problem by filling in the blank box provided. (A different *letter* in each box – answers may be given on a separate sheet.)

2. Write to Mr. Spencer explaining to him the reasons for your selection in each case.

Assignment 2

"Fair Deal"

A partnership firm is experiencing financial difficulties. The firm had a debt outstanding for £3000. The creditor promised the company that if £1000 was paid, the remaining balance would be forgotten. The partnership paid the £1000 and the apparent generosity of the creditor enabled the partnership to remain in business.

However, the creditor is now threatening to sue the company unless the remaining £2000 is paid. The partnership consulted a solicitor who has now written to them and advised against paying the debt because "whilst the common law gives no relief, 'equity' will almost certainly be granted . . .".

The members of the partnership are puzzled by this phrase and you have been called to the managing partner's office to explain to him what it means.

(If orally assessed, time allowed 4–5 minutes.)

Assignment 3

"Roger's Dilemma"

Roger, who is married with two young children, is presently employed as a clerical officer. Over the last three years he has developed his hobby of painting miniatures of domestic animals. He has been quite successful in selling these paintings to friends, neighbours and work colleagues, and he now wishes to put his talents on a proper business basis.

Roger's capital is as follows:

	£
Cash	500
Stock of completed miniatures	1200

Roger estimates that by giving up his full-time job he can produce about twenty new miniatures per week, which he would hope to sell at £12 each.

Explain to Roger about the different types of business unit and tell him your opinion about the wisdom of giving up his secure job to pursue his hobby.

Assignment 4

"Tanned for Life"

The following advertisement appeared in the *Daily Times* of 1 April 1982.

PERMANENT SOUTH SEA TAN!

*A mixture of the finest alkali oils has produced for the first time in the United Kingdom the genuine all-weather tan.

— *Full results assured*
— *Money back guarantee*
— *Easy to use*
— *Only £49.50 per bottle (incl. postage)*

*Cheques made payable to:

South Sea Co., 13 Nikket Street, London N 17

Allow 28 days for delivery

Before

After

Amilda Knitt saw the advertisement, sent her cheque for £49.50 and duly received the lotion. Although she followed the instructions correctly, her tan only lasted for three days.

She has written two letters to the South Sea Co. demanding her money back, but she has received no reply. She even tried to contact the managing director of the company, Mr. John Permanent, but he is always "unavailable".

You are one of her work colleagues and she has asked you:

1. To write a letter on her behalf to the company informing them, in the strongest possible terms, of their legal obligations.
2. To explain to her how she and other consumers are protected by law, particularly statute law, from firms like the South Sea Company.

Assignment 5

"Upholding Standards"

Prepare a numbered list of at least twelve standard form terms that might be contained in a standard form contract between *one* of the following types of organisation and a member of the public:

1. A bank, opening an account for a customer.
2. A football club, signing a new player.
3. A wholesaler, supplying goods to a retailer.
4. A nightclub, granting new membership.

Each term must relate and be relevant to the kind of business dealing that each particular organisation enters into with the public.

The contract must be headed and numbered appropriately and a real or imaginary name for the business may be used.

Assignment 6

"Star Trek"

. . . or The Lena Spock Story

"... so you see there I was employed by Kirk Enterprises Ltd – who were once part of the Klingon PLC Group – not any more (that was five years ago) – now they're completely unconnected – know what I mean? Anyhow, like I says, there I was minding my own business . . . eh? . . . minding my own business . . . working as secretary to the factory manager . . . no *not* Klingon . . . Kirk Enterprises . . . so Scott says to me, yeah he says to me 'Rita' he says. Scott? He was my boss – the factory manager – they used to call me Rita . . . everyone used to call me Rita although I'm Lena . . . he says to me 'Klingon's van is in the yard, go and sign for the invoice.' I says but I never sign the invoices, I says, five years I been here and I never sign invoices. He says 'Look Lena' (he never called me Lena before) he says 'Look Lena – I'm very busy. *That* is an order'. So . . . yeah . . . out I go – took me fags – out I go way around to the back of the yard – I've never been there before . . . lit a fag, reached the van . . . and *there* he was . . . this monkey-faced driver topping up his oil . . . turns round to me and says 'Hi sweetheart, hard of hearing?' Well! . . . I says, 'Drop dead!' and threw me fag (cigarette) at him and then . . . bang! . . . explosion . . . everything was alight . . . he was in hospital for three and a half weeks and they blamed *me* – sacked me the very same day it happened . . . and now this . . . this writ from Klingon – *they* say I'm to blame . . . something about paying damages. What do I do? I've got no money . . . I should never have been sent round to the back of the factory . . . and anyhow I want my job back . . . Scotty never wanted me to go – it was his bosses . . . *what* do I do?"

Instructions

1. Summarise the relevant facts in fifty words or less.
2. Consider the main legal problems arising.
3. Explain to Lena in clear, uncomplicated, and non-legal terms her rights, if any.

Assignment 7

"Memo from the MD"

Below is the reverse of a "memo" to a company accountant. Side 1 explained the economic and other reasons for having to make redundancies. Side 2 is a request to explain the meaning of redundancy, calculate redundancy payments and possibly make a *choice* to retain an employee (which may not be an exclusively legal problem). Put yourself in the accountant's position, and reply to the memo.

– PAGE 2 –

STRICTLY PRIVATE AND CONFIDENTIAL

MEMORANDUM

Continued:
. . . and so that is the rather sad state of the company's finances at the moment. With great regret the following employees will be made redundant:

(i) Mr. Gregory (warehouse); he is earning £85 per week and has been with the company for 8 years. He is aged 50. Both he and Stan are full-time.

(ii) Stan Phillips (machine room) aged 24, with us 6 years, earning £65 per week.

(iii) Doris, tea-lady, 15 hours per week, earning £1.46 per hour, with us 13 years since the age of "29".

(iv) Franky Brown (in the post room), 2 years with us and his first proper job since leaving school a couple of years ago, he's now 20 and earning £48 per week.

(v) Carl Pratt, my P.A., he's been here 3 years, is aged 31 and is getting £7500 annually.

So can you please have your reply with me a.s.a.p. What is our obligation to make redundancy payments? How much money is due to each of the above employees? If the total is less than £2000, I can afford to keep one of them on: who do you suggest and why?

JONATHAN PITNEY-PEWS M.D.

Assignment 8

"A Matter of Access"

Consider the illustration on page 213.

Extracts from a Standard Form.

1. What kind of obligation does a person enter when he signs this form and his application is accepted?

HIRE-PURCHASE AGREEMENT	SALE OF GOODS	STANDARD FORM CONTRACT	REGULATED AGREEMENT	DEBTOR-CREDITOR AGREEMENT	CREDIT TOKEN AGREEMENT

(Tick each and every box which is appropriate or submit on a separate sheet.)

2. Who are the parties to any obligation entered into?
3. In Clause 6 the bank says it "will prepare and send periodic statements..."; *if* the bank breaks this "condition" of use then what right does this give the signor of the document?
4. In Clause 11 the bank says it will "not be liable for the refusal of any retailer to honour the ... card"; how effective is this clause in view of the Unfair Contract Terms Act 1977?
5. When the applicant receives his card he fails to sign it and the card is stolen and misused to the sum of £85. What is the extent of the applicant's liability?
6. Suppose a card is issued to a person who signs the form, although he or she is aged 17; explain the legal position to the cardholder.

Assignment 9

"Thinking Big"

Harriet Smith is in partnership with her brother Reginald in a thriving motor vehicle dealership. The activities of the company include the buying and selling of all kinds of vehicles, including motor tricycles, bicycles, mopeds, agricultural tractors and even road-rollers. The company is expanding its arrangements with finance companies to enable purchasers to receive the benefit of instant credit authority and Harriet hopes that in the next year or so the company will be able to provide maintenance and service of all motor vehicles on the premises.

It is the intention of both partners that the status of the company is changed to enable the benefits of limited liability to be achieved. For this purpose Harriet has obtained a draft memorandum and articles of association (see page 214) but wishes to prepare a relevant main objects clause (clause 3a) to reflect the present and proposed activities of the motor vehicle dealership.

Meanwhile, Reginald has for some time expressed concern about the company's responsibilities and duties when it purchases motor vehicles for resale, only to subsequently discover or be informed that a third party is claiming "ownership" of a vehicle in the possession of the partnership.

Consequently the partnership has hired you to prepare, as appropriate:

1. A draft main objects clause for the future status of the firm.
2. A report outlining and explaining the rights of ownership in motor vehicles bought by the company *and* any advice you can suggest that will exempt or protect the company from persons so claiming ownership.

Enclose a "fee note" with your draft and report.

Assignment 10

"The Money Game"

L.S. Co. Ltd is in business manufacturing shoes. Lionel Scrivens is the managing director and holds ninety-nine shares at £1 each; the other shareholder is Emma Scrivens, who holds one share.

Lionel Scrivens has estimated the assets and liabilities of the company as follows:

Factory and office premises; value of twelve years remaining on lease, £85 000.

Four vans, each valued at £4000 – two on hire purchase.

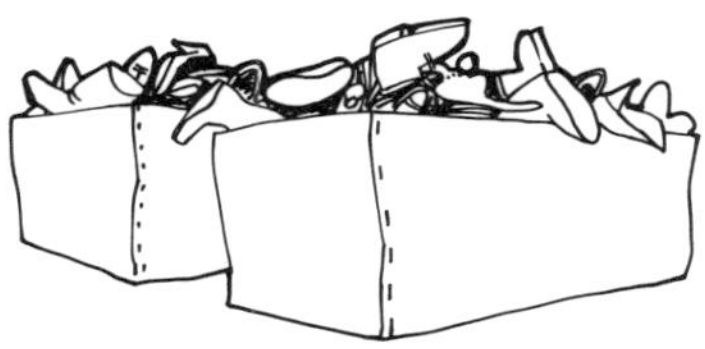

Shoes in stock value £17 000.

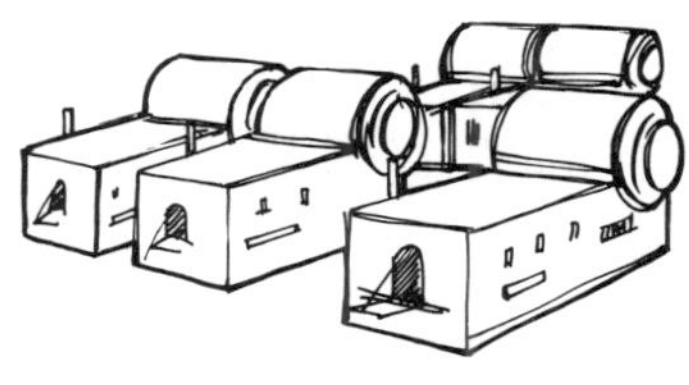

Five machines – three valued at £4500 and two valued at £7000 still being purchased on credit terms.

Tools – estimated value £4800.

Goodwill – valued at £25 000.

Office furniture – £3500.

Warehouse – valued at £21 000; L.S. Ltd owns the freehold.

£1000	£500
£2000	£1000

Four negotiable cheques not yet banked.

A "not transferable" cheque for

£5000

Sums due to the company from retailers:

£1100
£3500
£2500

Secured debenture (warehouse) due to L. Scrivens: £9000.

Debts of the company:	£
Payments due on machines	5000
H.P. payments outstanding on each van	2000
Overdraft at the bank – secured by charge (mortgage) on factory and office premises	45 000 (Limit £50 000)
Wages outstanding to employees	3000
Bills unpaid to creditors for two months	17 000

Instructions

Prepare a report on the current state of the company's affairs with particular reference to:

1. A valuation of the "real" property owned by the company.
2. A valuation of the "tangible" property owned by the company.
3. A valuation of the "intangible" property owned by the company.
4. A valuation of all the company's property which is freely transferable.

Calculations must be shown.

Assignment 11

"The Writing is on the Wall"

Ex-Imp (International) PLC, a large trading company with a huge turnover in goods, is very concerned about the large number of cheques issued by their accounts department which are subsequently misappropriated.

The company does not regard this state of affairs as being caused other than by the lack of knowledge of its accounts personnel. It has, therefore, requested the preparation of a wallchart to be pinned conspicuously in the accounts department. This wallchart must illustrate a cheque drafted in such a way that it gives the drawer the maximum protection and, as far as possible, makes sure that the money goes into the account of the person for whom the money is intended.

The parties to the cheque transaction must be defined precisely (using plain English) upon the wallchart, together with separate headings showing the responsibilities of the company's bankers and the lethal nature of an incorrectly drawn cheque.

Appendices

[45 & 46 VICT.] *Bills of Exchange Act,* 1882. [CH. **61.**]

CHAPTER 61.

An Act to codify the law relating to Bills of Exchange, Cheques, and Promissory Notes. [18th August 1882.] A.D. 1882.

Be it enacted by the Queen's most Excellent Majesty, by and with the advice and consent of the Lords Spiritual and Temporal, and Commons, in this present Parliament assembled, and by the authority of the same, as follows:

PART I.

PRELIMINARY.

1. This Act may be cited as the Bills of Exchange Act, 1882. Short title.

2. In this Act, unless the context otherwise requires. Interpretation of terms.

" Acceptance " means an acceptance completed by delivery or notification.

" Action " includes counter claim and set off.

" Banker " includes a body of persons whether incorporated or not who carry on the business of banking.

" Bankrupt " includes any person whose estate is vested in a trustee or assignee under the law for the time being in force relating to bankruptcy.

" Bearer " means the person in possession of a bill or note which is payable to bearer.

" Bill " means bill of exchange, and " note " means promissory note.

" Delivery " means transfer of possession, actual or constructive, from one person to another.

" Holder " means the payee or indorsee of a bill or note who is in possession of it, or the bearer thereof.

" Indorsement " means an indorsement completed by delivery.

" Issue " means the first delivery of a bill or note, complete in form to a person who takes it as a holder.

S.I. 1979 No. 959

THE UNFAIR DISMISSAL (VARIATION OF QUALIFYING PERIOD) ORDER 1979

S.I. 1979 No. 959

NOTE. — **Authority.** — This order was made on the 30th July 1979 by the Secretary of State under s. 149 (1) *(c)* of the Employment Protection (Consolidation) Act 1978, 48 Halsbury's Statutes (3rd Edn.) 608, and all other enabling powers.

Commencement. — 1st October 1979; see art. 1.

General. — This order increases to 52 weeks (from 26 weeks) the qualifying period for unfair dismissal complaints to an industrial tribunal, where the effective date of termination fell on or after the 1st October 1979.

1. Citation and commencement. — This Order may be cited as the Unfair Dismissal (Variation of Qualifying Period) Order 1979 and shall come into operation on 1st October 1979.

2. Variation of qualifying period. — Subject to Article 3, section 64 (1) *(a)* of the 1978 Act is varied so that for the reference to "twenty-six weeks" there is substituted a reference to "fifty-two weeks".

NOTE. — **Section 64 (1) (a) of the 1978 Act.** — *I.e.* s. 64 (1) *(e)* of the Employment Protection (Consolidation) Act 1978, 48 Halsbury's Statutes (3rd Edn.) 516.

3. Transitional and supplementary provisions. — (1) The variation specified in Article 2 shall have effect where the effective data of termination as defined in section 55 (4) or, where applicable, section 55 (5) of the 1978 Act falls after this Order comes into operation.

(2) In section 64 (2) of the 1978 Act, for the reference to the words "twenty-six weeks" appearing in section 64 (1) *(a)* there is substituted a reference to the words "fifty-two weeks".

NOTE. — **The 1978 Act.** — *I.e.* the Employment Protection (Consolidation) Act 1978; for ss. 55 (4) and (5) and 64 (2) thereto, see 48 Halsbury's Statutes (3rd Edn.) 504, 516.

A COMMON LAW DECISION

Allen v. Gulf Oil Refining Ltd

HOUSE OF LORDS
LORD WILBERFORCE, LORD DIPLOCK, LORD EDMUND-DAVIES, LORD KEITH OF KINKEL AND LORD ROSKILL

1st, 2nd, 3rd DECEMBER 1980, 29th JANUARY 1981

Nuisance — Defence — Statutory authority — Action for damages for nuisance arising out of construction and operation of oil refinery — Statute authorising oil company to acquire land compulsorily for construction of oil refinery — Oil company authorised to construct certain works and to construct and use certain subsidiary works in connection with refinery — Whether oil company able to rely on defence of statutory authority in action for nuisance — Gulf Oil Refining Act 1965 (c xxiv), ss 5, 15, 16.

By the Gulf Oil Refining Act 1965, an oil company ('Gulf Oil') were authorised to construct certain works in connection with an oil refinery they intended to establish at Milford Haven. The preamble to the Act recited that 'it is essential that further facilities for the importation of crude oil and petroleum products and for their refinement should be made available', and s 5 gave Gulf Oil power to acquire compulsorily land near Milford Haven 'for the purposes of [works authorised by s 15 of the Act] or for the construction of a refinery'. Section 15 authorised the construction of certain jetties and a branch railway line outside the boundary of the land. Section 16(1) authorised Gulf Oil to 'construct . . . and use' for the purposes of or in connection with the works authorised by s 15 certain subsidiary works, including, inter alia, railways, sidings etc. Section 16(3) provided for Gulf Oil to make reasonable compensation for any damage caused by the exercise of the power conferred by s 16(1). In 1967 Gulf Oil built a large refinery on the land referred to in the Act and which they had compulsorily acquired for the purpose, and constructed various jetties and railways in connection with it. The plaintiff, who lived in the near neighbourhood of the refinery, brought an action for damages or compensation against Gulf Oil, alleging that the operation of the refinery was a nuisance or alternatively that Gulf Oil were guilty of negligence in the method of construction and operation of the refinery. Gulf Oil resisted the claim by a plea of statutory authority. On a preliminary issue the judge ordered that Gulf Oil could rely on the 1965 Act as having authorised the construction and operation of the oil refinery. The plaintiff appealed to the Court of Appeal ([1979] 3 All ER 1008) which reversed the judge's decision. Gulf Oil appealed to the House of Lords.

Held (Lord Keith dissenting) — The preamble to the 1965 Act clearly showed that Parliament intended that a refinery, and not merely specifically authorised works such as jetties and railway lines, would be constructed on the land to be acquired, and such authority to construct a refinery expressly or impliedly carried with it authority to operate a refinery when constructed. It followed that Gulf Oil were entitled to statutory immunity in respect of any nuisance which was an inevitable result of constructing and operating on the site a refinery (but not necessarily inevitably resulting from the refinery in fact constructed) which conformed with Parliament's intention. Being a matter of defence, the fact that the nuisance was an inevitable result of a refinery on that site was a matter for Gulf Oil to prove. However, to the extent that the actual nuisance caused by the refinery in fact constructed exceeded the nuisance which inevitably resulted from any refinery on that site, the statutory immunity would not apply and Gulf Oil would be liable to the plaintiff. The appeal would therefore be allowed (see p 356 *g* and *j* to p 357 *b* and *g* to p 358 *f*, p 359 *f* and *j* to p 360 *b* and p 365 *f* to *j*, post).

Metropolitan Asylum District Managers v Hill [1881 — 5] All ER Rep 536 and *Manchester Corpn v Farnworth* [1929] All ER Rep 90 considered.

Decision of the Court of Appeal [1979] 3 All ER 1008 reversed.

EXTRACTS FROM A STANDARD FORM

CONDITIONS OF USE

1. The card supplied by the Bank from time to time under this agreement ("the ACCESS card") may be used only by the person to whom or for whose use it was issued ("the cardholder") and its use at all times is subject to the terms of the ACCESS Conditions of Use currently in force.

2. The ACCESS card is and remains the property of the Bank. It must be returned to the Bank upon request and it may be retained at any time by the Bank or by any person acting on behalf of the Bank.

3. The cardholder:
(i) must sign the ACCESS card immediately upon receipt;
(ii) in using the ACCESS card must not exceed the credit limit notified to him from time to time or to the person in whose name the account for the ACCESS card is maintained ("the principal cardholder"); and
(iii) may not use the ACCESS card before or after the period for which it is stated to be valid or after any notification of its cancellation or withdrawal given to him either by the Bank or by any person acting on behalf of the Bank.

4. The Bank will maintain an ACCESS account ("the account") for each principal cardholder and will charge to the account the amounts of all goods and services ("purchases") and of cash advances obtained by the cardholder under this agreement.

5. Interest will be charged at the rate of 2% per month on a daily basis equivalent to a maximum annual rate of 26.8%.

Cash advances will bear interest on a daily basis on the balance of the advance outstanding as from the date each advance is taken until full repayment is credited to the account.

No interest will be charged on the amounts of purchases repaid by the cardholder and credited to the account within 25 days of the date of the statement of account on which those purchases first appear. The daily balance of any such amounts outstanding at the end of the 25 days period will be charged interest from that statement data and will continue to be so charged until full repayment is credited to the account.

6. The Bank will prepare and will send periodic statements of accounts to the principal cardholder. The cardholder will pay to the Bank within 25 days from the date of each statement of account the minimum sum due and specified on the statement or any greater sum as the cardholder may choose. The minimum sum will be the larger of £5 or 5% of the outstanding balance shown on the statement.

7. Payments made by the cardholder to the Bank will be applied by the Bank on the date when they are credited to the account: first in payment of all interest shown on the latest and any previous statement; secondly towards payment of all cash advances shown on the latest and any previous statement; thirdly towards payment of all purchases shown on any previous statement; fourthly towards payment of all purchases shown on the latest statement; fifthly towards payment of any cash advances made but not then shown on any statement; and sixthly towards payment of any purchases made but not then shown on any statement.

8. The whole of the outstanding balance on the account shall become due and payable to the Bank on the bankruptcy or death of the cardholder or (at the Bank's discretion) if the cardholder is in breach of any of these Conditions of Use.

9. If the ACCESS card is lost or stolen the cardholder will notify the Bank's ACCESS Department immediately. If such notification is given orally it shall be treated as not taking effect if not confirmed in writing to the Bank's ACCESS Department within 7 days thereafter. Subject to such notification the maximum liability of the cardholder shall be £25 for loss to the Bank arising from use of the ACCESS card to any other person. The cardholder will nevertheless be liable to the Bank for any transaction effected by the use of the ACCESS card by any other person who acquired possession of it with the cardholder's consent before such notice is received as if he had used it personally.

10. On a written request to the Bank accompanied by the return of the ACCESS card together with any additional ACCESS cards for which he is liable the principal cardholder may terminate this agreement at any time without notice. The Bank may terminate this agreement with the cardholder at any time without notice by cancelling or refusing to renew the ACCESS card. Unless and until such termination takes place the Bank will provide a new ACCESS card for each cardholder from time to time.

11. The Bank will not be liable for the refusal of any retailer to accept or honour the ACCESS card. Where a retailer becomes liable to make any refund to a cardholder the Bank will credit the account with the amount to be refunded only on the receipt of a properly issued refund voucher or other appropriate verification of the refund by the retailer.

12. On the written request of a principal cardholder the Bank may issue an additional ACCESS card to any person nominated as an additional cardholder. The Conditions of Use apply to the use of an additional card and the principal cardholder shall be bound by and liable for its use in the same manner as if he had used it personally. In addition to its other rights and powers under this agreement the Bank may cancel an additional ACCESS card at any time at the written request of either the principal cardholder or an additional cardholder accompanied by the return of that card to the Bank.

13. The ACCESS card may be used outside the Scheduled Territories only within the limits imposed by the Exchange Control Authorities from time to time.

The Authorities will hold the cardholder responsible for any infringement of such limits.

14. The Bank reserves the right at all times to vary these Conditions of Use.

15. The Joint Credit Card Company Limited as an associated company of the Bank is the agent of the Bank for purposes of the ACCESS scheme and the cardholder agrees that the Bank may at any time disclose to the Company details of the account.

I confirm that I am not less than 18 years of age and the information given above is true and complete and that I have read and agreed to be bound by the Conditions of Use as set out overleaf and as may be amended from time to time. Where requested above I hereby authorise you to issue in accordance with the Conditions of Use as set out overleaf and as may be amended from time to time, an additional Access Card to the person named above who is not less than 18 years of age for use on my Access account.

Date____________________Signature of Applicant__________________

AS 78 6 (R Dec. 80)

The Companies Acts, 1948 to 1980

COMPANY LIMITED BY SHARES

Memorandum of Association

OF

B.E.C. COMPANY LIMITED

1. The name of the Company is "B.E.C. COMPANY LIMITED".

2. The Registered Office of the Company will be situate in England.

3. The objects for which the Company is established are:-

(a) To carry on business as printers, engravers, and lithographers of every kind and by every process and as artists, draughtsmen, designers and photographers and to manufacture and deal both wholesale and retail in stationery and paper of every description including cardboard, carbons, fancy and all other kinds of cards, calendars, envelopes, writing and drawing materials, implements and requisites, rubber and other stamps, cameras, photographic supplies, Company, Account and all other description of books and requisites of all kinds generally dealt with by printers and stationers and to carry on business as publishers, booksellers, bookbinders, producers and distributors, and as proprietors of newspapers, magazines, periodicals, books and other publications and as press, news, advertising, literary, dramatic, music, cinematographic and publicity agents, contractors and specialists, and further to carry on business as office equipment specialists and furnishers and to manufacture, repair and deal with both wholesale and retail in furniture, fittings, appliances, plant, machinery, equipment, implements and utensils, typewriters, duplicating, printing and calculating machines and dictaphones and of and in all kinds or types of supplies required for use in offices of every description and to carry on business as specialists for the like equipment and fitting out of shops, houses, hotels, theatres, churches and other buildings of every kind.

(b) To carry on any other business which, in the opinion of the Company, may be capable of being conveniently or profitably carried on in conjunction with or subsidiary to any other business of the Company and is calculated to enhance the value of the Company's property.

(c) To purchase or by any other means acquire freehold, leasehold or any other property for any estate or interest whatever, movable or immovable, or any interest in such property, and to sell, lease, let on hire, develop such property, or otherwise turn the same to the advantage of the Company.

(d) To apply for, register or by other means acquire any patents, patent rights, brevets d'invention, licences, trade marks, concessions and inventions and to use and turn to account the same or to develop, sell or assign the same or grant licences or privileges in respect thereof or otherwise turn the same to the advantage of the Company.

(e) To build, reconstruct or generally maintain buildings and works of all kinds, whether or not these are situate on the property of the Company.

(f) To invest and deal with the monies of the Company in such shares or upon such securities and in such manner as from time to time may be determined.

(g) To amalgamate with or to make any agreement or arrangement with or enter into partnership or joint purse agreement with any other company, firm or person carrying on business similar or complementary to the business of the Company or any part thereof.

(h) To subscribe for, take, purchase or otherwise acquire either for cash, shares or debentures in this Company or any other consideration any other company or business which, in the opinion of the Company, may be carried on so as directly or indirectly to benefit the Company.

(i) To sell or otherwise dispose of the whole or any part of the business or property of the Company for any consideration, shares or debentures as the Company may think fit.

(j) To lend money to customers, associates and others both corporate and incorporate and to guarantee the observance and performance of obligations and contracts by customers and others.

(k) To borrow or raise money in such manner as the Company thinks fit and secure the repayment thereof by the creation and issue of debentures, debenture stock, mortgages or in any other way.

(l) To pay or remunerate any person, firm or company for rendering services to the Company in the promotion of the Company or the placing and issue of shares, debentures, debenture stock or other securities of the Company.

(m) To support and subscribe to any funds and to subscribe to or assist in the promotion of any charitable, benevolent or public purpose or object for the benefit of the Company or its employees, directors or other officers past or present and to grant pensions to such persons or their dependents.

(n) To draw, make, accept, endorse, discount and execute bills, warrants, notes or other negotiable or transferable instruments.

(o) To assist in the promotion of or promote any company or undertaking which may appear likely to assist or benefit the Company and to place or guarantee the placing of, subscribe or underwrite or otherwise acquire any part of the stock, debentures, debenture stock or other obligations of such company.

(p) To promote by way of advertising the Company's products and services in any manner and to reward customers or potential customers and to promote or take part in any scheme likely to benefit the Company.

(q) To distribute in specie any of the shares, debentures or securities of the Company between the members of the Company in accordance with their rights.

(r) To do all such other things as may be deemed incidental or conducive to the attainment of the above objects or any of them.

All the foregoing objects shall be read and construed as separate and distinct objects and the generality of any such objects shall not be abridged or cut down by reference to any other object of the Company.

4. The liability of the members is limited.

5. The share capital of the Company is £1000 divided into 1000 shares of £1 each.

We, the several persons whose names, addresses and descriptions are subscribed, are desirous of being formed into a Company in pursuance of this Memorandum of Association, and we respectively agree to take the number of shares in the capital of the Company set opposite our respective names.

NAMES, ADDRESSES AND DESCRIPTIONS OF SUBSCRIBERS	Number of shares taken by each subscriber
MR. ANYBODY 33 Ludgate Hill, London, EC4M 7JQ. Company Director.	ONE
MR. A. N. BODY, 33 Ludgate Hill, London, EC4M 7JQ. Company Director.	ONE

DATED this 20th day of August, 1981.

WITNESS to the above signatures:

MRS. YET ANYBODY,
33 Ludgate Hill,
London, EC4M 7JQ.

Company Director.

The Companies Acts, 1948 to 1980

COMPANY LIMITED BY SHARES

Articles of Association

OF

B.E.C. COMPANY LIMITED

PRELIMINARY

1. Regulations 2, 3, 24, 53, 75, 88, 107, 108, 110 and 134 of Part I of Table A (hereinafter referred to as "Part I of Table A") shall not apply to the Company, but the Articles hereinafter contained together with the remaining regulations of Part I of Table A of the First Schedule of the Companies Act 1948 as amended by the Companies Act 1980 subject to the modifications hereinafter expressed, shall constitute the regulations of the Company.

CAPITAL

2. The initial share capital of the Company is £1000 divided into 1000 shares of £1 each.

3. The shares of the Company, whether forming part of the original capital or of any increased capital, may be allotted or otherwise disposed of to such persons and for such consideration and upon such terms as the Directors may determine subject, in the case of any shares forming part of any increased capital, to such directions as to the allotment or disposal thereof as may be given by the Company in general meeting at the time of the creation of such shares.

4. Subject to the provisions of Section 58 of the Act any Preference Shares may be issued on the terms that they are, or at the option of the Company are liable, to be redeemed.

TRANSFER OF SHARES

5. Any share may be transferred by a member to his or her spouse or lineal descendant and any share of a deceased member may be transferred to any such relation as aforesaid of the deceased member. Save as aforesaid the Directors, in their absolute discretion and without assigning any reason therefor, may decline to register the transfer of any share whether or not it is a fully paid share.

5.

6. The proviso to Regulation 32 of Part I of Table A shall not apply to the Company.

VOTES OF MEMBERS

7. Subject to any rights or restrictions for the time being attached to any class or classes of shares, on a show of hands every member present in person shall have one vote, and on a poll every member shall have one vote for each share of which he is the holder.

DIRECTORS

8. Regulations 80–87 of Part I of Table A apply except that Article 10 shall be substituted for sub-clauses (2) and (4) of Regulation 84 which shall be deleted.

9. A Director who has disclosed his interest in accordance with Regulation 84(1) of Part I of Table A and Section 199 of the Act may vote in respect of any contract, proposed contract or any arrangement in which he is interested directly or indirectly and such Director shall be counted in the quorum present at any meeting at which such contract or proposed contract or arrangement is being considered.

10. A Director may hold any other office or place of profit under the Company (other than the office of Auditor) in conjunction with his office of Director for such period and on such terms (as to remuneration and otherwise) as the Directors may determine.

11. Any Director may act by himself or his firm in a professional capacity for the Company, and he or his firm shall be entitled to remuneration for professional services as if he were not a Director; provided that nothing herein contained shall authorise a Director to act as Auditor for the Company.

12. The Company shall not be subject to Section 185 of the Act, and accordingly any person may be appointed or elected as a Director whatever his age, and no Director shall be required to vacate his office of Director by reason of his attaining or having attained the age of seventy years or any other age.

13. The office of a Director shall be vacated:

(1) If by notice in writing to the Company he resigns the office of Director.

(2) If he ceases to be a Director by virtue of Section 182 of the Act.

(3) If he becomes bankrupt or insolvent, or enters into an arrangement with his creditors.

(4) If he becomes of unsound mind.

(5) If he is prohibited from being a Director by any order made under Section 188 of the Act.

(6) If he is removed from office by a resolution duly passed under Section 184 of the Act.

BORROWING POWERS

14. The proviso to Regulation 79 of Part I of Table A shall not apply to the Company.

MANAGING DIRECTORS AND MANAGERS

15. The Directors may from time to time appoint one or more of their body to the office of Managing Director or Manager for such period and on such terms as they think fit and, subject to the terms of any agreement entered into in any particular case, may revoke such appointment. A Director so appointed, whilst holding such office, shall not be subject to retirement by rotation or be taken into account in determining the number of Directors to retire by rotation or the rotation of retirement of Directors, but his appointment, subject to the payment to him of such compensation or damages as may be payable to him by reason thereof, shall be automatically terminated if he cease from any cause to be a Director.

16. A Managing Director or Manager shall receive such remuneration (whether by way of salary, commission or participation in profits or partly in one way and partly in another) as the Directors may determine.

SECRETARY

17. The Secretary shall be appointed by the Directors for such term, at such remuneration and upon such conditions as they may think fit, and any Secretary so appointed may be removed by them. If at any time there shall be no Secretary or for any reason no Secretary capable of acting, the Directors may appoint an assistant or deputy Secretary.

NOTICES

18. Notice of every general meeting shall be given in manner authorised by Table A to every member except those members who are by these Articles disentitled from receiving such notices and those members who (having no registered address within the United Kingdom) have not supplied to the Company any address within the United Kingdom for the giving of notices to them.

FIRST DIRECTORS

19. The number of Directors shall not be more than ten but the Company in General Meeting may reduce or increase this limit. The first Director shall be MR. ANYBODY.

FIRST SECRETARY

20. The first Secretary of the Company shall be MR. A. N. BODY.

NAMES, ADDRESSES AND DESCRIPTIONS OF SUBSCRIBERS

MR. ANYBODY,
33 Ludgate Hill,
London, EC4M 7JQ.
Company Director.

MR. A. N. BODY,
33 Ludgate Hill,
London, EC4M 7JQ.
Company Director.

DATED this 20th day of August 1981.

WITNESS to the above signatures:

MRS. YET ANYBODY,
33 Ludgate Hill,
London, EC4M 7JQ.
Company Director.

Index